EUROPEAN AIR POWER

EUROPEAN AIR POWER

Challenges and Opportunities

Edited and with an introduction by

JOHN ANDREAS OLSEN

Potomac Books

An imprint of the University of Nebraska Press

Manufactured in the United States of America.

Library of Congress Cataloging-in-Publication Data
European air power: challenges and opportunities / edited and with an introduction by John Andreas Olsen.
pages cm
Includes bibliographical references and index.
ISBN 978-1-61234-681-6 (hardcover: alk. paper)
ISBN 978-1-61234-682-3 (pdf) 1. Air power—Europe. 2. Air forces—Europe. I. Olsen, John Andreas, 1968–, editor of compilation.
UG635.E85E86 2014
358.4'03094—dc23
2014000632

Set in Adobe Garamond Pro by Renni Johnson.

CONTENTS

Part 2. Nordic Air Powers

Part 3. Reflections: Where Do We Go from Here?

ILLUSTRATIONS

PROLOGUE: THE FIGHTER PILOT

Lt. Col. Jostein "Jaws" Grønflaten

The young aspiring student pilot was excited yet terrified. After lunch he would go "solo," his first flight without an instructor to guide him—or save his life if he messed up. In desperate need of some reassurance, he walked into the squadron bar to find an understanding soul to allay his concerns. There, draped in a scruffy flight suit with countless patches, wearing sunglasses despite the dim lighting, and firmly gripping a bottle of Jeremiah Weed, sat a crusty experienced fighter pilot. "How do you know there's a fighter pilot in the bar?" he shouted to the young arrival. Before the student pilot had time to utter a reply, the fighter pilot yelled out the answer to his own question: "Because he'll tell you!" Laughing hard at his own wit, he could barely stay on his chair.

The student pilot smiled politely and asked if he could sit down and ask a few questions.

"Sure, son, what's on your mind?"

"Well, sir, I'm flying my first solo after lunch, and although I'm really excited, I must admit I'm also a bit worried."

"Worried? About what? Flying isn't dangerous. Crashing is what's dangerous. We have a perfect track record in aviation: we have never left anyone up there! When in doubt, just hold on to your altitude. No one has ever collided with the sky. Just try to stay in the middle of the air. Don't go near the edges of it. The edges of the air can be recognized by the appearance of ground, buildings, sea, trees, and interstellar space. It is much more difficult to fly there. And in the ongoing battle between objects made of aluminum going hundreds of miles per hour and the ground going zero miles per hour, the ground has yet to lose.

"I will offer you some advice for free, son.

"Try to learn from the mistakes of others; you won't live long enough to make all of them yourself. Good judgment comes from experience. Unfortunately, experience usually comes from bad judgment. You start with a bag full of luck and an empty bag of experience. The trick is to fill the bag of experience before you empty the bag of luck.

"Always try to keep the number of landings you make equal the number of takeoffs you've made. A 'good' landing is one from which you can walk away. A 'great' landing is one after which the airplane is still usable. There are three simple rules for making a smooth landing. Unfortunately, no one knows what they are. Always try to put the landing gear down before you land. You will know you have landed with the gear up if it takes full power to taxi back to the parking ramp. If you are ever faced with a forced landing at night, turn on the landing lights to see the landing area. If you don't like what you see, turn them back off!

"And keep things simple. If you push the stick forward, the houses get bigger. If you pull the stick back, they get smaller—that is, unless you pull the stick all the way back; then they get bigger again.

"It is best to keep the pointed end of your aircraft going forward as much as possible.

"Fighter airplanes are the only planes worth flying. Propellers are there only to cool the pilot down—'cause when they stop spinning the pilot starts sweating. And don't bother flying anything with more than one engine. In a twin-engine aircraft the second engine is there only to supply the pilot with enough power to fly to the scene of the crash. If the wings of your aircraft are traveling faster than the fuselage, it is probably a helicopter and therefore unsafe, because helicopters can't fly; they're just so ugly the earth repels them. If something has not broken on your helicopter, it is about to.

"Remember that the radio is simply an electronic suggestion box for the pilot. Sometimes the only way to clear up a problem is to turn it off.

'Unskilled' pilots are always found in wreckage with one hand around the microphone. Flying the aircraft is more important than radioing your problem to a person on the ground incapable of understanding or doing anything about it. The only similarity between a pilot and an air traffic controller is if either one screws up, the pilot dies!

"And finally, young man, the three most useless things to a pilot are the altitude above you, the runway behind you, and the fuel at the pumps. The only time you have too much fuel is when you're on fire. Weather forecasts are just horoscopes with numbers, so look outside to determine what the weather is like. The pilot's ultimate responsibility is to fulfill the dreams of the countless millions of earthbound ancestors who could only stare skyward and wish. However, it's always better to be down on the ground wishing you were up in the air than up in the air wishing you were down on the ground.

"Any questions, son?" With that the fighter pilot ended his speech.

"No, sir," responded the young student pilot, eyes and mouth wide with awe. "This was very helpful. Thank you very much, sir."

"Anytime, son, anytime—and the best of luck on your solo!"

As he walked away, the young aviator thought, "I can either leave the bar, leave the squadron, drive off base, and never set foot on an airplane again. Ever. Or I can take the words of wisdom hidden in every sentence of that speech, make my own experiences, and someday maybe pass on my knowledge to a young fledgling who happens to be in the same shoes." The student pilot chose the latter, flew his solo, stayed away from the edges of the air, and made sure his number of landings equaled his number of takeoffs. He was well on his way to becoming a fighter pilot.

ACKNOWLEDGMENTS

What can European states afford to acquire and sustain in terms of air power? The answer depends on each country's specific geography, history, economy, and political-military orientation. This study examines the air power capabilities of eight air forces—four major European nations, including Turkey, and four Nordic countries—by combining conceptual and operational perspectives. It also provides contrasting reflections on the future of air power.

European Air Power: Challenges and Opportunities presents insight into the development of air power by those who are "in the know": independent analysts and serving air chiefs. Although primarily intended for readers who have a particular interest in the air power profession—especially serving and retired military personnel—this book should also be of interest to more general audiences that want to improve their understanding of air power as an instrument of national and international force.

I would like to thank all the authors for having accepted the book's overall framework and provided insight into their respective case studies. I am particularly grateful to the four Nordic air force chiefs, who took time from their busy schedules to commit their thoughts to paper. While all four generals played a direct role in developing their chapters, their respective staffs deserve a note of appreciation for seeing this project through.

I would like to acknowledge Lt. Col. Jostein Grønflaten for writing the prologue, which gives us an entertaining glimpse into the mind of an imaginary fighter pilot. I am deeply grateful to Margaret S. MacDonald for suggesting significant improvements to the manuscript and thankful to the Swedish National Defence College for sponsoring both the book and the conference based on it. My final note of appreciation goes to the publishing team, especially Bridget Barry and Sabrina Ehmke Sergeant.

INTRODUCTION

The Air Option

John Andreas Olsen

A brief review of the last twenty-five years of military operations suggests that air power dominates warfare. John A. Warden, widely acknowledged as the main architect of the theory underlying the air campaign that liberated Kuwait from Iraqi occupation in 1991, asserts, "Those who have air power overwhelm those who do not; those who do not have it spend their energies trying to get it, thwart it or escape it."[1] British strategist Colin S. Gray concludes that "airpower is one of history's most impressive success stories" and validates this assertion in his book *Airpower for Strategic Effect.*[2] Defense analyst Benjamin S. Lambeth demonstrates through a series of in-depth studies that the period between 1991 and 2003 was a triumphal time for air power and concludes that "airpower will inevitably be pivotal in future wars."[3]

Most analyses of modern air power have focused on the achievements of the United States, indisputably the world leader in air and space capabilities. By contrast, despite its technological sophistication and substantial size, European air power has received little attention, often being dismissed as a relic of the past or viewed as unimportant in comparison to American air power. Yet Operation Unified Protector, the 2011 North Atlantic Treaty Organization (NATO) intervention in Libya, showcased the important contributions of European air power. While U.S. involvement in the operation was crucial—particularly in terms of intelligence, command and control, air-to-air refueling, and airlift—both larger and relatively small European countries delivered effective combat strike sorties and performed essential noncombat functions that contributed significantly to the overthrow of Muammar Gaddafi's dictatorship.

Air Power: The Indispensable Element

Any assessment of modern air power should begin with Operation Desert Storm. The centerpiece of the military effort was an innovative air campaign that rendered the Iraqi leadership powerless and irrelevant within forty-eight hours of the initial attack. With few exceptions Saddam Hussein and his top commanders in Baghdad were unable to communicate with their security forces, commanders in the field, and the population at large. The devastating air campaign paralyzed the Iraqi regime, Republican Guard, and Iraqi Army at the political, military-strategic, operational, and tactical levels of war. Coalition ground forces performed admirably during the one hundred hours in which they engaged in combat, but in assessing the speed and scale of the victory, it is important to grasp the simple fact that the ground forces' achievements were, in large measure, made possible by the comprehensive air offensive.

Throughout the 1990s air power worked well under a variety of circumstances—from the open desert to populated urban areas in which strict rules of engagement constricted aerial missions. The internecine war in the former Yugoslavia that began in 1992 was horrific even by the standards of the twentieth century. Large-scale intervention on the ground was not an acceptable option for the international community, despite the worsening situation in Bosnia and Herzegovina as the conflict entered its third year. Most strategists concluded that it was the wrong war in the wrong place against the wrong sort of adversary for even air power to do much good.[4] Nevertheless, a two-week NATO air campaign in 1995 broke the Bosnian impasse. Operation Deliberate Force became the leading factor in bringing the Bosnian Serb regime to the negotiating table; the Dayton Accords paved the way for a political settlement that has lasted to this day.[5]

A similar situation prevailed four years later. In his endorsement of Operation Allied Force in March 1999, President Bill Clinton made it clear that the United States would not commit ground forces in Serbia or Kosovo; any military intervention would be executed through air power. After seventy-eight days of aerial bombardment, NATO succeeded in compelling President Slobodan Milošević to withdraw all his forces from Kosovo. Diplomatic efforts contributed to the solution, but air power again proved the leading military instrument, despite varying interpretations of the "true worth of air power,"[6] especially the value of precision weapons. Even though the mentioned air campaigns were hardly flawless, the decade represented, in short, a renaissance of air power.

At the start of the twenty-first century, air power took the lead in the initial phase of Operation Enduring Freedom, the joint and combined war against al Qaeda and the Taliban in Afghanistan, and then played a crucial role during the three weeks of major combat in Operation Iraqi Freedom in 2003. As those two conflicts assumed different forms, air power shifted from a leading to a supporting role. For more than a decade, air power has facilitated and aided land warfare, especially in the form of counterinsurgency operations, in Afghanistan and Iraq.

As debates over defense continue throughout Europe and North America, a dose of perspective is in order. On the one hand, air power did not single-handedly decide the conflicts between 1991 and 2003; it achieved its effects in synergy with other coercive tools and pressure. On the other hand, air power was and is considerably more important in counterinsurgency operations than most critics would care to admit. Even though one of the most influential doctrines to emerge lately—the U.S. Army's 2006 Field Manual 3-24 on counterinsurgency—largely neglects the importance of the aerial perspective, air power in fact performs so many roles and functions that no major military operation can do without it. For all the strength of ground and naval forces, it is almost inconceivable that a Western state or coalition of states would embark on any military venture, including a counterinsurgency campaign, without first ensuring control of the skies over the region of interest, without the situational awareness and overview that air power provides to military commanders, without significant precision strike capability, or without airlift to, from, and within the theater of operations.[7] In short, air power ensures that nations can operate with lower levels of risk, at higher levels of military effectiveness, anywhere in the world.

Still, it is important to have realistic expectations. Some claim that the mere existence of standoff, precision weaponry has changed the nature of warfare to the point at which any attack from the air should be able to destroy its intended targets without collateral damage. However, military intervention was, is, and will always be a human endeavor; it cannot achieve a perfection counter to the very nature of *Homo sapiens*. Strikes may be precise but can never avoid all unintended casualties, and their effects cannot be isolated from the various elements of fog, friction, and uncertainty inherent in warfare. The belief that military campaigns can be successfully prosecuted without human suffering is appealing, but politicians and the public cannot realistically apply peacetime standards to armed conflicts and hold the air power option to such unattainable standards.[8] Air power is strategically essential, but not risk free.

In short, air power is, and will remain, quintessentially a necessary, though not sufficient, condition for conflict resolution. Inflated expectations have led to the denigration of air power because it cannot impose a favorable result in volatile political and strategic environments with underlying dynamics that are impervious to any kind of armed force. Air power may contribute to conflict resolution, but its effects must relate to the broader political-military characteristics and nature of the specific conflict.

Operation Unified Protector offers a case in point. Air power represented the majority of the military operations in this intervention; indeed, NATO would not have agreed to intervene militarily to accomplish the mission defined in United Nations Resolution 1973 had it lacked the air option. First, most NATO members refused to consider sending ground forces into a civil war; second, NATO recognized that the air option would not involve huge allied casualties in the process of compelling a dictatorship to stop its violations of human rights. The fall of Gaddafi and his regime resulted not only from air power but also from significant political pressure and the combat actions of special forces on the ground and various groups of insurgents fighting the loyalists. The real successes and failures of the post-Gaddafi era will manifest themselves in decades to come. Overthrowing a dictatorship that has ruled for more than four decades is one thing; building up a state and society on the basis of democracy, individual liberty, and the rule of law is another. Although some aspects of air power performance in Operation Unified Protector could certainly be improved, much of the criticism actually focused, not on air power's effectiveness, but on the political decision to take military action and on NATO's subsequent inability to quickly turn a dictatorship into a democracy.

In addition to demonstrating that air power can play a significant role in civil wars, the intervention in Libya also illustrated that small and medium-sized nations can make considerable military contributions. As already mentioned, U.S. involvement in Operation Unified Protector was crucial, and France and the United Kingdom assumed the dominant role once NATO took responsibility for the mission, but relatively small countries, such as Belgium, Denmark, and Norway, contributed combat strike sorties.

American air power is, and will be for some time to come, in a class of its own. This study asks what European countries can accomplish through the air option, with or without the Americans. Most European air forces have gone through considerable restructuring and modernization so that they can undertake an increasing spectrum of ever more complex tasks. In the process the inevitable question has arisen: What kind of air power should any given state seek to have?

Framework for Analysis

The shape-deter-respond strategic construction, including four enduring air power capabilities and professional competence at its core, sets a framework for analysis (see figure). Such a framework constitutes a template for assessing what a state can and cannot achieve through air

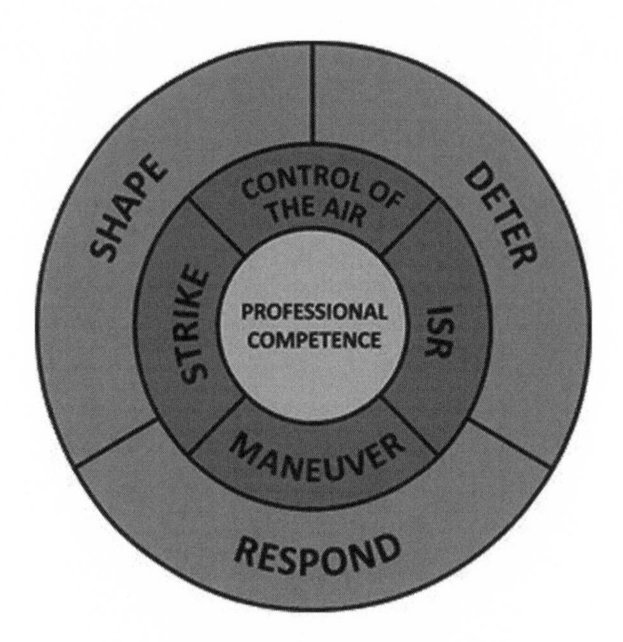

Framework for Analysis of the Air Option

power. Every state must decide where to position itself on this template and what that position means for resource allocation.

The first priority is to influence (shape) the geopolitical environment to advance the nation's interests and ambitions through the use of political, diplomatic, economic, social, cultural, and military means. Second, if shaping does not succeed, the nation might have to deter unwanted behavior. Finally, if deterrence fails, the nation might have to respond with a series of actions, with armed conflict and war representing the extreme end of the spectrum. Air power has unique functions in all these areas: to shape the environment, deter potential adversaries, and respond in operations to coerce or compel adversaries to adopt a course of action that aligns with the state's intent.

Within the shape-deter-respond framework, air power historically has delivered four basic capabilities: control of the air; situational awareness through intelligence, surveillance, and reconnaissance (ISR); strike (bombing); and maneuver (transportation and airlift).[9] Stated differently, any state that considers itself an "air power" must concern itself with performing four key tasks: ensuring air superiority, furnishing awareness, carrying out air-to-surface attack, and providing mobility. These tasks encompass numerous subsets, such as offensive and defensive counterair operations, maritime patrol, strategic attacks, interdiction, close air support, medical evacuation, and search and rescue.

To ensure that operational systems achieve the maximum effect, a nation needs an air force that understands and accepts that it exists to demonstrate the utility of air power. Thus, the air force must define air power competence, or professional mastery, by its contribution to the effectiveness of air power. True mastery of air power requires a proper balance among technological excellence, visionary leadership, and conceptual shrewdness.

European air forces—large, medium, and small—usually devote their attention to practical issues related to aircraft, weapon systems, and tactics rather than to leadership, command, theory, doctrine, strategy, or operational art. This tendency to focus on immediate challenges and the technology and equipment necessary to meet them, and to ignore the concepts and dynamics underlying those challenges, is the Achilles' heel of air forces. In their drive to achieve technological perfection, they generally underestimate the importance of mastering air power theory, of cultivating broader knowledge and insight into air power. Mastery of the air profession includes knowledge of the strategic history of air power, insight into air power's strengths and weaknesses, and the ability to think conceptually and strategically. It also includes the ability to communicate the nation's particular air power story.

As European air forces move from creating physical capacity to improving operational capability, the next step is to ensure professional competence at all levels of the organization. Improving the way airmen think about warfare is, in many ways, far more difficult than changing the equipment they use. And while individual insight is important, elevating this competence to the organizational and operational levels represents a challenge of an even higher order. All states need to acknowledge that air power has revolutionized warfare and to position their air forces accordingly.

European Air Power: Overview

This study examines the status of eight European air forces and their prospective air power capabilities.[10] It does so by reviewing contemporary national debates and the choices that different countries either have made or are in the process of making. It includes perspectives both from independent air power experts and from the leaders of four Nordic nations' air forces.

Within the identified national security framework of threats and challenges, and against the seemingly universal backdrop of lower budgets for defense, this study presents a range of views on what types of air power capabilities a state should have and what it can forsake. It explores how different air forces structure themselves to remain sustainable and efficient in accordance with their national strategic compasses.

Major European Air Powers

Part I of this book contains analyses of the air forces of four NATO members: France, Germany, Turkey, and the United Kingdom.[11] These are major powers in Europe today, each with comparable potential to allocate resources to military transformation. All four have or plan to acquire a modern fleet of fighter-bombers. Because of the multirole capabilities of modern jets (such as the Eurofighter, Gripen, and Rafale) and the fifth-generation fighter-bomber (the Joint Strike Fighter), the numbers and types of fighter-bombers a state owns effectively indicate combat capability. Part I illuminates commonalities and differences among the national air power debates in these four countries and identifies the choices that these countries confront. In assessing their air power ambitions for the future, all of these countries have considered directly or indirectly how to position themselves relative to U.S. air power.

In the first chapter Etienne de Durand presents the story of the French Air Force, which arguably led the world in air power during the first decade of manned flight and devoted great effort to developing successful air power capabilities during the First World War—yet failed to operate efficiently when once again put to the test against the Germans in 1940. The cycle has since been repeated in France, although in a different form: the French aircraft industry expanded, and the nation embraced its role as a nuclear power during the Cold War, only to find itself unprepared for the types of tasks that emerged during Operation Desert Storm. Yet since the 1990s the armée de l'Air has proved itself both in the Balkans and in various campaigns from Afghanistan to Libya and Mali.

Looking to the future, de Durand argues that declining defense budgets and the increased cost of state-of-the-art technology will make it difficult for the air force to become a service that covers the full spectrum of air power and can deal with the tasks that French politicians require of it. How few airframes are enough? De Durand concludes that the air force must choose between quantity and quality, between multirole capability and specialization, and between manned and unmanned platforms. While the proper balance will depend on an improved economy, the near term confronts the air force with the challenge of making the most of existing equipment.

Germany has recently undergone a comprehensive defense reform, the so-called Reorientation (*Neuausrichtung*), that calls upon the Luftwaffe to reduce its personnel by 30 percent. At the same time policy makers expect the German Air Force to take an ever more active role in joint missions with partner nations outside Europe. The study that resulted from the Reorientation, *Air Power 2030*, lays particular emphasis on four functions: air-surface integration, missile defense, military use of space, and unmanned aircraft. In chapter 2 Professor Holger H. Mey discusses the Luftwaffe's reorganization into three new commands and examines emerging operational demands, technological challenges, and the air force's need for cooperation with the German aerospace industry. Germany's geostrategic situation and its desire to operate in a multinational framework shape the priorities of its air force.

Like its counterparts throughout most of the Western world, the German Air Force will have to do more with less, but Mey is cautiously optimistic about the future. The Eurofighter offers substantial strike and ISR capability; overall surveillance capabilities are continuously improving as a foundation for command and control; the A400M, despite cuts in numbers, will provide a substantial air transport and air-to-air refueling capability for both aircraft and helicopters; and the Bundeswehr is developing a European unmanned aerial vehicle (UAV). Mey concludes that the future of German air power is perhaps not as bright as it could and should be but that the air force must work within the existing constraints, rather than pursue an unachievable ideal state. Germany's biggest obstacle to playing a considerable role in international operations today is political self-restraint, not operational capability.

In chapter 3 Dr. Christian F. Anrig asserts that the Turkish Air Force represents an air power to be taken seriously. Its planned acquisition of several squadrons of F-35s and its midlife upgrades of more than two hundred F-16s will give it considerable combat capabilities. In the post–Cold War era, Turkey has also obtained powerful force multipliers, such as tankers and airborne early warning and control systems. Together with the modernization of its strategic and tactical airlift capabilities, they ensure that Turkey is becoming a modern full-spectrum air force. Turkey also places strong emphasis on expanding its technological aerospace expertise and industrial base, thereby lessening its dependence on the United States and opening the door to new partners. In addition to these capabilities, the Turkish Air Force has gained considerable experience from modern counterinsurgency operations against separatist Kurds and has contributed to all of NATO's air campaigns since 1993.

Anrig paints a picture of a Eurasian country that confronts a more complex domestic and challenging geopolitical setting than most NATO members, has accumulated significant expertise through air combat operations inside and outside its borders, and has aerospace ambitions on par with or possibly exceeding those of both France and the United Kingdom. Those ambitions include the joint development and production of attack helicopters, further research and development of various unmanned platforms, including the expansion of a national satellite program. In contrast to the majority of NATO members, Turkey has actually increased its defense budget, and although the air force may receive less funding than the army, both can count on adequate resources, reinforcing Turkey's overall position as a serious military power.

In the fourth chapter Dr. Peter W. Gray first reviews the operations of the Royal Air Force (RAF) over the last twenty years and the resulting doctrinal implications and then focuses on the current debate in the United Kingdom regarding the future of the RAF. He presents a framework that includes the theoretical aspects of air power, subdivided into a process that considers political, economic, social, technological, legal, and environmental factors. All are of great importance to the "comprehensive approach" that the RAF seeks, but increased sensitivity to casualties, including those among enemy forces, lays ever more weight on legal aspects of air operations.

As the United Kingdom abandons the traditional approach of "reduction through salami slicing" to focus on strategic choices and real priorities in defense, it must redefine "operational art" so that it remains relevant in current and future operations. This requires the RAF to reconsider the debate over maritime patrol aircraft and the utility of carrier-borne air power and to examine the moral, legal, and ethical aspects, as well as the operational implications, of what Gray calls "the remoteness of warfare." Although various unmanned capabilities will receive increased attention, Gray argues that this represents a trend, not a fundamental change. Air power has traditionally been at the forefront of the United Kingdom's operational posture, and this leading role is likely to continue, simply because "air power will continue to offer policy makers and planners an effective and relatively cost-effective option for dealing with real-world events and contingences."

Nordic Air Powers

Part 2 of this book focuses on the Nordic countries of Norway, Denmark, Sweden, and Finland.[12] These countries have comparable populations and resources and, as small air power nations, must all make hard choices regarding where to direct their resources in terms of air power capabilities. Whereas part 1 of the book offers independent analyses, part 2 presents the perspectives of the serving air force chiefs in each country regarding their respective service's history, current status, and objectives for the future. These shorter chapters have a practical flavor and identify strategic, operational, and tactical directions and prioritized capabilities.

The people of the High North have much in common, but the geographic characteristics of their countries vary significantly and include flatland, mountains, forests, fjords, and lakes. With a combined population of approximately 25 million, the region has less than one-third of the population of Turkey; in area the Nordic countries approximate the territory of France, Germany, and the United Kingdom combined. This measure does not include Greenland, the world's biggest island and an autonomous country under Denmark, an area of significant geostrategic importance. The four countries cooperate in many areas and hold common exercises, despite different formal political and military arrangements. Both Denmark and Norway are founding members of NATO; Finland and Sweden do not belong to the alliance but are active in the Partnership for Peace program. Unlike the other three, Norway is not a member of the European Union (EU) but has contributed to EU battle groups.

One common denominator among the four Nordic air forces is that all have recently undergone and continue to pursue reforms that will allow each country to develop modern air power capabilities. Each country accords priority to roles that will give its political leaders and military commanders the desired flexibility to handle any given crisis at home and abroad—sometimes alone, sometimes as part of an international mission, but always with compatible technology and doctrine that enable a wide span of interoperability. Furthermore, all four chiefs are concerned with enabling their air forces to carry out a wider spectrum of roles and functions, and all emphasize the importance of the basic air power capabilities: control of the air, ISR, strike, and maneuver.

All air chiefs suggest that partnership and interoperability—in terms not only of compatible equipment but also of training, exercises, education, and doctrine—represent the way forward. Although the four leaders focus on operational platforms, they also emphasize the importance of ensuring that their airmen have operational skills, professional mastery, and the ability to lead in peace, crisis, and war. It is particularly noteworthy that these four air force leaders see the human dimension of their service as paramount for success—perhaps despite, but more likely because of, the latest technological developments. Each air force chief seeks to foster a well-organized, professional, and robust service that offers high availability and usability for their political leaders.

Reflections: Where Do We Go from Here?

Part 3 of this book offers contrasting viewpoints in the form of think pieces from prominent air power experts. Taking a step back to provide general reflections on the future of air power, Professor Martin van Creveld and Air Vice Marshal (ret.) R. A. Mason comment on challenges and opportunities for small and medium-sized air power nations.

Van Creveld argues that air power as traditionally understood is approaching its limits. He presents a short version of his recent book, *The Age of Airpower*, which suggests that the value of manned aircraft peaked during the Second World War and has since become less and less relevant to success in modern warfare. In addition, the unit cost of modern fighter-bombers is so high that few nations can afford a meaningful fleet; moreover, such aircraft cannot be decisive in an era characterized by intrastate insurgencies of various sorts. His conclusion is clear: for small and medium-sized states that believe they need an air force but "cannot afford the tens of billions needed to build and maintain a modern one," unmanned systems—whether missiles, satellites, or various forms of "drones"—represent the future. According to van Creveld, pilots have become increasingly unnecessary in an age of computer-driven, ground-controlled aircraft; instead, helicopters and unmanned aerial systems are the true representatives of the future projection of air power, not the fighters that have symbolized air power at least since the Battle of Britain.

R. A. Mason presents opposing views. He asserts that air power has remained as indispensable in current counterinsurgencies as in all other forms of warfare and that air power was decisive or dominant in every conflict involving European states in coalition with the United States between 1990 and the present. His main contention is that in a world of uncertainty, air power will continue to increase in importance as a political and military instrument across the spectrum of conflict. While acknowledging the growing salience of UAVs of various sorts, Mason argues that proposals to replace manned aircraft are shortsighted, ignoring much of the historical record and holding the inherent flexibility of air power hostage to the future. He notes that even space-based systems rely on satellite communications, which in turn are vulnerable to cyber attack. Thus, to ensure future Western military dominance and command of the air, Mason insists, "human responsiveness and ingenuity will remain indispensable." He concludes that the combination of the increased cost of modern aircraft and decreasing defense budgets means that the effectiveness of European air power will depend on interoperability within partnership: European states can apply air power effectively across the conflict spectrum in the twenty-first century, but only if they prepare fully in time of peace to operate as partners in crisis.

Prospects

One of the most valuable lessons of modern warfare is that air power remains such an important part of the political-military toolbox precisely because of its flexibility and adaptability: at times it is a game changer, at times a facilitator, and at times an adjunct to other types of force. Every conflict has its own unique challenges and special circumstances. The question, Should air power be regarded as the supported or supporting force? does not and cannot have a universal answer; air power can play both parts and often does so even in the same conflict. Air power can determine outcome, or it can be subordinate to other military actions based on the context of operations. None of the country-specific case studies suggests that "the time is fast approaching for a wake to be ordered for airpower."[13]

This book emphasizes the importance of cooperation, touches on pooling limited assets to achieve a greater effect, sheds light on full-service versus niche air forces, and deals with the dilemma of quantity versus quality. All European air powers must increasingly look to various forms of partnership and to interoperability. Ultimately, any nation-state must match its air power competence to its overall military-strategic orientation and to financial reality in order to prepare itself technologically, organizationally, and conceptually for current and future operations. The operational dimension represents the air forces' ends; the organizational, technological, and conceptual dimensions the means of achieving them.

As European states develop future air power capabilities, each must decide whether its air power should meet only national goals or whether it should have the capability and interoperability to participate in international scenarios as part of an alliance. Policy makers must consider whether the armed forces should perform support functions only—and what kind of support—or if they should develop and sustain a kinetic contribution in the form of real combat capabilities. Some European states have chosen to specialize in noncombat roles, whereas others are committed to building modern full-service air forces that include operational systems for combat, an effective and adaptive organizational structure, and highly skilled personnel. The book's eight case studies reveal that aircraft represent an important element of air power but emphasize the larger human and political dimensions of this technological wonder.

In closing, any student of air power could benefit from the advice of Richard P. Hallion: "What sustains us is guidance available from our past, which can both serve to inform and encourage our future efforts, as well as offer to us the perspective and insight to face contemporary challenges."[14] Western air powers have delivered astonishing military effects for decades, but to remain relevant, air forces must meet challenges and turn them into opportunities. If they can accept it, European air powers will play increasingly differentiated but ever more essential roles in the Western democracies' pursuit of security and prosperity.

ABBREVIATIONS

AAR	air-to-air refueling
AEW&C	airborne early warning and control
AGS	Alliance Ground Surveillance
AIRCOM	Air Command
AIS	Automatic Identification System
AKP	Justice and Development Party (Turkey)
AMRAAM	advanced medium-range air-to-air missile
AP	Air Publication
ASC	airborne surveillance and control
ASMP	Air-Sol Moyenne Portée
ASW	antisubmarine warfare
ATO	air tasking order
ATP	advanced targeting pod
AWACS	airborne warning and control system
BDA	battle damage assessment
BMD	ballistic missile defense
C2	command and control
C4ISR	command, control, communications, computers, intelligence, surveillance, and reconnaissance
CAFDA	Commandement aérien des forces de défense aérienne
CAOC	combined air operations center
CAP	combat air patrol
CAS	close air support

CIA	Central Intelligence Agency (United States)
CNN	Cable News Network
CPA	Commando parachutiste de l'air
CPMIEC	China Precision Machinery Import Export Corporation
CRC	control and reporting center
DEAD	destruction of enemy air defenses
DGA	Délégation générale de l'armement
DRM	Direction du renseignement militaire
EATC	European Air Transport Command
EBO	effects-based operations
ECR	electronic combat and reconnaissance
EEAW	European Participating Air Forces' Expeditionary Air Wing
EPAF	European Participating Air Forces
ER	enhanced range
EU	European Union
FAS	Forces aériennes stratégiques
FATAC	Force aérienne tactique
GDP	gross domestic product
GPS/INS	Global Positioning System/Inertial Navigation System
HALE	high-altitude long-endurance
HARM	high-speed antiradiation missile
HGK	Hassas Güdüm Kiti
HQ	headquarters
ICBM	intercontinental ballistic missiles
IDS	interdiction/strike
INADS	Integrated NATO Air Defense System
IOC	initial operating capability
ISAF	International Security and Assistance Force
ISR	intelligence, surveillance, and reconnaissance
ISTAR	intelligence, surveillance, target acquisition, and reconnaissance
JASSM	joint air-to-surface standoff missile
JDAM	joint direct attack munition
JFAC	Joint Force Air Component

JFACC	joint force air component commander
JSF	Joint Strike Fighter
JSOW	joint standoff weapon
KGK	Kanatlı Güdüm Kiti
LANTIRN	low-altitude navigation and targeting infrared for night
LGB	laser-guided bombs
MALE	medium-altitude long-endurance
MEADS	Medium Extended Air Defense System
MOD	Ministry of Defense
MRTT	multirole tanker transport
NAD	Norwegian Aeromedical Detachment
NADGE	NATO Air Defense Ground Environment
NAO	National Audit Office (UK)
NAOC	National Air Operations Center (Norway)
NASAMS	Norwegian Advanced Surface-to-Air Missile System
NATO	North Atlantic Treaty Organization
NCO	noncommissioned officer
NCTR	noncooperative target recognition
NRF	NATO Response Force
NTC	National Transitional Council (Libya)
OODA	observe-orient-decide-act
OUP	Operation Unified Protector
PAC	Patriot Advanced Capability
PfP	Partnership for Peace
PGM	precision-guided munition
PKK	Kurdistan Workers' Party (Turkey)
RAF	Royal Air Force
RAFCAPS	RAF Centre for Air Power Studies
RDAF	Royal Danish Air Force
RMA	revolution in military affairs
ROVER	Remotely Operated Video Enhanced Receiver
RPA	remotely piloted aircraft
RPV	remotely piloted vehicle
SAC	Strategic Airlift Capability

SACEUR	Supreme Allied Commander Europe
SAGE	Defense Industries Research and Development Institute (Turkey)
SALIS	Strategic Airlift Interim Solution
SAM	surface-to-air missile
SAR	synthetic aperture radar
SCAR	strike coordination and reconnaissance
SDB	small-diameter bombs
SDSR	Strategic Defence and Security Review (UK)
SEAD	suppression of enemy air defenses
SIGINT	signals intelligence
SLAM	standoff land attack missile
SOM	standoff missile
SSM	surface-to-surface missiles
TAI	Turkish Aerospace Industries
TBMD	theater ballistic missile defense
T-LORAMIDS	Turkish Long-Range Air and Missile Defense System
TRY	Turkish lira
TTPS	tactics, techniques, and procedures
TurAF	Turkish Air Force
UAS	unmanned aerial system
UAV	unmanned aerial vehicle
UK	United Kingdom
UN	United Nations
UOR	urgent operational requirement
USAF	U.S. Air Force
USSR	Union of Soviet Socialist Republics
V/STOL	vertical/short takeoff and landing
VPR	Verteidigungspolitische Richtlinien
WEU	Western European Union

I

EUROPEAN AIR POWERS

Air power is an unusually seductive form of military strength, in part because, like modern courtship, it appears to offer gratification without commitment. Francis Bacon wrote of command of the sea that he who has it "is at great liberty, and may take as much and as little of the Warre as he will," and a similar belief accounts for air power's attractiveness to those who favor modest uses of force overseas. Statesmen may think that they can use air attacks to engage in hostilities by increments, something ground combat does not permit. Furthermore, it appears that the imminent arrival of so-called nonlethal or disabling technologies may offer an even more appealing prospect: war without casualties.

ELIOT A. COHEN

ONE

French Air Power

Effectiveness through Constraints

Etienne de Durand

French air power has experienced a rich history of highs and lows since the beginning of manned flight. Accordingly, the French Air Force found it difficult to stabilize its identity until the advent of a national nuclear deterrent. This changed again with the end of the Cold War and the air force's recognition of its capability shortfalls following the U.S.-led campaign against Iraq in 1991. The need to modernize and adapt to the "age of intervention" has been crucially important because France has remained a significant international actor, willing to influence international events and ready to participate in military operations if need be.

Although adaptation has been slowed by the scarcity of available funding, France has in fact successfully completed this process. Over the past twenty years, French air power has modernized its hardware and operational practices in significant ways. At the level of theory or doctrine, however, the armée de l'Air has for the most part remained reluctant to articulate a clear vision of air power. Because of the legacy of history, the pressure of interservice rivalries, and the watchful control of nuclear strategy exercised by civilian authorities, the French Air Force has found it as difficult today as in the past to elaborate and publicize its own theory of war and victory. Given both intellectual timid-ity and the obvious disparity in resources between the French Air Force and the U.S. Air Force (USAF), the armée de l'Air charted a pragmatic middle course, reaping the benefits of technological innovation and modernizing as much as it could but without indulging in the overblown claims of some proponents of "military transformation." In other words, it has crafted a posture befitting a middle power that has global ambitions and an excellent technological base but limited resources.

As successive operations from Kosovo to Libya and Mali attest, the overall results have been positive. All these efforts will have been fruitless, however, if the worst effects of the economic and budgetary crisis come to pass. Demilitarization under financial pressure has now replaced the Luftwaffe, the Soviet Union, or some yet unknown technological breakthrough as the clearest threat to the continued relevance of French, and indeed European, air power.

A History of Contrasts

From 1918 to 1940 the armée de l'Air went from being the leading air force in the world to being a prime cause of French defeat, only to reinvent itself, after a period of transition, as an agent of nuclear deterrence. The cyclical nature of French air power's history has had deep repercussions for the military culture of the armée de l'Air.

The Rise and Fall of French Wings

It is hard to find a clearer example of rapid rise and steep decline than that provided by French air power in the two world wars, with the glorious debut of French aviation during the Marne battle and the triumphs of Verdun and 1918 and the infamous defeat of the armée de l'Air in 1940.

Outstripping American air power, French air power was highly ambitious from its inception in the pioneering work of Clément Ader onward and made good on its claims throughout World War I. French planes spotted Alexander von Kluck's columns in September 1914, thus facilitating the French counterattack on the Marne that stopped the German advance. Reconnaissance remained a central function of French air power during the entire war, with half the total number of planes dedicated to that mission in 1918.

For all the belligerents, the Great War presented an opportunity to develop and put into practice, at least in a rudimentary fashion, the whole spectrum of air missions, from reconnaissance to "strategic" bombing (i.e., bombing well beyond the front lines) and from air superiority to battlefield interdiction.[1] The French were often at the forefront of this flurry of tactical and technical innovation. Verdun, for instance, not only was the longest and bloodiest battle in history but also happened to be the first air battle; the French massed fifteen squadrons to contend against the Germans for dominance in the air. Beginning in 1916, the French recognized air superiority as a prerequisite for any significant air operation.[2] By the end of the war, the French high command under Gen. Philippe Pétain, though made up of army generals, had come to two main conclusions. First, aviation ought to be employed en masse and should gain air superiority. Second, aviation not only had great tactical impact because of reconnaissance, aerial spotting for artillery, and close air support (CAS) for infantry, but could also be potentially decisive, as battlefield interdiction made it possible to degrade enemy communications and slow down their reinforcements, thus facilitating the work of ground units.[3] The importance accorded to reconnaissance and interdiction seems eerily prescient, as it foreshadowed respectively German Blitzkrieg tactics in World War II and the modern insistence on intelligence, surveillance, and reconnaissance (ISR).

This intellectual insight was matched by the accomplishments of French air power at the matériel level, as France proved able not only to spur technological innovations and launch countless prototypes but also to mass-produce the best among these designs. France ended the war with the most powerful air force in the world, comprising 90,000 personnel and 331 squadrons totaling more than 3,700 operational planes, all supported by a dynamic aviation industry.[4] At the symbolic level Word War I saw the emergence of a whole series of positive images associated with air power, from the heroic duels between aces that turned fighter pilots into modern "aerial knights" to the notion of mechanized warfare with planes and tanks substituting for personnel and helping to preserve precious French lives.[5]

These realizations notwithstanding, the French aeronautical industry was fragmented, and the air arm of the army was not centrally organized but rather divided according to different missions and command structures—an arrangement that was viable only because of the size of the 1918 air force. As in other countries, peace led to a brutal downsizing of the aviation industry, which the government had not consolidated into a synergistic whole, while army and navy officers soon forgot the military utility of aviation amid the budgetary quarrels of the 1920s. With the benefit of hindsight, it seems that the command arrangements of the victorious French forces, as well as the industrial system of 1918, were brittle. The abject failure of 1940 was thus a product of organizational weaknesses already present in 1918 that were reinforced during the interwar period.

During the 1920s France failed to maintain and preserve its edge in the air. A series of doctrinal and budgetary disputes constricted the development of French air power. This stagnation was compounded by the absence of a dynamic program of industrial and military modernization, which began only in 1937—too late. The first failure was industrial, as successive French governments proved incapable of organizing the numerous aeronautical companies into a coherent industry endowed with the critical mass and ability to innovate, to mass-produce successful prototypes, and to compete in international markets. The second failure occurred at the military level and stemmed from a complete lack of doctrinal and institutional stability. Between 1911 and 1933 the armée de l'Air was reorganized no fewer than fourteen times and completely changed its doctrine several times. As doctrine was linked to the institutional status of the armée de l'Air vis-à-vis its sister services, the actors involved could not address the issue in a dispassionate way. In France, as elsewhere, the need for massed forces to gain air superiority and even Giulio Douhet's theory of strategic bombing were popular ideas among airmen, but the rest of the military regarded these concepts as self-interested falsehoods designed to promote institutional independence of the air arm rather than properly support ground or naval forces according to their needs.

Faced with economic and budgetary troubles, civilian decision makers and the air force leadership spent the interwar period vacillating between promoting the air force as an independent service and acquiescing to a subordinate role to the army and navy as a supporting arm (*arme de coopération*). Even the elevation of French military aviation to the dignity of an independent service in 1933 did not end the debate, as the newly created air force reemphasized the joint dimension and cooperation with the army beginning in 1937. This doctrinal hesitation not only revealed interservice rivalries and the underlying financial tensions that aggravated them but also sharply reflected the country's historic strategic quandary. As both a maritime and a continental power, France would be logically tempted by strategic bombing (all the more so given its promise of quick and bloodless victory after the tremendous losses suffered during the Great War), while the proximity of the German land menace also forced French policy makers into giving priority to air-ground coordination. France simply did not have the financial resources to undergird both of these divergent aspirations.

For all these reasons French military aviation lagged behind that of other nations in both number and quality at the end of the 1930s. Rearmament began in earnest only in 1937 and needed two years to reach a satisfactory level. By then the Second World War had started, and France would have required a few more years to catch up to Germany in terms of organization and equipment. Consequently, the armée de l'Air was no match for the Luftwaffe and moreover had to fight at the worst possible time, caught—like the army—in the midst of its transition to full recovery and modernization.[6] In particular, the French Air Force proved unable to properly spot and attack German troop concentrations in the Ardennes prior to the May 10, 1940, offensive; its fighters could not dispute German air superiority or even protect French troops in the Sedan area; and its attack planes finally proved incapable of hindering the German crossing of the Meuse. In a very real sense, France first lost the 1940 campaign in the air.[7]

The procrastination of the 1930s, the subordination of the air force to the army, the leadership's indecisiveness during the campaign, and the guilt and bitterness over the "strange defeat" left a deep mark on the armée de l'Air. In the postwar period this led to a distinct preference for action and a strong aversion to intellectual debates, the doctrinal often being confused with the doctrinaire.[8] The immediate postwar years until 1960 represented a transition period that did not fundamentally alter this legacy. The armée de l'Air was torn between the Fourth Republic's efforts at nurturing the rebirth of the French aerospace industry; its own dreams of modernization, with the new possibilities offered by heavy bombers and nuclear weapons; and the grimmer reality of day-to-day missions flown on outdated American planes during the decolonization wars of the time—first in Indochina and then in Algeria.

Although underappreciated at the time, the lessons that the French Air Force drew from these wars and the tactics it pioneered have remained relevant to this day. In Indochina the French faced a determined if elusive enemy, apt to hide itself and take full advantage of difficult terrain covered with jungle. The armée de l'Air learned that CAS was effective only when supported by special reconnaissance aircraft. Conversely, interdiction and "strategic" bombing did not work at all. The French were also hindered by limited resources, trying as they were to cover the whole of Indochina with three bomber groups, two reconnaissance squadrons, and two fighter squadrons (augmented to four in 1954). They also lacked ammunition suited to fight dispersed light infantry, qualified personnel for photo interpretation, and most of all, a coherent grid of airstrips and airfields. French forces progressively made up for these various deficiencies toward the end of the war, yet the Vietminh was faster in acquiring and fielding potent antiaircraft artillery. Despite all these issues, the interrogation of enemy prisoners confirmed that they feared aviation above all.[9]

Algeria also validated the primacy of reconnaissance in a counterinsurgency context. This time around the French had undisputed air superiority against a much weaker but even more elusive enemy. In reaction they made extensive use of helicopters and broke new and fertile ground by devising vertical envelopment tactics, imitated a few years later by the Americans in Vietnam. Unfortunately, most of this accumulated experience was lost; as soon as the "revolutionary wars" of the 1950s and 1960s ended, the French Air Force returned to what it considered its real business: high-intensity war.

Preeminence through Subordination: Nuclear Air Power

From 1962 to 1990 the Cold War environment in Europe and French policy as set by Charles de Gaulle dictated that air defense and nuclear deterrence would be the main missions of the armée de l'Air, which allowed the air force to stabilize its identity. The Soviet threat turned air defense into a natural priority. De Gaulle's decision to leave the integrated military structures of the North Atlantic Treaty Organization (NATO) in 1966 did not really affect this priority, as accords signed soon afterward coordinated French and NATO air defense. In fact, throughout the Cold War the armée de l'Air remained more in contact, and therefore more interoperable, with allied forces than were the navy and especially the army.

However, de Gaulle's original decision to develop an independent nuclear deterrent—which led to a confrontation with the United States and the 1966 withdrawal from NATO's integrated structures—did have a tremendous impact on the armée de l'Air and deeply affected its culture, as the service became tasked with implementing the deterrent. The nuclear mission was accorded top priority not only by civilian authorities but also by the air force's leadership, which became deeply committed to the nuclear game. Nuclear weapons indeed determined the air force's strategic nature in three different ways: as the "absolute weapon" in and of themselves, as the armed hand of the president, and as a concrete mission that uniquely justified and manifested the armée de l'Air's independence vis-à-vis its sister services.

The price that the air force paid in return was complete subordination to civilian authority, including on matters of nuclear doctrine, as well as the final renunciation of strategic bombing and similar claims to a war-winning role specific to air power. Despite the advocacy of a few influential air force generals, such as Pierre Gallois, the air force as such had little say in nuclear strategy and simply implemented the civil authorities' policies. Whatever the private misgivings of its members, the armée de l'Air as a military institution was therefore silent. This initially resulted from de Gaulle's defiant attitude toward the military, the armée de l'Air included, since its leadership was heavily represented in the attempted 1961 coup in Algiers. In a broader sense, however, the entire military found itself largely excluded not only from the nuclear realm but also from strategic matters in general since these issues were inevitably linked to the possibility of escalation and therefore to nuclear deterrence and civilian control.[10]

As a uniquely destructive, dangerous, and therefore political weapon, the bomb was subject to particularly stringent supervision by civilian leaders in almost all nuclear-armed countries. In France the specifics of the national posture crafted by de Gaulle strongly reinforced this strategic dimension and the ensuing control of the military. From the beginning France rejected notions such as flexible response, limited nuclear war, conventional deterrence, and even extended deterrence.[11] Invoked only to protect the vital interests of the nation, the French *force de frappe* had a single goal under de Gaulle and retains that role today: to deliver a "final warning" and then, if warning fails, to visit unacceptable damage on the enemy by destroying the equivalent of "one France." This posture of pure deterrence by punishment erects a firewall between peace and war: it defines the bomb as "the weapon of peace" whose sole purpose is to prevent wars, not to win them. As long as the threat of French retaliation remains credible, disparities in conventional military power, whether in numbers or technology, are irrelevant; deterrence holds and war is impossible.[12]

The twin primacies of nuclear deterrence over war and of civilian authority over military expertise impelled the air force to abandon its vision of strategic bombing entirely. This occurred first because the leadership could not understand how bombing could in any meaningful sense be "strategic" if it was not nuclear. Second, and more important, any speculation about actual war would have implied doubts about the national deterrence posture and, incidentally, about civilian preeminence in strategic affairs. In addition, for the public the word "bombing" conjured up images of the destruction of many French cities in the course of the Second World War. As a consequence French political and military authorities have systematically, and to this day, eschewed the word "bombing," preferring "strikes" instead. In this sense nuclear weapons embodied both strategic bombing as a decisive tool and the impossibility of using air power as a war-winning strategy; the "theological" dream of air power had dissipated while coming true.

This contradiction notwithstanding, the armée de l'Air fully embraced its nuclear mission, buying its most advanced aircraft and saving its best pilots for its nuclear component, the Forces aériennes stratégiques (FAS). The FAS fielded its first nuclear squadron of Mirage IV bombers in 1964 and retained them for two decades, progressively phasing them out of their nuclear role in the 1990s. They were replaced first by Mirage 2000Ns and then by Rafales armed with the Air-Sol Moyenne Portée (ASMP), a nuclear-tipped, air-to-ground cruise missile. A force of eighteen intermediate-range ballistic missiles located on the Plateau d'Albion was added in 1971, progressively modernized, and finally abandoned in 1996 as a unilateral disarmament gesture by President Jacques Chirac.

Throughout the period the priority accorded to the nuclear mission negatively affected the modernization of the conventional forces. This impacted the viability of several projects proposed by industry and also degraded the operational performance of the nonnuclear forces: the Force aérienne tactique (FATAC) for tactical forces and the Commandement aérien des forces de défense aérienne (CAFDA) for air defense. During Operation Desert Storm, for instance, only the Mirage 2000N was all-weather capable, but the planes were kept in France for the deterrence mission. Apart from the Mirage III, designed in the late 1950s, which owed part of its fame to Israeli achievements in 1967, French-built planes such as the Jaguar and Mirage F-1 saw action only in minor French operations in Africa and were not widely exported. At the end of the Cold War, only the Mirage 2000 could boast an overall technological and commercial success comparable to that of the Mirage III. In the end, although the period from the 1960s to the 2000s unquestionably proved a time of great development for France's air power and its aerospace industry, the lack of sufficient funding prevented successive governments from fully modernizing conventional forces and from catching up with U.S. technological and tactical developments of the 1970s.[13]

The French Air Force's rich but troubled history during the twentieth century translated into a distinct military culture. As a community the armée de l'Air has been dominated by fighter pilots bent on air superiority and distrustful of theoretical discussions. The institution has consequently encouraged improvisation as well as industrial and technological innovations, often favoring a policy of developing prototypes, but has refrained from engaging in awkward debates over doctrine and strategy. The French population and elites have supported the generic concept of air power, but only up to a point and far less than the concept of nuclear deterrence.

The Theory and Practice of French Air Power in the Intervention Age

The two decades that separated the 1991 Gulf War from the interventions in Libya and Mali were a time of tremendous change for the French military. The Soviet Union—the raison d'être for the military's overall format, force structure, and strategic posture—had disappeared, but multiplying crises that called for intervention led French authorities to professionalize the military and rebalance its procurement priorities between nuclear and conventional forces. In this framework the modernization of air power received special political attention despite inadequate budgets. Once the French Air Force had digested the unpleasant surprises of the Desert Storm campaign, it successfully adapted to the practical demands of the "intervention age": frequent military operations by Western, often U.S.-led coalitions that enjoyed a preponderance of power but were constrained by the political restrictions inherent in limited war. Conversely, the French military remained mostly unmoved by the ideology of transformation as advocated in the United States, while the armée de l'Air continued to wall itself off in "doctrinal silence" despite its considerable achievements.

Shock in the Gulf

The 1991 Gulf War not only marked the end of the bipolar world order but also signaled the dawn of a new strategic age, often referred to as the post–Cold War era but, as noted previously, more appropriately characterized as an age of intervention. Involving a U.S.-led international coalition intervening against a single "rogue state" via a limited conventional clash, Desert Storm bore many of the hallmarks typical of contemporary conflicts: it was expeditionary; it was asymmetrical, at least in terms of power and capabilities; and it installed Washington and the American military in their new roles of global security provider and military model. Finally, it brilliantly demonstrated the centrality of air power and helped launch the revolution in military affairs (RMA) school of thought.

In addition to these general characteristics, the 1991 war proved a wake-up call for French political authorities, the French military, and particularly the air force.[14] To begin with, the performance of the armée de l'Air was not very impressive. Having been prevented from participating in operational planning (to safeguard French independence, as defined by President François Mitterrand); lacking all-weather capable aircraft, laser-guided bombs (LGBs), and cruise missiles; and having its best equipment confined to the nuclear watch in France, the armée de l'Air was at a distinct disadvantage and was completely taken by surprise by the realities of the Gulf War. Since Iraq was a great importer of French weapon systems, the French prepared to fight in planes that the enemy possessed as well. As a result, most French air superiority fighters (Mirage 2000s) guarded the southern flank of the Saudi peninsula. Meanwhile, the Jaguar attack planes involved in the initial daylight attacks against Al Jaber Air Base suffered so much damage from Iraqi antiaircraft artillery fire that the coalition deemed it best not to deploy them anymore.[15] For what was supposedly one of the best air forces in the West, this was quite disappointing.

Not only the military but also the upper ranks in the Ministry of Defense (MOD) and the political leadership learned a great deal from the Gulf War experience. French political elites realized the extent of France's dependence on the United States for satellite communications and strategic intelligence. French forces had no way of independently checking the information they received. After the 1991 war, possessing "national technical means" became a quasi-obsession. At the military level the lessons to be dissected and acted upon were equally important and more numerous. The armée de l'Air had experienced firsthand the power generated by a modern command, control, planning, and battle management system and its associated procedures, such as the air tasking order (ATO). Tactically, French airmen observed the devastating effect of precision strikes and the positive implications of standoff attacks in terms of force protection and casualty avoidance and even caught a glimpse of the importance of ISR and battle damage assessment (BDA). More generally, Desert Storm was for the armée de l'Air a defining if negative moment, through which it rediscovered war and the old theology of air power as a winning weapon, with Col. John A. Warden III and precision strikes replacing Douhet and classic strategic bombing theory.

Desert Storm demonstrated to French authorities in no uncertain terms that the strategic environment was changing fast and that adaptation was necessary.[16] Strategically, the disappearance of the Soviet Union that same year confirmed the reduced salience of nuclear weapons on the international stage, while operations over Iraq, Somalia, and Bosnia-Herzegovina all revealed the newfound centrality of coercive air power in successful peace-keeping operations. In this new age, intervention had displaced deterrence as the currency of international influence.

Realizing at the same time that genuine capability gaps now existed between the United States and its European allies and that these gaps mattered much more than before, Defense Minister Pierre Joxe was quick to react and embarked on a series of far-reaching, though discreet, reforms directly after the 1991 conflict. The MOD regrouped diverse branches into a new military intelligence directorate (Direction du renseignement militaire, or DRM), launched France's first military space program with the optical Helios satellites, and took steps first to acquire U.S. LGBs and fit them on French planes and then to develop the nation's own precision-guided munitions (PGMs). More generally, the air force decided to opt for quality rather than quantity by reducing the overall number of its planes, officially abandoning the long-held objective of maintaining 450 combat-ready planes—an ambition that in truth had already been eroded in the 1980s by the lack of adequate funding and the slowing pace of modernization.[17] By the time of the conflict in Kosovo—or in a mere eight years—the armée de l'Air had indeed caught up to the USAF as it existed in 1991, except that U.S. technology and operational practice had evolved in the meantime, for instance, with bombs guided by the Global Positioning System (GPS) complementing LGBs as necessary, such as in situations of degraded visibility.

The Failure of Transformation as Ideology and the Doctrinal Silence of the French Air Force

The new possibilities offered by air power were naturally deeply alluring to airmen everywhere, including within the armée de l'Air, as they seemed to herald a true revolution in warfare while demonstrating or restoring the primacy of air power.[18] Yet French airmen were prevented from advocating these ideas widely and even from publicly and strongly supporting them within the defense establishment. By and large, the ideology of transformation, much like the earlier discourse on strategic bombing, failed to take root in France.

As discussed previously, bad memories of World War II combined with civilian preeminence over nuclear matters had made it anathema to speak of any nonnuclear theory of air power as "strategic." Absent a national tradition of strategic bombing that predated nuclear weapons and of a strategic culture strongly oriented toward technology, like that of the United States, it is no wonder that France initially met the RMA with skepticism.[19] Aside from the national procurement agency (Délégation générale de l'armement, or DGA) and some branches of the military—the armée de l'Air especially—France did not accept military transformation either as a reality or as an objective, and the concept received little attention in the national media or within decision-making circles. Actually, French strategic culture and a traditional measure of political defiance vis-à-vis the United States ensured that reactions to the RMA were mostly critical.[20] In this respect the traditional antagonism between proponents of land power and advocates of air power was probably the most salient manifestation of transformation as ideology in the French strategic debate of the 1990s and 2000s.[21] As in other, comparable nations, the two sides traded arguments based on examples such as the Kosovo War, the 2006 war in Lebanon, and most recently, the conflicts in Afghanistan, Libya, and then Mali. The armée de l'Air was probably on the winning side in the 1990s but stood more on the defensive during the "counterinsurgency decade" that followed, at least until the NATO operations in Libya. Yet budgetary problems made these disagreements more acute than they would have been on purely intellectual grounds.

Interservice rivalries and, more important, national strategic culture ensured that there simply was no public space for articulating a theory of air power as a war-winning asset in its own right. John Warden's theory has remained popular in the armée de l'Air to this day, but this timid revival of air theories failed to gain wide acceptance beyond select communities of airmen and a few specialized publications, and it was often perceived within defense circles as a transparent attempt to promote institutional primacy in the wake of the Gulf and Kosovo Wars.[22]

As a result of this absence of theory and of the legacy of the 1930s, the armée de l'Air has distinguished itself from other Western air forces for almost five decades by its remarkable "doctrinal silence," apart from minor and mostly internal documents.[23] After failed attempts in 1998 and 2003, the armée de l'Air in 2008 finally released the Air Force Concept, more or less on a par with the USAF capstone document, at the initiative of Gen. Stéphane Abrial, then the air force chief of staff. Unlike the Royal Air Force, for which the decade between 1998 and

2008 was a period of doctrinal plenty, the French Air Force found it internally and externally difficult to define and articulate its vision for the future. Debates over doctrine, when not stifled outright, took place strictly within the service. This, in turn, made it difficult to consider out-of-the-box alternatives to the existing aircraft inventory, such as bombers, either as low-end "bomb trucks" or as high-end defense-penetrating advanced platforms. In this respect the influence of indigenous industry partly explains the primacy of multirole fighters, the choice of versatility and broad-spectrum capabilities over specialized families of planes, and the initial absence of official interest in innovations such as stealth aircraft or unmanned aerial vehicles (UAVs).

Transformation in Practice: The Normalization of the Armée de l'Air

The French Air Force has been racing against time since the 1990s. It had to modernize by phasing out its old planes and buying the Rafale, and it also had to adapt to the new context of U.S.-led international coalitions and to incorporate technological innovations that lay at the heart of interoperability (Link 16, modern sensors, PGMs) and therefore of strategic influence. The air force had to accomplish this despite an indifferent public and often distracted decision makers, who on the one hand did not always properly fund the transformation of French air power, while on the other frequently committed French forces to international operations. Despite insufficient budgets and the failure of transformation as an ideological flagship, the armée de l'Air managed in practice to participate successfully in Western interventions and to complete a significant part of its planned modernization.

Transforming for expeditionary coalition warfare depended on a minimal level of political support, which the air force obtained for two main reasons. First, French authorities may have been impervious to the ideology of transformation, but they recognized fairly early the potential of air power as a political tool. The flexibility and versatility inherent in air power, the ability of standoff precision attacks to limit both exposure and collateral damage, the importance of air power for reconnaissance and for the collection of national-level intelligence, and the strategic freedom of maneuver that accrued from these capabilities all received a much warmer reception than technological prowess per se.[24] Second, the political leadership had always regarded the French Air Force as intrinsically linked to the aeronautics industry, itself perceived as a national priority of the highest order for reasons of strategic and technological independence. The track record of French air operations of the past twenty years only reinforced this political support.

The Kosovo War proved that France had taken the lessons of 1991 to heart. Less than a decade had elapsed since the disappointing performance of French air power in the Persian Gulf, yet the armée de l'Air became the second-greatest contributor to Operation Allied Force after the USAF. France provided 98 planes (76 combat planes) out of a total of 786 allied planes and conducted 12 percent of the offensive sorties, 20 percent of the reconnaissance sorties, and 8.5 percent of the total number of sorties.[25] The French contribution almost matched that of Italy and the United Kingdom combined. Of course, the armée de l'Air offered few assets for electronic reconnaissance or air defense and none at all for airborne command and control or suppression of enemy air defenses (SEAD). It also had to mobilize most of its all-weather-capable attack aircraft (the Mirage 2000D) for night operations, using pairs of older Jaguars or Super Etendards for daytime operations. The low number of laser-designating pods and the absence of SEAD capabilities and of noncooperative target recognition (NCTR) systems on board the Mirage 2000s fitted with Radar Doppler Impulse (RDI), unlike the later Mirage 2000-5, represented real constraints on the French Air Force. Most of all, French political authorities sorely regretted not having yet fielded cruise missiles, as deploying even a few of them seemed to have opened to the British the possibility of participating in U.S. strategic planning prior to the operation.

Despite these limitations French participation was regarded as a political and military success, erasing the bad memories of 1991. Afghanistan, by contrast, always remained a minor operation for the armée de l'Air, involving on average six of its planes, though sometimes up to a dozen or more. Accordingly, that conflict received much less public and political attention. Since France did not take part in the U.S.-led intervention against Iraq, however, Afghanistan offered the only opportunity for the French Air Force to familiarize itself with new U.S. procedures for CAS and fire integration and gave the air force its first recent experience of air operations in a counterinsurgency setting. During the Afghanistan mission the armée de l'Air increased its experience with UAVs, deploying its Harfang (derived from the Israeli Heron) to the theater, and also acquired Remotely Operated Video Enhanced Receiver (ROVER) systems.[26]

Yet the heyday of the current French Air Force, and its most telling achievement, came in 2011 with the intervention over Libya. By the end of August, French air power, of which naval aviation represented a third, had contributed forty-five hundred sorties, accounting for 25 percent of all coalition sorties and 35 percent of strike sorties.[27] This highly significant contribution essentially remained at the same level until the conflict ended two months later. By then French planes had conducted fifty-six hundred sorties in the same proportions as before and had in addition launched more than forty helicopter raids that destroyed six hundred targets and represented 90 percent of coalition helicopter strikes.[28] These figures more or less match NATO accounts, which acknowledged a total of 26,530 sorties, including 9,710 strike sorties, for Operation Unified Protector.[29]

Beyond numbers or the opening air strikes on Benghazi on March 19, what really matters is that France, along with Great Britain, played a key part and was on the front line during the whole seven months of the operation.[30] Of course, the USAF played a crucial enabling role, first by clearing Libyan air defense systems during the SEAD part of Operation Odyssey Dawn and second by providing ISR assets and tankers throughout the campaign. Yet France and Britain accepted their role as the nations with the greatest political and military exposure, going so far as to engage in dynamic targeting, to put helicopters in harm's way, to deliver weapons to the rebels, and to deploy special forces on the ground.[31] France also mobilized most of its intelligence assets and a good portion of its naval capabilities. Dispatching thirty sorties per day over a period of months as part of an enduring operation, France probably committed most of its available air power to the operation, excluding the minimum numbers needed for air defense, nuclear deterrence, and a few residual deployments elsewhere. The French Air Force and naval aviation also used SCALP-EG cruise missiles for the first time and committed Rafale planes in nonpermissive situations, thus demonstrating the platform's self-protection capability and versatility.

Despite all these significant successes, the modernized French Air Force of today still lags behind the USAF on several important counts. Libya highlighted several capability gaps and shortcomings in specialized personnel, such as intelligence specialists and targeteers, but even more in equipment. Transport and refueling aircraft, SEAD capabilities, UAVs, and ISR assets in general were all in short supply, and in these areas France relied heavily on American help. In 2013 Operation Serval in Mali revealed the same weaknesses, with the exception of SEAD missions, which were not required. French progress was sometimes hampered by a lack of sufficient assets for transportation, refueling, and persistent ISR. While the Gulf War showed French authorities the pressing need to invest in strategic intelligence collection, the difficulties encountered in Libya and Mali highlighted the importance of tactical intelligence for ISR, BDA, and the ability to engage targets of opportunity. Together, these two operations have made a strong case for acquiring medium-altitude long-endurance (MALE) drones.

Mali especially showed beyond doubt the necessity of improving real-time ISR and dynamic targeting operations and of learning to deal with small, nonindustrial targets, such as groups of individuals. It also proved that air power could help a limited initial number of special operators (including some from the armée de l'Air) to first halt and then, with the help of French forces prepositioned in Chad and other African countries and of reinforcements from France, defeat a much larger contingent of heavily armed insurgents riding in hundreds of pickup trucks. Beyond the crucial first days, air power was also instrumental in supporting a fast counteroffensive carried out by a few thousand troops. With a total of 2,300 sorties from January to April 2013, including 530 strikes and CAS missions, airplanes and helicopters from the air force and the army together provided a constant umbrella of reconnaissance and protection to the French ground offensive.[32] Sometimes by protecting the flank of advancing French columns through "push CAS," sometimes by supporting airborne and air assault operations, and always by engaging the enemy with precision strikes directed by forward air controllers from the Commando parachutiste de l'air (CPA) 10 or 20, air power truly paved the way for Operation Serval and probably helped redefine how strategic raids should be conducted in the early twenty-first century.[33]

Bleak Horizons

In spite of some glaring deficiencies, the armée de l'Air has essentially succeeded in making the transition from a Cold War service focused on nuclear deterrence and air defense to a first-class expeditionary and multirole force. Yet despite these considerable achievements, it is now in danger of suffering a significant decline: either reverting to secondary status or becoming a hollow force. Like its sister services, it is hitting a financial wall, whose effects it will not be able to surmount until the end of the decade, if ever.

Doctrine, technology, personnel development—all these elements are crucial in creating a competent air force, yet they remain dependent variables to the one truly decisive criterion: capital investment. In a service as dependent on technology as a modern air force, the old saying of the French kings "pas d'argent, pas de Suisses" (no money, no Swiss mercenaries) is more true than ever. Always a rich man's sport, air power has of late become even more expensive at a time when public finances across the West suffer severe restrictions. Rather than the rise of a peer competitor or even the spread of advanced integrated air defense systems, French air power first and foremost faces the risk of self-destruction through overpricing. This is compounded by the aggregation of delays, program reductions, and other debatable or downright poor decisions made during the past twenty years.

Table 1. Order of Battle of the French Air Force, 2012

Role	Total	Aircraft
Strategic forces		
Fighter ground attack	45	25 Mirage 2000N; 20 Rafale B F3
Tanker/transport	11	11 C-135FR
Tanker	3	3 KC-135 Stratotanker
Combat brigade		
Air defense fighter	73 (c. 50)*	22 Mirage 2000-5; 12 Mirage 2000-B; 39 Mirage 2000-C
Fighter ground attack	143 (c. 120)* (+68)	61 Mirage 2000-D; 6 Mirage F-1B; 22 Mirage F1-CT (all of them being retired); 17 Rafale B F3, 37 Rafale C F3(+ Navy: 34 Rafale M F3, 34 Super Etendard Modernisé)
ISR (ASW)	29 (+15)	29 Mirage F-1CR; (+ Navy: 15 Atlantique 2)
Electronic intelligence	2	2 C-160G Gabriel (ESM)
Training and aggressor assets	91 (80)*	91 Alpha Jet
UAV/ISR/Heavy	4	4 Harfang
Air mobility brigade		
Tanker/transport	20	20 C-160 NG Transall
Transport	107	14 Hercules; 24 C-160 Transall; 24 CN-235M; 5 DHC-6-300, 25 EMB-121, 9 TBM-700, 6 Airbus
Air space control brigade		
AEW&C	4(+3)	4 E-3F Sentry(+ Navy: 3 E-2C Hawkeye)
Air training command		
Training	48	5 CAP 10; 18 Grob G120A-F; 25 TB-30 Epsilon

Source: Military Balance 2013 (London: IISS, 2013). Based on 2012 figures.

*Indicates 2013 figures taking into account retiring aircraft.

None of this is specific to France or indeed Europe, as the same trends can be observed throughout the West. They simply hit middle powers, such as Britain and France, the hardest because up to now these nations had still tried to maintain a top-quality yet full-spectrum force. Whereas the United States, enjoying a large quantitative cushion and a significant qualitative edge, occupies a category of its own, smaller air forces have already accepted the need for specialization or deep cuts in numbers. Accordingly, the fate of the armée de l'Air, which might essentially dwindle from a current force of almost three hundred combat planes to fewer than two hundred, could presage future trends for Western air power in general, as table 1 illustrates.

Between a Rock and a Hard Place

There is something profoundly unfair in the current and future situation of the armée de l'Air. Just when it has not only shown its ability to reform, adapt, and innovate as an organization but also proved its worth on the battlefield, the French Air Force may receive an especially severe blow.

Although made much worse and more acute by the current financial and economic crisis, this budgetary squeeze was long in the making and has many causes. Defense, at least in European countries, has been in a structural state of financial deficit since the end of the Cold War because of the combined effect of diminishing budgets, large inherited infrastructure, and the growing cost of weapon systems; the phenomenon of "military inflation" has been made even worse by the pace of technological innovation during the past twenty years. In France, defense accounted for 3.3 percent of the gross domestic product (GDP) in 1990, but that share has been roughly halved over the course of two decades and could fall further in the future. Meanwhile, the per unit cost of modern planes, such as the Rafale, has been multiplied by a factor of two or three in comparison to that of the previous generation (Mirage 2000); the difference would probably be even greater if research and development costs were included.[34] The increasing pace of overall technological progress; the cost of adapting innovative technologies to military requirements, with equipment produced in small numbers; and finally, the complexities of system integration have resulted in an acceleration of Norman Augustine's sixteenth law, according to which the unit cost of new military aircraft grows exponentially as defense budgets grow linearly. Accordingly, military modernization has turned into a ruinously expensive business. Declining resources and soaring prices have thus combined to squeeze defense capabilities and put the military services under unprecedented strain.

At the same time air power has become the weapon of choice politically and the tool of first resort to manage international crises. The coupling of air platforms and modern information technology has allowed for unprecedented levels of precision, speed, and standoff attacks that ensure a high degree of control over collateral damage and almost no casualties among friendly forces. No longer confined to its origins as a weapon of total war, air power has proved its mettle as a tool of crisis management.[35] Despite its mounting costs air power has indeed remained a tempting proposition and has probably become even more alluring after a decade of frustrating occupation in Afghanistan.

Beyond their traditional missions, such as air defense, European air forces have tried to acquire new and significant capabilities and to refine existing ones, whether for interdiction, CAS, space, or ISR—especially persistent surveillance. Deploying the full panoply of old and new toys, such as PGMs and drones, thus became mandatory for leading European air forces, such as the armée de l'Air, precisely when lowered resources made it more and more difficult to catch up with the innovations pioneered by the USAF. This problem was compounded not only by the imperative of modernizing at an accelerated pace but also by the demands of readiness engendered by the proliferation of operations in terms of training, spare parts, munitions, and C4ISR (command, control, communications, computers, intelligence, surveillance, and reconnaissance). European forces in essence had to choose among modernization, recapitalization, and readiness, according to their available resources and national priorities. Faced with this difficult dilemma throughout the late 1990s and early 2000s, France chose to sacrifice recapitalization, financing modernization and readiness through expedients (for instance, temporarily equipping only a low fraction of the force with modern pods) and a reduction of equipment and personnel. In other words, the armée de l'Air, like all other Western air forces, traded off quantity (numbers) for quality (technology).

Recapitalization would naturally have proved impossible on a plane-by-plane basis, given the size of Cold War arsenals and the reduced level of resources in the years that have followed. Yet policy makers deliberately accelerated this trend. The government's 2008 "White Paper on Defense and National Security" explicitly advocated a significant downsizing of the French military: fifty-four thousand jobs were to be cut between 2008 and 2015 to finance modernization.[36] Once the cuts were effected, the gains resulting from the reduction in infrastructure and personnel costs were to be reinvested in the procurement portion of the budget, raising it to around €17 billion a year. Explicitly presented as a trade-off, this bargain was supposed to ease the military's acceptance of the cuts. As a result the armée de l'Air lost 25 percent of its workforce and twelve bases between 2008 and 2012.[37] Base closures and personnel reductions were scheduled to end in 2015, but the new 2013 white paper and programming law (*Loi de programmation militaire*) have decreed otherwise: the armée de l'Air will have to close a few more bases and to cut its personnel numbers by a few thousands. Thus the downward trend of the past twenty years seems to have no end in sight.

Hitting the Budgetary Wall

The financial and economic crisis that has struck Europe has greatly worsened the situation. As the second-largest economy in the euro zone, France has had to underwrite the single currency by supporting the ailing economies of southern Europe, but the nation must now bring its own deficit back to manageable levels. Scrutinized by the European Commission, its European partners (Germany in particular), and international markets, France has had no choice but to embark on an austerity program designed to balance the budget by 2017. This has translated into an unprecedented effort at trimming public expenditures—an effort that does not spare defense. As of this writing defense will be asked to contribute with an annual budget frozen at €31.4 billion until 2016 at best, which means that it will be reduced each year by inflation. In total the cuts will amount to 8 percent or more of the budgets as previously planned. In addition, part of the yearly budget will depend on extraordinary resources (sales of wave bands or real estate) that might fail to materialize. What is beyond doubt is that the defense budget will contract in real terms, dipping below 1.5 percent of GDP (pensions excluded) for at least a few years, and that the 2013–15 period will be especially hard.

Accordingly, the air force will have to revise the modernization plans laid out in 2008, perhaps drastically so. This revision will probably involve both postponements of acquisitions and reductions in absolute numbers. As envisioned in 2008, the armée de l'Air would have boasted a sizable inventory in 2020, comprising mainly 230 Rafales, 67 Mirage 2000Ds, 50 A400M strategic airlift assets, 14 multirole tanker transport (MRTT) aircraft, and a dozen MALE drones. The air force will not reach those levels in that time frame, and probably not ever. The 2013 white paper thus states that French air power will comprise 225 fighter planes (naval aviation included), 12 tankers, 12 MALE drones, and around 50 transport aircraft—without ever specifying the type of planes or the time frame, which probably indicates that modernization will be slower than originally planned.[38] More generally, modernization across the board and through constant innovation will be unsustainable with such a reduced level of resources, even when stretched out over three decades or more. Given the accumulated delays, deferred bills, and underfinanced capabilities, the effect of the economic crisis and resulting budgetary adjustment will in all likelihood be severe.

For the past twenty years, the armée de l'Air has held its own in terms of readiness and modernization, slowly sacrificing recapitalization in the process. With the crisis the air force must solve an even more difficult equation, as it will prove impossible to finance even two out of the three components. First, the 50 percent reduction that took place between the Cold War force of six hundred planes and today's three hundred may be followed by a further 20 percent to 30 percent reduction. It is not clear that at the end of the process, the armée de l'Air will be able to field more than two hundred planes in the longer term or even that the more versatile and capable Rafale, acquired in such low numbers, will cover as broad a spectrum of missions as the air force covered at the end of the Cold War. Second, the modernization and readiness of even this much smaller force will not be sustainable across the board.

How Few Are Enough?

The arguments in favor of sacrificing quantity for quality are well known. Although these arguments apply to all the military services, navies and air forces—relying as they do on technological superiority—seem especially prone to accepting such trade-offs. It is also true that strict numerical comparisons are misleading, as ratios do not look so unfavorable when operational functions are compared. In other words, a multirole plane such as the Rafale is worth several planes of previous generations. In air-to-air combat a 4.5-generation plane or better can engage several older-generation planes, and this rough standard is perhaps even more applicable at the operational level, since the ISR and ground attack capabilities of the Rafale were previously covered by several different types of older planes.

Yet the reality is less straightforward when viewed from a strategic perspective, as it should be. Indeed, when successive reductions bring a significant air force down to around two hundred planes, especially taking into account the spectrum of mandatory missions, a threshold effect manifests itself. As a former chief of the French Air Staff readily admitted before a parliamentary commission, quantity does matter, even for such a high-technology service as an air force.[39] The lower the total number of planes, however capable they may be, the truer this becomes. This law of threshold effects is even more salient for the air services of middle powers that cannot afford the quantitative order of battle cushion that would ensure a safety net, yet have a mandate to cover the full range of missions. In the French case it is not clear how the air force could absorb another 25 percent or so reduction and remain capable of performing the tasks demanded of it today. Once the requirements of nuclear deterrence, homeland defense and safety (*posture permanente de sécurité*), and training are taken into account, the remaining budget is inadequate to sustain the capabilities required for expeditionary missions, whether steady-state or exceptional. Even assuming that some future stabilization operations could do without any air cover, the total number of aircraft that could be freed up for a single major operation remains equally at risk of becoming insignificant.

The 2008 white paper called for seventy planes to be available for the high-intensity phase of an operation, amounting to perhaps a hundred sorties a day. This is admittedly not much, when compared to the fifteen hundred sorties a day of the 1991 Gulf War or the nine hundred daily sorties that characterized the most intensive phase of Allied Force in 1999. As previously noted, the Libya operation never reached those levels, which was probably good for the French Air Force, given the duration of the campaign. If the overall French aircraft inventory were to fall by 25 percent, however, the reduction would directly and disproportionately affect the number of planes available for expeditionary operations, as nuclear deterrence and safety missions normally take precedence. Even assuming both a degree of overlap between the planes earmarked for these different missions and a willingness to accept a certain level of risk regarding the protection of French air space or even deterrence, the French Air Force would still have far fewer "actionable" aircraft left, thus degrading either readiness or the level of ambition for expeditionary missions (the number of missions the French can simultaneously conduct and their capabilities in those missions). Indeed the "operational contract" of the armée de l'Air for a single major operation has been set by the 2013 white paper at forty-five planes, which amounts to a 35 percent reduction.[40]

The solution would then seem rather straightforward: instead of modernizing the force across the board, which can be financed only by a further reduction in the overall inventory, it would seem logical to buy fewer Rafales and use the money saved to retain a greater number of older planes, for instance—as the 2008 white paper envisaged—the Mirage 2000D, whose airframe is fairly recent. Yet this short- to midterm solution might run afoul of long-term priorities, as it could endanger the continued production of the Rafale. In turn this would jeopardize the viability and possibly the independence of the armée de l'Air, which would be unable to rely on a domestic source to provide spare parts or increase production if a worsening international environment required a rapid buildup. In other words, the short-term operational needs of the air force and the longer-term interests of the defense industry may not be entirely compatible, and a delicate balancing act will be needed.

Discriminate Dominance

These concerns about the defense industrial base notwithstanding, it has become apparent that modernization across the board with multirole platforms is beyond reach. Accordingly, the way ahead for French air power, and possibly for Western air power in general, will involve mixed fleets, with varying proportions of modern and older planes, differentiated training for pilots, and overall specialization, in order to preserve the "tip of the spear" while retaining numbers that are not so low that they restrict the ability to conduct several missions simultaneously. This reintroduction of a degree of specialization might be regarded either as a return to the past, signaling the failure of the choices made during the past twenty years, or as the only possible way forward, ideally able to deliver an acceptable balance between quality and quantity and allowing for "discriminate dominance."

Given the per unit cost of acquiring, operating, and maintaining modern aircraft, it seems quite sensible to fund a limited number of high-end planes while also retaining in the fleet a good number of workhorses from older generations. Even the United States has decided to buy only a limited number of F-22s and in parallel to keep a much larger number of older planes. It is not even clear that the F-35 will not in the end follow the same path, even though it was conceived of as an "advanced workhorse." In the case of France, retaining part of the

Mirage 2000D fleet seems justifiable on three grounds. First, the cost of modernizing some Mirage 2000Ds (or Mirage 2000-5s) on average would amount to only a fraction of the cost of procuring new Rafales, depending on the extent of modernization sought and whether or not these planes are equipped with minimal air-to-air (2000D) or air-to-ground (2000-5) capabilities.[41] Consequently, reducing the overall number of Rafales by a few units, either by cutting the planned acquisition of a new batch or by slowing procurement, could allow the armée de l'Air to upgrade several dozen Mirages, thus preserving overall numbers and somewhat mitigating the worst threshold effects described previously. Second, as the Mirage 2000 is cheaper to operate, it seems ideally suited to low-risk missions and secondary tasks, including protection of the homeland from terrorist attacks that follow the 9/11 model.

In turn these routine tasks that do not demand cutting-edge technology or training make it possible to tailor pilot training. It is expensive to train pilots for the most demanding missions or phases of an operation. Typically, "opening" the theater through SEAD or destruction of enemy air defenses (DEAD) operations or an attack in depth requires the best possible machines and pilots, lest the mission fail or entail unacceptable costs. However, not all the capabilities deployed for a given operation must meet the most demanding standards; after all, as soon as the enemy air defense system has been overcome, workhorses should be capable of handling ordinary strikes or air superiority missions. If need be, as in the case of a long campaign, such as the conflict in Libya or Kosovo, the training of pilots in the second tier could be accelerated so that they are progressively brought up to the standards of those in the first tier.[42] Called "differentiation" in the 2013 defense white paper, this logic is now officially accepted.[43] Extending the use of simulation and relying on reserves offer other possible avenues for savings.

Conclusion

Even assuming that the economic and budgetary situation of France improves so that the armée de l'Air is not subjected to flat or declining budgets over a long period, the service will still have to develop a course of action, acquisition plans, and budgets for operations and maintenance that are financially sustainable over time. The phenomenon known as "military inflation," whereby the cost of each new generation of equipment increases faster than the cost of goods subject to general inflation, means that the air forces of middle powers will be unable to afford technological superiority across the board and at all times. These air forces will have to choose not only between quality and quantity but also between multirole capability and specialization (for air superiority or ground attack) or degrees thereof. Choices regarding when to pursue or forgo the marginal gains of technological superiority will also present themselves with regard to the range of missions given to UAVs and unmanned combat air systems and the appropriate mix of manned and unmanned platforms. Given that a surge in defense spending seems highly unlikely even after France has overcome the worst of the present economic crisis, smart and realistic planning is indispensable. For the armée de l'Air and several of its peers, judicious choices might preserve the future, whereas poor decisions will rapidly lead to terminal decline, keeping in mind that below a certain minimum level of resources, no solution, however ingenious, can be effective.

TWO

German Air Power

Ready to Participate in Joint and Combined Operations

Holger H. Mey

Germany's central location in Europe has always shaped the country's strategic thinking and German Air Force (Luftwaffe) planning, including after the end of the Cold War. Unlike France and Great Britain, Germany has neither aircraft carriers nor naval landing forces (marines). As a major land power in the center of Europe, Germany used to see itself as the only large European nation with a clear focus on the European, as opposed to the global, theater of operations. Now that Germany is "surrounded by friends," its defense policy has only slowly begun to reflect the reality of a more distant European periphery of unstable regions, from the former Soviet Union to the Middle East and North Africa. Today the Luftwaffe operates beyond German territory, both within and outside Europe. Its missions range from air policing in the Baltic states to transport and surveillance in the Balkans and around the Mediterranean, air operations in Afghanistan, Patriot deployments along the Turkish-Syrian border, and support to French operations in Mali. Of course, the Luftwaffe continues to secure German air space 24/7 within the integrated air defenses of the North Atlantic Treaty Organization (NATO).

By 2030 European air space is expected to be three times as congested as it is today. More accurate and longer range missiles are proliferating at an alarming rate, and nuclear weapons are affecting the strategic calculations of global actors in new ways.[1] German air power faces new challenges, difficult decisions, and disruptive technologies that present both new threats and new opportunities. At the same time the financial crisis and competing budget priorities put defense spending lower on the nation's agenda. The future of German air power will be about learning to do more with less.

The Luftwaffe believes its role is growing disproportionately to those of the other services. Its forward-looking 2012 mission statement, *Air Power 2030*, articulated the expectation that Germany's air force will take on a far larger number of tasks in the future as an important allied and joint partner, if not as an independent force. Throughout the ongoing transformation of the Luftwaffe, discussions have centered on the future. Four areas of competence that continue to receive particular attention in these discussions, and that this chapter will explore further, are air-surface integration, missile defense, the military use of space, and unmanned aircraft.[2] All of these focus areas bring their own sets of dilemmas and conceptual challenges.

As the Luftwaffe undergoes yet another in a long series of reorganizations, it must perform a rigorous analysis to determine its appropriate roles. However, interservice, interagency, and international competition complicate any effort to achieve a more rational division of labor among the military services. At the same time, as jointness has gained greater legitimacy, these rivalries have shifted from the realms of doctrine and strategy to a more narrow focus on increasingly scarce resources. Indeed, shrinking defense budgets and improving network technologies make the possibility of greater integration ever more attractive and necessary.

As important as systematic thinking is a keen understanding of emerging opportunities and emerging threats. On the one hand, new technologies and new international common interests will allow a more rational sharing of burdens. On the other hand, new airborne threats create unprecedented organizational, doctrinal, and technological demands. From unmanned aerial vehicles (UAVs) to cyber attacks to satellite disruption, the Luftwaffe confronts a constantly changing threat environment. At the same time German air power must also contend with the changing capabilities of its allies and neighbors—including their acquisition of the U.S. F-35 Joint Strike Fighter. Germany must keep pace in order to maintain its influence within NATO.

NATO has demonstrated that it offers enduring value in moving even intransigent members toward greater cooperation and exertion. European roles and geography have also motivated cooperation, as evidenced by the increasing interdependence of British and French air and naval power. Anglo-French cooperation in Libya and Mali did not go unnoticed in the Luftwaffe. Whether Germany will ever employ air power in such a manner remains uncertain, although the Luftwaffe can, if asked to do so, generate a sortie rate equivalent to that of the British or the French. However, this remains strictly a political decision.

Conceptual Background

Air power is an increasingly mobile, extremely flexible, and (thanks to air refueling) long-range capability that can use many of the same assets for multiple purposes to enable a rapidly broadening spectrum of operations. Germany, highly endowed with scientific, engineering, and system-integration skills, has a special ability to add to the totality of NATO air and space power. If understood well and applied appropriately, air power will also become an increasingly essential element of Bundeswehr military operations, whether for defense, expeditionary operations, or global engagement.

With regard to the international campaign in Afghanistan, some critics, particularly in Germany, have argued that the role of air power has been limited. They point out that, for instance, for the price of one Eurofighter the armed forces could have bought a large number of armored fighting and transport vehicles, which were badly needed—unlike the Eurofighter, which was allegedly useless in such a conflict. More generally, until a few years ago critics contended that traditional ("classical") military power, including air power, was of little use in combating terrorists or in asymmetric conflicts. Such thinking fails to consider the new possibilities for air power in supporting ground forces—and the added capability that air power gives ground forces to achieve their objectives.

Air, land, and naval forces sometimes oversell their value. They often disregarded the principles of jointness. In reality, air power does not make ground forces largely irrelevant, nor can ground forces perform their tasks without air coverage. Hence, transport aircraft, such as the A400M, and fighter aircraft, such as the Eurofighter (Typhoon), are not just "air force programs" but actually "army programs" in the sense that they serve (or enable) ground operations; they are, in the true sense, joint programs of the armed forces.

The Luftwaffe has come to recognize that emphasizing the role and importance of NATO ground forces will actually strengthen the role of air power. Indeed, air power proved extremely important in a wide range of military missions in Afghanistan and elsewhere. At the same time Luftwaffe planners became familiar with the challenge of providing the Bundeswehr contingent in Afghanistan with its own full-spectrum air support. The other services seem to appreciate the Luftwaffe's newfound roles.

As the Libyan engagement has shown, "Western" air power can be a most appropriate and useful instrument in the context of so-called asymmetric conflicts. Yet it succeeded (and even then only after six months) only because NATO nations decided to arm the insurgents and sent in special forces to teach the untrained rebels how to become a skilled military force that could exploit favorable air situations on the ground.

Much has been made of asymmetric conflict and the challenges it poses to traditional Western military thinking. The truth is that all violent human conflicts have been, and will always be, in one way or another asymmetric. War is all about maximizing one's own strengths and exploiting the opponent's weaknesses. Successful strategy includes asymmetric responses. The Western response to terrorists flying civilian airliners into tall buildings, for instance, cannot be to fly civilian airliners into the enemy's buildings; toppling the governments hosting the terrorists, after unsuccessfully requesting that those governments turn them in, is a more appropriate response.[3] When tens of thousands of Albanian refugees descended on Italy, Italy responded not by sending its own people as refugees to Albania but by intervening to stabilize a failing state (Operation Alba). Understanding one's opponent helps. So does understanding one's partners and allies. Understanding oneself, including one's own weaknesses and strengths, is of tremendous importance; making the most of one's own asymmetric advantages is even more essential.

Many countries cannot easily develop a skilled military; historically, many never have. When it comes to classical war fighting, Western states have usually enjoyed impressive superiority. For non-Western states that challenge or even threaten Western interests, the question arises, why confront the West by investing in mechanized divisions or fighter wings—that is, capabilities in which the West, in many if not most cases, so far enjoys clear-cut superiority? Why not invest in areas that appear to have a more promising return on investment when it comes to competition with the West? If it is difficult to field an impressive number of skilled heavy divisions and high-tech fighter wings, why not recruit microbiologists and computer hackers? This approach looks even more attractive if the enemy studies the potential weaknesses of Western societies: concerns about their own casualties and dependence on (highly vulnerable) critical infrastructure. Logically then, non-Western governments would generate a greater return on investment in weapons of mass destruction and cyber warriors. Would the West really have bombed a foreign capital in the Balkans for seventy-eight days if President Slobodan Milošević had possessed nuclear weapons and long-range delivery vehicles?

Peer competitors, in contrast, will most likely challenge Western dominance in every area of influence. China, for instance, is not only investing huge sums in cyber warfare (and espionage) but also in its navy, fifth-generation fighter planes, and ballistic missiles. It would be unrealistic to assume that these efforts merely reflect a "me too" attitude rather than a cold-blooded analysis of how to increase China's own scope for maneuver while reducing the options available to its opponent or peer competitor, the United States.

Air power is important for Germany and other Western countries because it plays a vital role in supporting ground forces and in helping to prevent the opponent from prevailing. More fundamentally, air power is important because it gives the West the ability to act asymmetrically to its own advantage, particularly through the application of superior air power in joint and combined operations.

Germany's Enduring Geostrategic Situation

Any analysis of national capabilities—and why those capabilities have taken a particular form—must begin with the geography of the country in question. While many new elements have recently come to play a more prominent role in foreign and security deliberations—as current deployments abroad suggest—Germany remains a land power in the heart of Europe with maritime interests (in contrast, for instance, to Great Britain, which traditionally is a sea power with interests on the Continent and beyond). Clearly, those categories seem outdated, but only to an extent. A variety of traditional factors, such as the number and size of neighboring countries, availability and access to resources, and open sea lines of communication, still determine Germany's specific role in the world order and in particular Germany's interests. Fundamentally, Germany's prosperity increasingly depends on a globalized world, but Germany alone lacks the military reach to affect events beyond the European periphery—other than as a member of alliances and together with partners.[4]

Like other NATO members, Germany subscribes to the alliance risk assessment that places heavy emphasis on "likely" scenarios. While this is quite understandable given limited resources, this approach tends to downplay the potential damage caused by unlikely but dangerous contingencies. Security policy must cope with risks and not just probabilities. Risk is a product of the likelihood that a scenario might happen multiplied by the level of damage that could result if it did happen (the so-called low probability / high impact scenarios). As an analogy, homeowners do not purchase fire insurance because their houses are likely to burn down but because of the consequences if the houses did. Hence, responsible security policy must be risk oriented and not focused only on probabilities. German security interests are a result of the country's history, geographic location, international political and economic relations, and resource dependency as a center of high technology and an exporting nation with few natural resources. These interests are not static but can change in and along with international constellations and associated developments.[5]

During the Cold War the threat of invasion by Warsaw Pact troops placed top priority on territorial defense within NATO. The German armed forces emphasized strong ground troops, maritime capabilities, particularly littoral warfare (Baltic Sea, North Sea), and air forces that—together with the air forces of Germany's allies—could (with air-based and ground-based air defenses) counter ten thousand or so sorties by the Warsaw Pact on day one and achieve air superiority. Those air forces would also have had to provide air support for ground forces (close air support and tactical mobility) and to contribute to NATO's shared nuclear capability in multiple ways, for instance, by participating in planning, sharing risks, and supplying proven platforms, such as dual-capable aircraft.

Now, although geography continues to play a role, threats such as cyber crime and the potential of cyber war, international terrorism, and certain capabilities of air power—particularly in its currently extreme form of ballistic missiles—have modified this general truth somewhat. The speed and range of air systems bring time and distance into a new relationship. For instance, air power changes the role of geography by making distances to conflict areas, buffer zones, and other factors less relevant. However, the implications still depend largely on the context, the specific nature of the conflict, and the concrete circumstances. In any case the classical categories of land power and sea power, while still of some (and often underestimated) importance, become less salient.

Germany's geostrategic situation has changed little despite all the factors that may make geography less important. Today, as in the past, the European periphery remains a focus of German concern. The wording of the 2011 binding defense policy guidance (Verteidigungspolitische Richtlinien, or VPR), which set the parameters of the Bundeswehr's Reorientation (*Neuausrichtung*), shows a defense force focused on security challenges that despite new directions, do not look totally different from those of two decades ago. The VPR defines German security interests in general terms, to include the following: "preventing, mitigating and managing crises and conflicts that endanger the security of Germany and its allies; advocating and implementing positions on foreign and security policy in an assertive and credible way; strengthening transatlantic and European security and partnerships; advocating the universality of human rights and principles of democracy, promoting global respect for international law, and reducing the gap between the rich and the poor regions of the world; [and] facilitating free and unrestricted world trade as well as free access to the high seas and to natural resources."[6] Given those general terms the VPR could embody the policies of many other countries and hence does not look specifically German. It also set three overarching objectives that indicate both Germany's aims and its dilemmas: "Safeguarding National Interests, Assuming International Responsibility, Shaping Security Together."[7]

In 2010 then defense minister Karl-Theodor zu Guttenberg initiated a Bundeswehr reform that Thomas de Maizière, in office from March 2011 to December 2013, continued to push forward. Some considered the Reorientation of the Bundeswehr as significant as any reform of the German armed forces since the reunification of Germany in 1990.[8] Like previous reorganizations, the Reorientation has proceeded from an assessment of Germany's security environment, even as it is also very much driven by ongoing budget considerations.

Since the early 1990s and the end of the Cold War, the tasks of the Bundeswehr have included both NATO Article V territorial-collective defense and wider ranging, more global activities known now (for instance, in a 1994 white paper on defense) as "international conflict prevention and crisis management" (*internationale Konfliktverhütung und*

Krisenbewältigung).[9] Thus, more than twenty years after reunification, Germany continues to define its strategic interests along both national and European collective defense lines. Fundamental to this is the imperative to bear responsibility as part of an international community—which, of course, is related to the self-interest of a stable and prosperous global environment of free trade and access to resources and markets.

Germany's military involvement in distant conflicts has increased significantly, with over seven thousand German soldiers until recently serving abroad, including in areas where, a few decades ago, nobody in post–World War II Germany would have considered intervening. Foreign deployment of troops, including Luftwaffe personnel and equipment, has become almost routine. Twenty years ago the Bundeswehr did not view itself as an *Einsatzarmee* (a deployed army, or an army in combat). Today it does, despite Berlin's decision not to participate in NATO's Operation Unified Protector over Libya in 2011. This was a sovereign political decision, similar to decisions by Germany's allies in other instances; for example, France decided not to join the Afghanistan operation when it began and then disengaged early, and Britain decided to cease deploying its forces in the Balkans. Now, the term *Einsatz* (deployed in combat missions) appears again and again in Bundeswehr planning documents. The Bundeswehr has gained valuable experience from its deployments, while also suffering losses and overcoming equipment shortfalls in the field. Currently, the Bundeswehr focuses far more on contending with current challenges than on planning for possible long-term threats.

While deployments have grown, overall military spending has declined. Defense spending for 2012 was €31.87 billion,[10] or 1.4 percent of gross domestic product (GDP),[11] reflecting a slight decline from 1.5 percent over the past decade. Spending is slated to drop further by 2015.[12] Therefore, the German military and the Luftwaffe in particular are undergoing a dramatic shift toward improving deployment capacity without adequate funding to do so. For Berlin, saving the euro through the European Stability Mechanism has become more important than funding the Bundeswehr, which is, to some extent, understandable given the consequences of a breakdown of Europe's financial system and its implications for defense budgets.

The Impact of Reorientation on the Luftwaffe

Twenty years after the end of the Cold War and ten years after the first major deployments abroad, the Bundeswehr is still a shrinking military. Indeed, with conscription ending only in 2011, some of the most significant changes have now occured as the Bundeswehr declines from 255,000 to 185,000 military personnel and from 76,000 to 55,000 civilian workers. On September 20, 2011, German defense minister Thomas de Maizière announced that the Luftwaffe would decrease from around 36,000 to 22,550 airmen and civilians.[13] It is not clear yet how the Bundeswehr in general, or the Luftwaffe in particular, can fulfill all of its demanding tasks with fewer and fewer people. Modern technology might help but is no deus ex machina.

As the Bundeswehr shrinks, the Ministry of Defense effort to do more with less has led to a strategic focus on providing some capability in all areas rather than in-depth capability in a few—and on working more closely with allies and partners to compensate for national shortfalls. In the VPR Defense Minister de Maizière directed the Bundeswehr to cover the entire spectrum of conflict so that smaller national partners can add niche contributions across a broad range of Bundeswehr capabilities. De Maizière specifically calls for "breadth before depth" even at the cost of lower "sustainability" (*Durchhaltevermögen*), noting, "We cannot be completely prepared for every contingency, but we should not be completely unprepared for any contingency."[14] The Luftwaffe, in this context, formally speaks of "differentiated sustainability" (*differenzierte Durchhaltefähigkeit*).

The Luftwaffe has also made an effort to reassert its own importance in the competition for resources. The air force chief of staff, Lt. Gen. Karl Müllner, released an analysis of Germany's national interests and German air power's ability to support these interests in the decades to come. Setting the Luftwaffe's future course, *Air Power 2030* "represents the orientation system and its derivatives for the orientation and configuration of the air force in the coming decades" and puts forward a holistic approach that focuses on the network (*Verbund*) of "reconnaissance-command-effect-support" (*Aufklärung-Führung-Wirkung-Unterstützung*).[15] "Team Luftwaffe," as the analysis calls the air force, would provide a range of classic and novel air power services to all who need them—particularly in the expanding area of satellites and drones. Altogether, *Air Power 2030* has placed the Luftwaffe and its partners at the center of a modern, forward-looking, comprehensive definition of the importance of air and space power in an increasingly networked, multipolar world.

Today's political circumstances in Central Europe clearly do not require a Luftwaffe of Cold War size. What is less clear, though, is that current and future missions will require significantly fewer aircraft in the respective theaters of operation. In the days of the Cold War, the main mission for the Luftwaffe, together with its allies, was to establish air superiority over its own territory after an attack by Warsaw Pact aircraft. Today and in the future, a more likely objective is unchallenged air dominance over an area of operations, which is unlikely to be the homeland. For example, NATO's Operation Unified Protector over Libya was a limited operation in a comparatively benign air environment. NATO's stocks of precision-guided munitions were quickly depleted, and only significant U.S. contributions allowed the campaign to continue until it achieved its aims.[16]

As newer systems arrive in fewer numbers and more slowly, the Luftwaffe has phased out or reduced the numbers of aircraft that served on the front line in the Cold War and then in over a decade of deployments abroad. These include the air-superiority F-4 Phantom and the workhorse of tactical air transport, the Transall C-160. The Luftwaffe currently has no plan to phase out the Tornado entirely as long as Germany's political leadership does not decide on a follow on. There will be no replacement for political reasons. Air defense has moved from Nike-Hercules and Hawk to Patriot III missiles and Mantis cannons with dramatic improvements in both radars and command and control. As missile defense becomes a central mission for NATO and Germany, the speed and efficiency of a coordinated response will become more important. While these new systems will bring added capability, the total number of planned procurements has steadily declined. With the Reorientation the number of German Eurofighters on order will go down to 140 from 180 and the number of A400Ms acquired will be 40 rather than 60. Nevertheless, the Luftwaffe continues to expand its reach while also upgrading Germany's contribution to NATO air defense. A Luftwaffe with high-quality assets is the good news; far fewer numbers of aircraft and challenging changes is the bad news.

The Luftwaffe was already in a difficult position before the 2011 *Neuausrichtung*. Like all Bundeswehr services, the Luftwaffe was trapped by long-term procurement commitments. Military specifications defined when the original development decision was made did not necessarily reflect current and future requirements. Performance shortfalls, cost overruns, and delays on a number of these long-term major projects—some caused by industry, some by the customer—created additional challenges. The Luftwaffe identified modularity and bundling of core capacities as the way to remain operational with fewer and fewer resources. "Smart defense" and "pooling and sharing" had become politically guiding themes for creating synergies under difficult circumstances. These are, however, political deliberations and not ideas entertained by the Luftwaffe.

Under the Reorientation previous reform plans have evolved into a comprehensive and ongoing reorganization of the Luftwaffe—an attempt to rebalance overall capabilities with an emphasis on the four areas mentioned previously: air-surface integration, missile defense, the military use of space, and unmanned aircraft. As one industry analyst put it, "On the basis of own experiences from deployments and the experiences of allied forces, the main focus in the capability profile shifted from fighting against the enemy's ability to conduct air war to supporting air operations like air transport, reconnaissance and close air support."[17] While in some exceptional cases air power might be used alone, in most cases air power will be employed, in one way or another, in joint operations.

New Commands

With the creation of the Air Force Command in October 2012, the Luftwaffe took the first step in its reorganization. The year 2013 saw the establishment of further new competence-based subcommands, and most changes are expected to be completed by 2017. Ending the division structure should remove layers of the management hierarchy and free personnel for tasks, such as incorporating and operating new unmanned systems into the Luftwaffe's arsenal sometime in the future.

Lieutenant General Müllner called the Reorientation of Team Luftwaffe "the most comprehensive change in its history."[18] The Reorientation changed Müllner's own role as the top Luftwaffe officer—the chief, or in German terminology, the "inspector," of the air force. Although the inspector will remain the primary Luftwaffe adviser to the government, he will no longer have administrative responsibilities within the Ministry of Defense; he will have only command responsibilities—and more of them than before.[19] With this change, the Luftwaffe command headquarters (HQ) will move out of the Ministry of Defense to Berlin-Gatow Air Base near the Joint Operations Command (Einsatzführungskommando) for all German military operations at Potsdam.[20] Three competence-based subcommands—Air Operations Command (Zentrum Luftoperation), Air Force Operational Forces Command (Kommando Einsatzverbände Luftwaffe), and Air Force Support Forces Command (Kommando Unterstützungsverbände Luftwaffe)—now replace the previous, more layered air division organization.

Air Operations Command will direct all German air operations and organize Luftwaffe roles in NATO's integrated command and air defense architecture. Located on the Dutch-German border (at Kalkar/Uedem), the command will manage Luftwaffe cooperation with NATO, including the nearby NATO Combined Air Operations Center in Uedem.

Ongoing NATO reorganization will affect the Luftwaffe significantly. A major challenge for Air Operations Command is establishing the Joint Force Air Component (JFAC) HQ as a "framework nation." This designation implies both that air power must always be viewed in a "joint" context and that the "air component" needs its own NATO Air HQ capability. Initiated at the NATO 2010 Summit in Lisbon, this reform transfers more of the NATO command structure to dual-hatted national NATO military structures. As a result national militaries now have a greater role in establishing NATO commands, including the necessary technologies and personnel for planning and executing combined and joint military operations. NATO would run larger operations through its own top Air Command (AIRCOM) JFAC HQ in Ramstein, Germany, while "smaller joint operations" could be run from any of the five national NATO JFAC HQs: in the United States, the United Kingdom, Germany, France, and Italy. Nominally, the German JFAC HQ should be able to plan and command a six-month air campaign with up to 350 sorties a day. Such a campaign would nevertheless remain highly dependent on U.S. capabilities, as was apparent in NATO's Operation Unified Protector, which averaged 120 sorties per day over six months.

Improving the Luftwaffe's ability to plan air operations while at the same time establishing Germany's JFAC HQ will not be easy. *Air Power 2030* states, "Qualitative improvement of joint effects and combined interoperability is more important than the optimization of equipment or sub-systems."[21] Leadership in partnership is thus the central focus. Training backup personnel across the Luftwaffe will be important so that they can transfer to the command in case of crisis. This new focus on running a JFAC HQ command also reflects the belief that synergies there will allow the Luftwaffe to fully realize its potential. Integrated joint planning and execution of air operations will be a core task of the new NATO JFAC HQ.

Playing a new role in the NATO air operations process offers many opportunities for the Luftwaffe in cooperation with countries such as France or Britain, but the Luftwaffe also understands and accepts that the combined capabilities of all those countries cannot operate without the United States in any other than small contingencies. The Air Operations Command will thus also focus on giving Germany competence and influence in NATO's multinational commands. *Air Power 2030* underlined the importance of being able to shape NATO decisions:

"The Air Force must maintain its strong role in the Alliance structure, on the one hand to introduce its legitimate interests into the Alliance, on the other hand to introduce and ensure the implementation of relevant aspects of NATO in the national area."[22] Germany clearly wants a seat at the table.

Aspiration is one thing, but competence and capability are another. Although the Luftwaffe does not lack competence, capability is tied to budget, and both are irrelevant if the government lacks the political will to bring the country's (limited) military power to bear.

The Luftwaffe's national responsibilities and competencies come together in what might be called the National Air Operations Center (Operationszentrale der Luftwaffe). In essence, this center will, among a wide variety of tasks, coordinate Germany's important role in the Integrated NATO Air Defense System (INADS). The INADS Command has moved to NATO's Air Command at Ramstein Air Base in Germany in conjunction with the establishment there of a new command for ballistic missile defense (BMD). Ramstein, in the Rhineland Palatinate on the border with France, is the largest U.S. air base abroad. The Luftwaffe wants to become a competent and influential presence in these Ramstein commands, and the Air Operations Command sees this as an important and growing responsibility. As it evolves, the Air Operations Command will need the ability to quickly shift its focus from planning and commanding ongoing operations to building up the NATO JFAC to improving command capabilities and training opportunities.[23]

The Air Force Operational Forces Command will manage the actual force, consisting of seven aircraft wings (*Geschwader*) and one air defense wing. The command is responsible for maintaining the wings and providing tailored, modular force packages as needed. Run out of Cologne/Wahn, the Air Force Operational Forces Command divides its areas of responsibility into air and ground, with most aircraft deployed in the north to facilitate training. These include three Eurofighter wings, one fighter-bomber wing, one reconnaissance wing, one air transport wing, and one helicopter wing. The Luftwaffe is fielding three multirole Eurofighter wings, each with two squadrons, for a total of 140 Eurofighter Typhoons. A fighter-bomber wing fielding Tornado interdiction/strike (IDS) planes will remain in service at Büchel Air Base. The three previous air transport wings are merging into a single wing based at Wunstorf Air Base, which will field forty A400M Atlas transport planes. Reconnaissance Wing 51, where the electronic combat and reconnaissance (ECR) Tornados are based, will remain in service and add one UAV squadron to its Tornado IDS/ECR squadron.[24] Furthermore, the Luftwaffe stations its ground-based Air Defense Wing 1 in Husum.

Air Force Support Forces Command is responsible for logistics, training, and aircraft certification and will play an important role in ensuring the future capability of the Luftwaffe. This command includes Germany's large aerospace testing complex in Manching, near Munich—an important development center for meeting the Luftwaffe's advanced technology requirements. The command also has responsibility for cooperation with commercial enterprises, as illustrated by its proximity to Airbus Defence and Space. Modification and certification of UAVs are among the many joint endeavors at the Manching complex.

New Operational Demands and Technological Challenges

The Luftwaffe faces new operational demands and technological challenges in a number of significant areas. First, it must expand its role in air defense, at both the national and NATO levels, to encompass BMD. Second, air transport remains a serious challenge for the Bundeswehr, which relies on rented Russian and Ukrainian aircraft to transport matériel to Afghanistan while it waits for delivery of new, capable, and technologically complex Airbus A400M transport planes. Third, surveillance, whether conducted by space assets or by lower altitude UAVs, presents a particularly important area for improvement. Fourth, air-ground integration has become the focus of Eurofighter development, as the aircraft is increasingly assigned an advanced strike role. Finally, the Luftwaffe is struggling with all the dilemmas created by proliferating unmanned aircraft technologies. Germany tends to strive for a leading role in the development of a European UAV (the Future European medium-altitude long-endurance [MALE] UAV). At the same time Berlin is considering the purchase of a foreign-made UAV as a bridging solution—a model that can be armed to serve immediate and near-term requirements and can enable the Luftwaffe to gain operational experience.

The Luftwaffe certainly sees evolving operational demands in the area of national and NATO air defense, which is no simple mission and is also essential to any global engagement. Here the Reorientation ambitiously calls upon the Luftwaffe to develop an ability to deploy two large air force packages simultaneously. Each package would perform multiple tasks and have to be sustainable over longer periods.

> In the future the Luftwaffe will be able to provide up to two flying task forces with deployment modules for airstrike, including close air support, flying air defense, tactical reconnaissance, suppression of enemy air defenses (SEAD), and unmanned surveillance and reconnaissance in up to two operational areas (though for only a limited time in the second area). Additionally, the Luftwaffe will supply up to two antiaircraft missile task forces and mixed air transport packages that include capabilities for strategic air transport, aerial refueling, and tactical and strategic transportation of casualties. In addition, the German Air Force must maintain and sustain one operational air base in theater and, for a limited time, provide Luftwaffe security personnel to maintain airfield security.[25]

Deploying such a broad spectrum of new capabilities challenges the numerically shrinking Luftwaffe. Thus, according to *Air Power 2030*, "multi-role capability and open-system architectures" will be essential.[26] Here too the Luftwaffe knows, "multi-role" and "open-system" cannot entirely compensate for a lack of mass or money (as planning officials are painfully aware).

Air Defense in a Multinational Framework

As Germany modernizes its air defenses, it is also developing competence in missile defense so that the Luftwaffe can play an expanding role in NATO's nascent BMD capability. German planners recognize that U.S. encouragement and technology have allowed NATO to move toward a comprehensive missile defense system. Not surprisingly, the Luftwaffe sees NATO's 2010 Lisbon decision as making missile defense "a new core mission" for the alliance. Missile defense brings a new and important dimension to Europe's relationship with the United States and opens up partnership options with non-NATO countries as well. At its May 2012 summit in Chicago, NATO announced that an interim capability BMD was operational and had been placed under the authority of NATO Air Command at Ramstein Air Base.[27] Currently, NATO's multinational approach anticipates a final operating capability by 2020 that would integrate the U.S. "phased adaptive approach" for missile defense in Europe "to provide full coverage and protection for all NATO European populations, territory and forces."[28] The extent to which the recent threats posed by North Korea will lead the United States to rethink its European missile defense plans and to shift its emphasis from Europe to Northeast Asia remains to be seen.

Lt. Gen. Friedrich Wilhelm Ploeger, a retired Luftwaffe officer and in his last function deputy commander of NATO Allied Air Command, emphasized that ballistic missiles of greater range and accuracy are becoming available to an increasing number of actors. Ploeger believed NATO's new mission to protect territory, population, and deployed forces "has the potential to be a transatlantic link [*Klammer*] of strategic importance."[29] Nevertheless, the Luftwaffe should expect its influence to be proportional to its own overall contribution.

Germany is part of a seven-nation group running Patriot missile batteries that now come under the command of the nascent Ramstein missile defense headquarters. The country is currently building up from the Patriot III capability (limited terminal-phase defense against incoming missiles with ranges of up to a thousand kilometers) by acquiring additional radars, data networks, command and control capabilities, and U.S. Navy Aegis missile ships in the Mediterranean. Ploeger stated that he would like to see the European partners play a greater role in providing technology for this NATO project: "The system needs to be enhanced by contributions from other Alliance partners with sensors and effectors."[30] The partner nations must also do everything necessary to ensure the new command structure at Ramstein is up to the task of making the split-second decisions required by missile defense.

Ploeger also noted that Russia poses a major political challenge to NATO missile defense. He argued that transparency and exchange on early warning are important but so are national sovereignty and "collective defense" without Russian interference: "BMD does not replace nuclear deterrence, it enhances it."[31]

As the Luftwaffe comes up to speed on missile defense, it must take over the air defense role previously filled by the German Army, including the introduction of the new air defense cannon Mantis.[32] The German air defense architecture has also had to adapt to the U.S. withdrawal from the three-nation Medium Extended Air Defense System (MEADS), announced in 2011. The two other partners, Germany and Italy, will now attempt to build on existing battle management and state-of-the-art 360-degree radar coverage capabilities. The emphasis will be on integrating the various systems into one common command so that they can "plug and fight." In the meantime it appears that the United States will fulfill its contractual obligation to finish the development phase of MEADS.

Planning is also under way to upgrade the missile defense capability of the German Navy—the Frigate Class 124 system (which has been in operation since 2009)—and thus add a valuable component to NATO's overall missile and air defense architecture.[33] Continuing efforts are adapting the widely used air-to-air guided missile IRIS-T to serve as a surface-to-air missile that can be linked to a wide variety of sensor networks. The reconfigured IRIS surface-launched medium-range missile is scheduled to enter service in 2014.[34]

Air defense now extends well beyond Germany and Europe, as illustrated by the recent deployment of Patriot surface-to-air missiles in Turkey. The Luftwaffe continues to focus on air-defense deployability. As such, restructuring German air defense architecture is ongoing and in consultation with international partners and industry.[35]

Air Transport: Growing Demand, Declining Assets

The Luftwaffe is expanding its spectrum of air mobility tasks even as budgetary realities force it to cut the number of new A400M systems that it will receive. Airlift plays a role across the entire range of Bundeswehr activities throughout a deployment, and the Reorientation's emphasis on deployed forces has generated significant demand for strategic and tactical airlift. The VPR calls on the Bundeswehr to sustain up to ten thousand deployed soldiers indefinitely. Although the Luftwaffe runs the air transport wing, the Armed Forces Support Command plans the logistics to create this level of mobility. National, multinational, and commercial partners are all essential, and leasing aircraft and ships has been a central aspect of Germany's deployments over the past decade. The Luftwaffe could, and probably will, do more to optimize European A400M logistics and operations supply.

With no long-range and oversized cargo air transport of its own and the continuing need to carry troops and matériel to Afghanistan, Germany initiated the Strategic Airlift Interim Solution (SALIS) in 2006.[36] Already in the year 2000, Germany chaired the respective NATO working group on oversized air cargo, which then, in 2006, lead to the setup of SALIS. This multinational airlift consortium is chartering six giant Russian and Ukrainian Antonov An-124-100 transport aircraft to meet shortfalls in NATO's long-range oversized airlift capabilities. In December 2012 the partners extended the agreement until 2014. SALIS should not be confused with the Strategic Airlift Capability (SAC), a consortium of twelve nations that pools resources to purchase and operate Boeing C-17 Globemaster III aircraft for joint strategic airlift purposes. Germany is not part of the SAC group, which is based in Hungary and includes ten NATO nations (Bulgaria, Estonia, Hungary, Lithuania, the Netherlands, Norway, Poland, Romania, Slovenia, and the United States) and two Partnership for Peace nations (Finland and Sweden).

Germany long pushed for the establishment of the European Air Transport Command (EATC). The command became operational in 2010 with the integration of German national air transport command and planning structures into the new four-nation EATC. The members—Germany, France, Belgium, and the Netherlands (which does not participate in the A400M program)—have established an "open" approach that they hope will offer a model for other pooling arrangements. With three out of four EATC members soon to acquire the A400M and Spain and Luxemburg intending to become members, there is hope that new partners might see more incentive to join the "club."[37]

Continually Improving Surveillance

The German deployment to Afghanistan created an urgent need for reliable and continuous surveillance and reconnaissance. From 2006 to 2010 the German multirole reconnaissance Tornado performed this role in Afghanistan and in doing so made a significant contribution to NATO's optical intelligence, surveillance, and reconnaissance capability in the area of operations.[38] As of 2010 the Luftwaffe has also operated leased Heron I UAVs out of Mazar-i-Sharif in northern Afghanistan, and by the end of 2013, it had logged more than sixteen thousand flying hours. The Bundeswehr has extended this important contract with industry through October 2014. New satellite communications have added operational range to the Heron I, and German industry has provided tailored capabilities and support.[39] As Germany moves to acquire its own MALE UAV, interest has grown in arming the platform, as will be discussed later. In addition, Germany intended to introduce the Euro Hawk—which has sensors for signals intelligence—and the associated ground stations. The Luftwaffe's four Euro Hawk systems were planned to reach initial operating capability (IOC) by 2015,[40] but the future of the program is in doubt because of recent revelations that the costs of certification are much higher than anticipated. Furthermore, the U.S. decision to halt the acquisition of Global Hawks raises questions about the costs of supply and logistics support for the Euro Hawk.

The Euro Hawk's sibling, the Global Hawk, will serve as the platform for NATO's Alliance Ground Surveillance (AGS). After almost two decades of deliberations, NATO agreed in 2012 to fund the development and delivery of an AGS system consisting of five Global Hawks and their respective control systems and costing €1.2 billion, of which Germany will pay €400 million. European companies will work with a U.S. contractor to achieve IOC by 2016. The NATO aircraft will be stationed in Sigonella, Sicily, and be capable of providing surveillance from, and of, two different theaters of operation. A European company will build the mobile ground segment for these units.[41] Again, given budgetary constraints and increasing cost, nothing can be taken for granted. Consequently, Germany has moved from describing its contribution to NATO AGS in terms of a specific platform to stating its intention to contribute with Luftwaffe personnel and some other unspecified capabilities.

Space, from surveillance and communication to navigation, represents a growing area of focus for the Luftwaffe. Germany plays a central role in numerous European space projects, including Galileo (which is not a Luftwaffe program) and the European Space Agency.[42] In 2011 the Luftwaffe established the national Space Situational Awareness Center to oversee the operations of the German government's satellites, and the center has expanded steadily ever since. *Air Power 2030* underlined the importance of improving Luftwaffe competence in this area: "With the development and growing use of outer space the Luftwaffe has continually increased its expertise, which it must continue to do, not only to protect space-based systems, but also to provide better quality information support to the policy-making processes and the entire military operation."[43]

The Luftwaffe is the designated center of excellence for establishing holistic, capability-oriented, and joint military space utilization. The Luftwaffe wants to shape Bundeswehr utilization of space, especially with regard to the protection and operation of five Bundeswehr SAR-Lupe synthetic aperture radar satellites (not operated by the Luftwaffe). The Luftwaffe seeks to close capability gaps and build up new capabilities in the area of space situational awareness and early warning / missile defense. While it supports European activities, the Luftwaffe has traditionally sought close cooperation with the United States in the ongoing buildup and expansion of the Space Situational Awareness Center.

Support for Ground Forces

Nations have frequently employed air power in support of ground forces, especially over the past decade. Sometimes these ground forces have been Western forces operating together with local governments against insurgents and irregular militias, as in Afghanistan, Pakistan, Iraq, Yemen, Somalia, and most recently, Mali. At other times Western air power has aided bands of irregulars fighting against their governments, from the Kosovo Liberation Army to the Northern Alliance to the militias that toppled Muammar Gaddafi. Although air forces remain fundamentally configured for war between nations, experience has underlined the importance of the ability to employ air power in subnational conflicts and particularly in complex urban environments.

Until recently air power was something of a blunt instrument, with a comparatively high risk of inflicting collateral damage, including losses to friendly fire. Precision munitions and improved target acquisition have slowly changed this situation, allowing air-delivered missiles to be targeted even against specific individuals. More important, air power has offered the reconnaissance and surveillance capabilities that allow high-value targets to be tracked for hours or even days. Few small-unit operations nowadays lack real-time overhead surveillance and signals intelligence. Close air support has become more reliable as technologies have enabled air and ground forces to display the same maps, pictures, and targets on their respective screens, even as audio connections have also improved. At the same time rear-echelon analysts can track multiple vehicles, individuals, and sources to identify insurgent networks and operating patterns. The German staff at NATO Air HQ has written that "airpower is a fundamental precondition for a military contribution that can spare the population and the infrastructure while fighting insurgents."[44]

Whereas air power remains important for all operations on the ground, counterinsurgency operations remain primarily a mission for ground forces. Air power will, however, play an increasingly important role in such missions. For example, air power has significantly improved the possibilities for logistic support via precision air drop / point-of-use delivery. This reduces the need for land infrastructure, such as airfields, and for ground vehicles, as well as the associated danger of attacks. Sustaining even a small force in the field creates the demand for significant strategic and tactical air transport. Finally, increasing air-ground integration has been accompanied by cross-training of forward air controllers, including rotations through different services, simulations, and exercises to enhance the efficiency of joint and combined operations. Germany is now working at full speed to develop the competence necessary for this highly challenging mission.

The Luftwaffe's current and future combat aircraft inventories were not designed for ground support as a primary mission. Instead, Germany's F-4 Phantoms and Eurofighters were intended primarily to ensure air superiority and to excel in air-to-air combat. Long-range interdiction and SEAD complemented these roles. Support for troops in contact had seemed infeasible until precision-guided munitions became available. Now, as technology has improved and the demand has grown, the Luftwaffe is reorienting many of its aircraft toward a much larger ground-support role. The Luftwaffe is particularly interested in ensuring that more of the Eurofighters acquire an advanced ground-support capability and that the air force will be better integrated into the planning and execution of ground operations. Air chief Karl Müllner has insisted that "the Luftwaffe calls for all Eurofighters to be made multirole" and identified three important capabilities in addition to air defense: "precision strike, manned reconnaissance and electronic warfare."[45] A four-nation group is developing "role adjustment" for the aircraft, including integration of capabilities for dropping the GBU-48 precision bomb. Müllner noted that modifying Tranche 2 or 3 aircraft to make them multirole would be easier than adapting the Tranche 1 planes; Germany could export the Tranche 1 planes to partner countries, a plan that Great Britain is already implementing. Müllner hoped that the Eurofighter would have an initial multirole capability by 2015. Afghanistan has shown how important this is, since "we should be able to provide the protection and security of our soldiers."[46]

This need for a multirole aircraft recalls the tanker truck incident in 2009, when Bundeswehr colonel Georg Klein requested an air strike against two tanker trucks stolen by the Taliban near Kunduz. Klein feared that the Taliban would use the tankers to penetrate the camp perimeter, but he did not have his own reconnaissance or quick-reaction force. In response to his call but against the pilots' clearly articulated reservations, American F-15Es dropped bombs that killed a large number of civilians, causing a great outcry and political turbulence in Germany. This fueled the political will to acquire German national aerial reconnaissance and target acquisition capabilities. Such experiences have emphasized the need to carefully calibrate the use of force. *Air Power 2030* reminded its readers, "The complexity of the operational theater, which also includes an increasingly urban environment, requires stand-off capability, precision and an orientation towards achieving the desired effect for the overall conduct of operations while excluding any unwanted side effects."[47]

The overall strategic and political environment requires the Luftwaffe to have better information and deliver more precise effects related to ground operations. The Luftwaffe had formerly defined air-ground integration as one of its four future focus points. The Reorientation has placed even more emphasis on air-ground integration, with the Luftwaffe seeking not just coordination but "synchronization."[48] Joint fire support with video links to ground forces has already been added to the Tornado; Luftwaffe presence in joint staffs has increased. Air-surface warfare (naval aviation) now falls within the Luftwaffe's purview. The new Mantis antiaircraft cannon, with its antimortar and antiartillery capability, will be transferred from the army to the Luftwaffe, placing the Luftwaffe in the role of providing tactical air defense for ground units deployed abroad and reinforcing the consolidation of air defense for support of ground forces in the Luftwaffe's hands.

The Eurofighter design has been evolving since it was first envisioned more than three decades ago. Today, against the background of experience in Afghanistan and Iraq, the program's follow-on tranches center primarily on giving the fighter improved ground-support capabilities.

Germany has decided to reduce its initial order of 180 Eurofighters to 140 and is planning to keep 85 Tornados in service through 2025 and beyond, with 49 of them serving in an IDS and reconnaissance mode. The two Tornado squadrons, one based in Büchel, are also tasked with the "nuclear participation" role (*nukleare Teilhabe*), a nuclear-sharing role that the Federal Republic of Germany has performed since the late 1950s. Up to forty-six Tornados are technically capable of carrying the American B-61 nuclear bomb. Such dual-capable-aircraft arrangements already exist between the United States and Germany, as well as between the United States and Belgium, the Netherlands, Italy, Greece, and Turkey. In Germany, this nuclear-sharing role has repeatedly generated controversy. Indeed, all possible coalition partners of Angela Merkel's Christian Democratic Union (the Free Democratic Party, the Social Democratic Party, and the Greens) have programs calling for the removal of U.S. nuclear bombs from Germany. Should the Tornados one day be retired, the question will arise as to which (if any) German aircraft should take on this role—particularly if demand for aircraft in a ground-support role continues to grow.

Debate over Next-Generation UAVs

Luftwaffe chief Lt. Gen. Müllner has argued that in the future UAVs will play an "important, if not dominant role."[49] Reflecting on the experience with Heron 1 in Afghanistan, he has concluded that the Bundeswehr would no longer conduct major operations without UAVs. This perception is broadly shared within the Luftwaffe and by the German political leadership.

Unmanned aircraft technology attracts great interest across government and business in high-tech Germany. The Bundeswehr has accumulated more than a decade of experience in successfully operating short-range UAVs, in particular the KZO, which has a range of five hundred kilometers and three hours' flying time. The Luftwaffe, in contrast to the German Army, began to operate UAVs only in 2010 and then did so quite suddenly when it decided to lease four Heron 1s. At that time the German military incorporated certain upgrades to both the aircraft and the accompanying ground stations. The Heron Is are provided by Luftwaffe Reconnaissance Wing 51 "Immelmann," serviced by a German defense company; they have operated under the command of Germany's International Security and Assistance Force (ISAF) North HQ at Mazar-i-Sharif Airfield. The aircraft can operate at an altitude of up to ten thousand meters for sixteen hours and have been upgraded with a satellite connection that allows for command and control via a beyond-line-of-sight communication link and for optical and infrared video, which also can be fed directly to units on the ground.[50]

Germany is still trying to decide what kind of MALE UAV it ultimately wants to acquire. At the moment the Luftwaffe cites three "phases" in the way ahead. The current situation, considered an "interim solution," consists of leasing the Heron I and operating it with a private company through 2014, with a possible extension through 2016. At the same time the German Ministry of Defense is pursuing a "European development solution" that could reach IOC by 2020 or 2021—assuming timely development and procurement decisions. Germany would play a leadership role in such a program, emphasizing a wide range of military and nonmilitary applications for the UAV.

Germany will need a bridging solution to cover the period between the end of the Heron I lease and the availability of the Future European MALE UAV. Various options are under consideration, with the most likely choice being either a more advanced Heron TP that can carry missiles or the U.S.-made Predator B. Some in Germany have argued for continuing the Heron solution, augmented by the more advanced Heron TP, as licensing issues have largely been resolved; they see the Heron TP as the less costly and less risky solution. Others have suggested that a German company could cooperate with a U.S. firm to carry out the minor modifications to the Predator B necessary to meet specific Bundeswehr requirements, with the German company providing certification, maintenance, and operational support. Many have argued that because Britain and Italy are already operating the Predator B, Germany's adoption of the UAV would facilitate a common European capability.[51] The *Süddeutsche Zeitung* reported that Luftwaffe chief

Müllner also favored the Predator B,[52] whereas some members of Parliament and officials in the Ministries of Defense and Economics have favored the Heron bridging solution.

To meet the Bundeswehr requirement for a high-altitude long-endurance (HALE) UAV, Germany initially decided to buy four U.S. RQ-4E Euro Hawks, with important sensor components and ground stations coming from a German prime contractor at an estimated cost of €1.2 billion. The Euro Hawk is a version of the RQ-4B (Block 20) Global Hawk that will replace signals intelligence capabilities provided by the Breguet Atlantic aircraft BR-1150M. The initial Euro Hawk flight tests in Germany with the German signals intelligence (SIGINT) payload on board took place at the beginning of 2013. Those tests were conducted on the basis of a preliminary type certificate provided by the German certification authorities. After several flight tests over German territory, the successful "acceptance flight" took place in the third quarter of 2013. This ended the development contract. At that time, the Euro Hawk remained in "flight-worthy condition" and could have been flown for further operational testing. It could have been even used for intelligence-gathering missions in crises areas.

The prototype of the Euro Hawk has always been considered "just" a capability demonstrator. Nevertheless, it was intended to be transferred to Reconnaissance Wing 51 "Immelmann" in Schleswig-Jagel.[53] At least that was the plan. As mentioned previously, decisions are final only when "the ink on the contract is dry," and even then the contract might be canceled.

The German air chief Lt. Gen. Müllner has demanded a quick decision about the next phase after the Heron 1 lease ends in 2014. Finally, with regard to training and career advancement, Müllner has noted that UAV operators will need licenses and certifications similar to those required of pilots operating manned aircraft. His call for "equal qualifications, equal chances" implied that UAV operators should not suffer career disadvantages.[54]

In contrast to the widespread agreement about the value of UAVs in general, the issue of armed UAVs remains contentious. *Spiegel Online* reported at the beginning of January 2013 that the German government has now formally called for the acquisition of an armed UAV. However, rules of engagement and the legal issues related to using drones to kill individuals on a foreign battlefield will certainly generate controversy within a German public highly sensitive to the issue of targeted killings.[55]

Cooperation with the Aerospace Industry

The growing technological complexity of air power poses a challenge to the vital cooperation between government and industry. Planning complex, often politically sensitive, multiyear (or multidecade) weapons projects requires interaction between military and industry personnel at multiple levels and in multiple forums. Global, transatlantic, European, and national interests all come to bear, as investments in national security always have economic and employment implications. Bundeswehr operational deployments abroad have been accompanied by an effort to more closely involve industry in meeting urgent operational requirements from the field. In particular, the Luftwaffe has tried to involve its fifteen thousand reservists in a more collaborative relationship with industry.[56] The Luftwaffe also seeks to maintain the competence to assess and, if possible, use cutting-edge technological developments that could fundamentally change the nature of air power. *Air Power 2030* noted, "Robotization, automatization, and digitization open until recently unimaginable possibilities. As a user of advanced technology, these developments have many influences in the Luftwaffe."[57]

Germany certainly has a strong industrial base when it comes to aerospace technologies. World-famous companies such as Airbus Defence and Space, MBDA, Rheinmetall, Diehl, and Thales Deutschland all are either German companies or have a strong presence in Germany. German technical competence will be central to the Luftwaffe's doing more with less in the future. Various industrial associations and lobbying organizations actively support Luftwaffe and aerospace interests in the German political process. However, not surprisingly, the current period is not a boom time for the German aerospace industry.

Conclusion: The Limits of Doing More with Less

Many factors, from the geostrategic to the technological to the political, will determine the future of German air power. Conceptual considerations regarding the changing role of air power indicate that ground-support operations will grow in importance for the Luftwaffe, even as air power's limitations—against targets in built-up, populated areas—remain significant. The enduring nature of Germany's geostrategic position means the country will have to find a balance between its important air power role in securing the European continent and its need to join with allies and partners on operations in more distant areas. The Bundeswehr Reorientation brings fundamental changes to the Luftwaffe, including a 30 percent reduction in personnel, a significantly flatter command hierarchy, and a greater role in NATO commands.

German air power must contend with new operational demands and technological challenges that raise difficult issues in regard to NATO and national air defense, air transport, air-ground integration, and a future unmanned aircraft. First, as the Luftwaffe expands its air defense role in a multinational framework to include missile defense, it will have to cope with significant new technologies, particularly with the U.S. focus on establishing a BMD for Europe, while considering the extent to which the Bundeswehr should have a concrete operational role in NATO missile defense. Second, the Luftwaffe's air transport capabilities are being cut even as demands increase. The Luftwaffe has great expectations that the A400M can meet a wide range of needs, from transport to air-to-air refueling of both aircraft and helicopters, even if fewer aircraft will be delivered than initially hoped. Third, urgent operational needs in the field and the availability of new technologies—including the leased Israeli Heron drones used in Afghanistan—have resulted in continually improving surveillance capabilities. Germany is also engaged in continuing efforts to develop a greater space-based surveillance capacity. Fourth, Luftwaffe support for ground forces demands new technology, new doctrine, and new organizational structures as the Eurofighter is assigned a significant strike and ground-support role while Germany continues to pursue better joint training and communications. Fifth, the Bundeswehr wants its own armed UAV. This requirement received official support from the Angela Merkel government in 2013, even as discussions continued regarding the role of such a drone and the morality of firing missiles from unmanned aircraft. Finally, the Luftwaffe continues to place high hopes on innovative cooperation with the aerospace industry as a way to do more with less and to ensure that Germany does not lose irreplaceable industrial capacities.

Luftwaffe planning occurs within a multinational framework. NATO sets the standards. German armed forces represent a single set of capabilities that can be used within any coalition in which policy makers want them to operate. Integration into NATO forces and also into future European structures is axiomatic, and the Luftwaffe will continually develop greater interoperability with those coalition forces. But other coalitions might emerge in the future. NATO, like Germany, emphasizes partnership and outreach to additional countries. Thus, the Luftwaffe may well be called upon to cooperate with an increasing number of partners in the future. As a consequence the Luftwaffe must retain some flexibility to adapt to changing interoperability needs for future joint, combined, and multilateral operations.

Clearly, Western thinking has shifted from seeing air power as a strategic "hammer" to wield—or defend against—to seeing it as the enabler of multispectrum, multimission, distributed operations. Whether the counterinsurgency model, with its assumption of "free" air superiority, will continue to drive Luftwaffe decisions in the decade ahead is another question. What plans should the Luftwaffe make regarding emerging peer competitors? Here, too, the Luftwaffe offers an answer: the great advantage of air power is that many of the same assets can perform many different tasks.

Germany will continue to view air power as a central and prudent investment that provides the flexibility necessary to meet evolving global demands and challenges. The Luftwaffe can achieve much, assuming the political will necessary to overcome the compartmentalized, service-oriented thinking that stands in the way of fully exploiting or even pushing new technologies for more effective joint, combined, and multilateral operations. All the same, the Luftwaffe does not confine its vision for the future of German air power to greater interoperability with ground forces and partner nations but also seeks to define the unique role that German air power should play in a globalizing NATO challenged as much by irregulars, cyber attacks, and the proliferation of weapons of mass destruction as by classic military opponents with their divisions of armor, fleets of ships, and squadrons of combat aircraft.[58]

THREE

Turkish Air Power

Toward Full-Spectrum Aerospace Forces

Christian F. Anrig

In the foreseeable future the Türk Hava Kuvvetleri (Turkish Air Force) is expected to operate the second-largest fleet of advanced North Atlantic Treaty Organization (NATO) fighter-bombers after the U.S. Air Force (USAF). In addition to the planned acquisition of a hundred Lockheed Martin F-35A Lightning II Joint Strike Fighters (JSFs), Turkey took delivery of more than 250 F-16 fighter-bombers, a substantial number of which have been earmarked for a midlife update. The Peace Onyx III program will bring them to a common avionics configuration by the end of 2015. Among other changes the planned upgrades include an advanced multimode radar, a helmet-mounted cueing system, and the Link 16 secure data link.[1] The Turkish Air Force (TurAF) received the last newly built F-16 Block 50 plus fighter-bomber in December 2012.[2] Not only is the Turkish F-16 fighter-bomber fleet state of the art, but it can also employ an impressive array of modern air-to-air and air-to-ground weapons, including over-the-horizon, all-weather standoff cruise missiles.[3]

Turkey has also acquired powerful force enablers. Despite being a member of the NATO Airborne Early Warning and Control (AEW&C) Force established in the early 1980s, the TurAF is—at the time of writing—building up its own AEW&C capability by bringing four Boeing 737 AEW&C aircraft into service.[4] In the mid-1990s seven KC-135R Stratotankers entered the TurAF's arsenal.[5] Although seven tankers is by no means comparable to USAF levels and corresponds only to approximately half of the air-to-air refueling (AAR) capacity of France and of the United Kingdom, the number is nonetheless substantial in both NATO and international terms. With the added AEW&C capability, these tankers provide the TurAF with force enablers that only a few air forces can boast. Although Turkey is primarily a regional security player, the TurAF nevertheless has a sizable transport fleet that includes thirteen C-130B/E Hercules and sixteen C-160D Transall transport aircraft, as well as other airframes.[6]

Over the last two decades, Turkish defense planners have confronted the challenge of balancing the buildup of these conventional capabilities with the requirements for counterinsurgency warfare. Since the mid-1980s Turkey's campaign against the separatist Kurdistan Workers' Party (PKK) has shaped Ankara's grand and military strategy. Ankara's campaign against the PKK not only influenced Turkey's foreign policy but also had a significant impact on force structuring. Thus, the government has at times prioritized equipment specifically dedicated to counterinsurgency warfare over conventional capabilities.

To operate its large inventory of equipment, the TurAF employs some sixty thousand personnel, approximately half of them conscripts.[7] Generally, its pilots and other personnel must meet high training standards and have significant expertise in operating the F-16. Thus, the TurAF has provided F-16 training to foreign air forces, in particular the United Arab Emirates Air Force.[8] The TurAF also demonstrated its emphasis on skills and training by opening a regional combat-readiness center near the Turkish city of Konya in June 2001 for air-to-air and air-to-ground training. Fitted with simulated surface-to-air missile (SAM) batteries, threat generators, and tactical firing areas, the center is also available to NATO members and other friendly air forces.[9] The training range annually hosts foreign air forces for the Anatolian Eagle exercise. Turkish squadrons generally specialize in one specific role. Besides the primary air-to-air and air-to-ground combat roles, the TurAF also has a suppression of enemy air defenses (SEAD) squadron and dedicated reconnaissance squadrons. A mixed F-16/F-4 squadron specializes in weapons and tactics.

In the post–Cold War era the TurAF has translated its training standards into real operational output. Alongside its NATO counterparts, the TurAF has been involved in a number of major Western air campaigns and has proved itself to be a force employable across the full spectrum. Yet Turkish decision makers have so far emphasized narrow rules of engagement, quite in contrast to Turkish counterinsurgency operations against the PKK in southeastern Turkey and northern Iraq.

While the TurAF hones its operational skills, Turkey's industrial base has gradually expanded its aerospace expertise. The majority of the more than 250 F-16 Fighting Falcons delivered to the TurAF were coproduced in Turkey.[10] In the last decade Ankara has also embarked on a dual-track acquisition strategy. Although Turkey—the only Muslim-majority NATO member—has access to some of the latest Western defense technology, it has started to develop indigenous expertise and to decrease the country's dependence on foreign suppliers.

This thrust toward mastering aerospace technology is in line with the words of the founder of the modern Turkish Republic, Mustafa Kemal Atatürk: "All our aircraft and their engines are required to be manufactured in our country and the air war industry to be developed on that basis."[11] In an irony of history, Prime Minister Recep Tayyip Erdoğan's Justice and Development Party (AKP) has raised Turkey's ambition of achieving autarchy in defense matters to an unprecedented level. AKP leaders have gradually undermined some fundamentals of Atatürk's secular and pro-Western legacy, known as Kemalism. But in the last decade the TurAF has been developing in line with Erdoğan's and the AKP's ambitions. While retaining close relations with the West, the TurAF is on the verge of becoming a full-spectrum air force capable of independently pursuing Turkish foreign policy goals.

This chapter first describes Turkey's changing strategic setting as it relates to the TurAF's development. It then scrutinizes the TurAF's employment in real operations. Its distinct roles reflect Ankara's unique strategic ambitions. Finally, the chapter examines Turkey's aerospace goals and procurement programs.

The Strategic Setting

Located at the fault line of international politics, Turkey has confronted a plethora of external and internal challenges. In 1996, for instance, open hostilities between Greece and Turkey almost escalated into conventional war over the islet of Imia/Kardak. As a result of the détente process initiated in 1999, Turkish-Greek relations have improved considerably. These days Ankara views Athens as much less of a security challenge.[12] As a consequence Greek military potential has become less of a driver for the development of Turkish air power than it used to be. Because examining Turkey's strategic setting in its entirety lies outside the scope of this chapter, the discussion here focuses on aspects that are likely to shape Turkish air power.

At the outset of the post–Cold War era, the first Gulf War had a major impact on Turkey's relationship with the United States, Ankara's main supplier of air power matériel. In particular, Washington's approach to Middle Eastern affairs exacerbated Ankara's fight against the PKK, whereas Iran and Syria began to support Turkey's counterinsurgency campaign. Domestically, the AKP's strategic ambitions have influenced Turkey's unprecedented thrust toward autarchy in aerospace matters. Finally, Ankara's strategic relationship with Israel has had far-reaching corollaries for the development of Turkish air power in the last two decades. While Israel initially provided Turkey with an alternative source of state-of-the-art technology, the chasm between Israel and Turkey accelerated Ankara's thrust toward self-reliance.

Turkey and the United States

Despite Turkey's crucial geostrategic position during the Cold War, extreme tension periodically arose between Washington and Ankara. For instance, after Turkey's intervention in—or, depending on the vantage point, invasion of—Cyprus in mid-1974, Congress passed two bills to impose an arms embargo and cease military assistance. The Carter administration finally lifted the embargo after realizing that problematic relations with Turkey harmed Western security interests.[13] The embargo episode continues to color contemporary Turkish attitudes toward the United States.[14]

In the post–Cold War era, Turkey's unstable neighborhood has continued to add to the country's strategic importance. In 2008 a Rand report underlined the country's significance as a hub for U.S. operations in Iraq; more than 70 percent of U.S. military personnel and matériel passed through Turkish territory.[15] Yet both the 1991 Gulf War and the 2003 invasion of Iraq proved critical catalysts for Ankara's reengagement with the Middle East as a complementary and alternative foreign policy option to its pro-Western alignment.

Seizing the 1991 Gulf War as an opportunity to demonstrate Turkey's continuing importance and to foster defense ties with Washington, then president Turgut Özal unswervingly supported the U.S.-led campaign—against the advice of many of his top civilian and military advisers. Yet his hopes did not materialize, and Turkey's relationship with the West hardly improved. Instead, the Gulf War—besides causing losses in trade revenues with Iraq—significantly impeded Turkey's efforts at combating PKK militants, who henceforth used northern Iraq as a logistical base for attacks on Turkish territory.[16]

During Secretary of State Madeleine Albright's 1999 visit to Turkey, then prime minister Mesut Yilmaz raised reservations about Turkey's role in an invasion of Iraq. He highlighted a number of specific concerns, including the possible creation of a Kurdish state. Before the 2003 invasion of Iraq, Erdoğan, then head of the newly formed AKP and expected to become prime minister, was invited to Washington and to the White House. On that occasion he once more made it clear to U.S. decision makers that he did not want Turkey to be the only Muslim state to join the U.S.-led invasion of Iraq. But given the ongoing American force buildup near and in Turkey itself, U.S. decision makers continued their efforts to obtain a solid commitment from Turkey—to no avail.[17]

In early March 2003 the Turkish Parliament by a narrow margin refused to grant the U.S. military the right to use Turkey as a staging post for operations in northern Iraq. Since a reconsideration of the vote was not an option, the United States sought permission to use Turkish air space for air raids against Iraq. The Turkish government immediately granted this request.[18] During Operation Iraqi Freedom carrier-based strikes from the Mediterranean used Turkish air space, but no combat missions were allowed to be flown from Incirlik Air Base, the hub for Operation Northern Watch.[19] As late as March 2009, Turkish defense analysts referred to the U.S.-Turkish relationship as still somewhat frayed by the 2003 disagreements.[20]

The PKK: Ankara's Litmus Test

From its beginning in 1984 to the end of the last decade, the Kurdish insurgency was reported to have claimed in excess of forty thousand lives and thus had become a significant issue for Ankara.[21] The corollaries of Desert Storm hampered Turkey's counterinsurgency against the PKK, as northern Iraq provided a local venue for PKK training camps. Whereas division-level cross-border interventions were still possible in the 1990s,[22] the U.S.-led invasion of Iraq in 2003 and the resulting strained relations between Ankara and Washington made large-scale Turkish operations into northern Iraq impossible. In fact, Operation Iraqi Freedom realized some of Ankara's worst fears; in particular, the Kurdish drive for autonomy and eventual formal independence had gained unprecedented momentum.[23] Moreover, the PKK withdrew from a unilateral cease-fire in the aftermath of the invasion.[24]

With the Kurds as the most loyal backers of U.S. policy in Iraq and with U.S. forces stretched thin, Washington did not answer the Erdoğan government's repeated requests for military assistance to destroy PKK training camps in northern Iraq. By exacerbating one of Ankara's most crucial problems, Washington's actions fueled negative attitudes toward the United States.[25] Only from late 2007 onward did U.S. support in Turkey's efforts to eradicate PKK camps significantly ease the relationship between Ankara and Washington.[26]

In contrast, both Syria and Iran began to tackle the "PKK problem" proactively in the last decade, significantly improving Ankara's relations with Tehran and Damascus. Immediately prior to this warming, relations reached a crisis point in 1998, when Ankara threatened to invade Syria if it continued to harbor PKK leader Abdullah Öcalan.[27] Syria reacted by expelling Öcalan and forcing the PKK to relocate its headquarters to the mountains of northern Iraq.[28] Moreover, the U.S.-led invasion of Iraq proved a catalyst for closer relations. Concerned that an economically robust Kurdish government in northern Iraq could stimulate nationalism among its own Kurdish minority, Damascus sought closer ties with Ankara.[29] Yet more recently, as Syrian president Bashar al-Assad's regime took up arms against his own Sunni population, relations between the two countries dramatically worsened against the background of the Arab Spring.

Turkish-Iranian relations experienced an upswing during Erdoğan's visit to Tehran in July 2004. The countries signed a security cooperation agreement branding the PKK a terrorist organization and set out to cooperate in border protection.[30] Tehran also began attacking PKK-affiliated bases.[31] As of 2010 Iran was the only country to extradite PKK militants to Turkey.[32] Tehran's new behavior was in complete contrast to its behavior of the 1980s and 1990s, when it supported PKK efforts with the aim of destabilizing Turkey.[33] As a consequence coordinated action against the PKK largely overshadowed Ankara's concerns over Iran's growing regional influence or the prospect of Iran possessing nuclear weapons.[34] Although Ankara remains concerned about the long-term security implications of a nuclear-armed Iran, Turkey—despite intense pressure from the United States—joined Brazil in voting against fresh sanctions on Tehran at a United Nations Security Council meeting on June 9, 2010.[35] Turkish officials also unsuccessfully attempted to veto the deployment of elements of NATO's proposed missile-defense umbrella on Turkish soil at NATO's Lisbon summit on November 19–20, 2010, but they managed to avoid any explicit reference to Iran as a threat.[36]

The AKP's Rise to Power

Much of the AKP's core membership originated from hard-line Islamist parties banned by the Constitutional Court for allegedly eroding the

1. Mirage 2000D fighter jet, Operation Serval, *French Air Force*

2. Mirage III fighter jet, *French Air Force*

3. Rafale fighter jet, Operation Unified Protector, *French Air Force*

4. Mirage 2000N fighter jet refueling with a Boeing C-135, *French Air Force*

5. Rafale fighter jet, Operation Unified Protector, *French Air Force*

6. Rafale fighter jet, Operation Serval, *French Air Force*

7. Airbus A400M airlift, *German Air Force*

8. Panavia Tornado multirole fighter, *German Air Force*

9. NHIndustries NH-90, *German Air Force*

10. Eurocopter Tiger, *German Air Force*

11. Eurofighter Typhoon, *German Air Force*

12. RQ-4E Euro Hawk, *German Air Force*

13. F-16C, Turkish Air Force, *Serge Van Heertum*

14. Boeing 737 AEW&C aircraft, *Turkish Air Force*

15. F-4E Phantom, Turkish Air Force, *Serge Van Heertum*

16. C-130E Hercules and C-160D Transall, Turkish Air Force, *Serge Van Heertum*

17. KC-135R tanker aircraft and F-16C fighter-bombers, *Turkish Air Force*

18. F-16 Block 50 plus, *Turkish Air Force*

19. Tornado GR4 armed with Storm Shadow, *Royal Air Force*

20. C-130J Hercules, *Royal Air Force*

21. MQ-9 Reaper remotely piloted air system, *Royal Air Force*

22. C-17A Globemaster III, *Royal Air Force*

23. Eurofighter Typhoon FGR4, *Royal Air Force*

24. Sentinel R1/ASTOR ISTAR Platform, *Royal Air Force*

principle of secularism enshrined in the Turkish constitution. Yet although the AKP did not seek an Islamic state based on the sharia, it did want to build a more Islamic society. From its vantage point, the narrow interpretation of secularism had to be eased, a case in point being the ban on women's wearing headscarves at the university.[37]

In the 2002 election the AKP won 34.4 percent of the popular vote, giving it 363 seats in the 550-member assembly. As the new prime minister, Erdoğan set as his highest priorities fostering economic recovery from the 2001 recession and passing sufficient democratic reforms to open accession negotiations with the European Union (EU).[38] In the subsequent elections of 2007 and 2011, the AKP increased its electoral percentage to 46.6 percent and then to 49.9 percent. In fact, the AKP became the first Turkish political party in more than half a century to remain in power for a third successive term.[39] Steadily increasing its public support, the AKP's success was also an expression of Turkey's new self-image as a regional power more independent from the West. In line with this development, a conservative and nationalist elite has gradually displaced the previous secular and pro-Western Kemalist elite. The new AKP leadership is both more religious and more inclined to embrace Turkey's Ottoman past.[40]

The AKP's grand strategic ambition is to reestablish Turkey as a regional fulcrum, not by restoring political hegemony over the former Ottoman territories, but by tying those countries to Turkey through bilateral relations. Under this policy, while Turkey would seek to maintain good political and economic ties with the West, it would also be elevated as a hub in its own right between the two cultural hemispheres.[41] Accordingly, and despite its Muslim-leaning attitude, Erdoğan's government initiated official accession negotiations with the EU in October 2005.[42] However, while the EU remained ambivalent about Turkish membership, popular support in Turkey for EU membership had started to significantly dwindle. By 2010 the topic of EU membership had almost vanished from the public discourse, and the government remained disinclined to implement the required reforms.[43] Despite this seeming lack of interest, Erdoğan further attempted to harness support for Turkey's EU membership, for instance, in his discussions with German chancellor Angela Merkel during her visit to Ankara in February 2013.[44]

The armed forces saw themselves as the ultimate guardians of Atatürk's secular legacy,[45] and they fiercely opposed the AKP's rise on the basis that it undermined the military's ideological foundation. In 2007, during Turkey's presidential elections, the chief of the Turkish General Staff implicitly threatened to topple the government. In the face of strong popular support for the AKP, this heavy-handed attempt failed, and the military's public prestige and political leverage suffered severe damage.[46] The days when the military could oust democratically elected governments in coups—as had happened in 1960, 1971, 1980, and 1997—had definitely passed.[47]

Having consolidated its power base, Erdoğan's government set out to reshape the military leadership. Large numbers of serving and retired officers, including generals and admirals, were detained on charges of alleged military plots to stage coups.[48] On July 29, 2011, the chief of the Turkish General Staff and the individual service commanders resigned to protest court cases against hundreds of active and retired officers.[49] Some evidence suggests that arrests and resignations of high-ranking TurAF officers weakened the air force's leadership.[50]

Turkey and Israel

In the aftermath of the 1991 Gulf War, Ankara recognized the need for strategic diversification. Essentially for reasons of mutual convenience, Turkey and Israel in 1996 began to maintain a close relationship that provided each country with tangible benefits. The partnership allowed Israel to break out of its regional isolation and to put pressure on Syria, at the time also Ankara's archfoe. For Turkey, Israel presented an alternative avenue for obtaining modern defense technology.[51] This was particularly important in light of frequent restrictions by the U.S. Congress on weapons sales to Turkey.[52]

The alliance of the non-Arab states with the most formidable military forces in the region fundamentally altered the balance of power in the Middle East and presented Syria, Iraq, and Iran with a significant threat. In 1998 Israel's defense minister, Yitzhak Mordechai, publicly underlined this new reality: "When we lock hands we form a powerful fist. . . . Our relationship is a strategic one."[53] The same year, the Turkish ambassador to the United States was reported to have stated that Turkey would consider allowing Israel to use Turkish air space for retaliation against Iraq, which had threatened to launch missiles against Israel.[54] Almost a decade later, on September 6, 2007, the Israeli Air Force did indeed use Turkish air space—albeit without permission—to attack a suspected Syrian nuclear reactor.[55]

Turkish-Israeli relations also resulted in cooperative air combat training. In late 1998 the threat of a TurAF air strike had stopped the Greek Cypriots from deploying Russian-delivered S-300 long-range antiaircraft missiles in the divided island. Allegedly, Turkish pilots had trained in the Negev Desert to take out the missile sites.[56] The first major combined exercise, code-named Anatolian Eagle, was held at the TurAF combat-readiness center near the Turkish city of Konya in June 2001. Complementing significant contributions from Israel and Turkey, the USAF participated with six F-16s.[57]

In the aftermath of the AKP's rise to power in 2002, however, Turkish-Israeli relations gradually deteriorated, and Erdoğan's government began to adopt a pro-Palestinian policy. Israel's 2006 Lebanon campaign further strained Turkish-Israeli relations, with Erdoğan sharply condemning the Israeli attacks.[58] On December 27, 2008, Israel launched Operation Cast Lead—a three-week military offensive in the Gaza Strip. The operation brought about the first substantial rift in Turkish-Israeli relations, directly affecting cooperation at the military level.[59] In October 2009 Ankara excluded the Israeli Air Force from participating in Anatolian Eagle. In protest, the United States and Italy also boycotted the exercise. In a sign of the strained civil-military relations at the time, the Turkish General Staff issued a statement holding Turkish foreign minister Ahmet Davutoğlu responsible.[60]

The following year the Chinese Air Force deployed Sukhoi Su-27 Flankers through Pakistan and Iran to Turkey. The Sino-Turkish

Anatolian Eagle exercise marked the first time that China had ever taken part in a combined exercise in a NATO member country. Turkish officials denied rumors that the TurAF's advanced F-16s had participated in the exercise; because of U.S. objections, the TurAF reportedly used its older F-4 fighter-bombers.[61] Given Sino-Turkish disagreements over the status of the Uighur Muslim minority in Xinjiang,[62] it would be excessive to suggest that a new strategic axis was formed between the two countries. Instead, Anatolian Eagle 2010 particularly emphasized Turkey's wish to acquire a modern fighter-bomber outside U.S. influence—an issue that this chapter will examine in the section on procurement.

The final break between Israel and Turkey occurred on May 31, 2010, when Israeli commandos stormed a flotilla of ships, led by a Turkish Islamist nongovernmental organization, that was attempting to break Israel's embargo on Gaza. In the assault eight Turkish citizens and one Turkish-American were killed, and several more were wounded.[63] After the Israeli government rebuffed Ankara's demands for an official apology, Turkey decided on September 2, 2011, to suspend all military agreements with Israel.[64] Furthermore, Washington's muted response to the incident undermined U.S.-Turkish relations.[65]

The Turkish Air Force in Real Operations

While the TurAF proactively took part in the Balkan air campaigns, its contributions to U.S.-led campaigns in the Middle East were more of a supportive nature. In the context of the Arab Spring, Turkey also participated in NATO's operations over Libya and has been heavily affected by Syria's civil war. Most important, counterinsurgency operations in southeastern Turkey and northern Iraq have absorbed significant TurAF resources since the mid-1980s.

Besides these major operations, the TurAF has joined in selected NATO operations. In 2006, for instance, the TurAF deployed fighter aircraft to the Baltic to conduct NATO air policing missions and contributed a C-130 transport aircraft to NATO's support for the African Union mission in Darfur.[66] The Kabul airport command missions of 2002 and

2005, in which the TurAF performed primarily force-enabling tasks, were perfectly in line with Turkey's restrained approach to operations in Afghanistan.[67]

The Balkan Air Wars

Turkey's first contribution to out-of-area operations in the post–Cold War era did not involve its fighter-bomber fleet, but its transport aircraft. After a French Air Force C-130 Hercules had opened the air bridge into Sarajevo in late June 1992, Turkey participated in the multinational effort to relieve the besieged city. Within two months the international airlift armada clocked in excess of a thousand sorties into Sarajevo. On September 3 the shootdown of an Italian Air Force Alenia G-222—which lacked a self-protection suite—caused a hiatus in the constant stream of transport aircraft. As a consequence the United Nations high commissioner for refugees shut down airlift operations for more than a month. Five NATO air forces—from Britain, Canada, France, Germany, and the United States—resumed the airlift effort in late 1992, providing relief during the critical winter months.[68] Turkey did not join them.

This seemingly insignificant episode during the summer of 1992 revealed a paradigm of Turkey's post–Cold War intervention policy that has—with slight differences in style—remained constant. Operating alongside Western powers, Turkey contributes forces within narrow national constraints and with calculated risk. A year after the initial airlift efforts into Sarajevo, on April 20, 1993, TurAF F-16C fighter-bombers took part in Operation Deny Flight, designed to impose a no-fly zone over Bosnia-Herzegovina. The Turkish jet aircraft arrived eight days after Deny Flight's first combat air patrols on April 12.[69]

Subsequently, the TurAF contributed to Operation Deliberate Force, NATO's brief air campaign in August and September 1995, which was instrumental in bringing about the Dayton Accords and a fragile peace in Bosnia-Herzegovina. Like the German contingent,[70] the Turkish detachment operated under specific national constraints. Thus, Turkish fighter-bombers were primarily restricted to flying combat air patrol

(CAP) sorties. Only if required would they support a multinational rapid reaction force, which had previously been inserted to protect the United Nations Protection Force's potential withdrawal. Taking account of these restrictions, the eighteen TurAF F-16C fighter-bombers assigned to Operation Deliberate Force primarily conducted air-to-air missions flying four to six CAP sorties per day for a total of seventy sorties, accounting for 24 percent of the Deliberate Force CAP volume.[71] In addition, the Turkish detachment executed four strike missions.[72]

In Bosnia-Herzegovina TurAF detachments operated under national constraints that reflected not only deliberate policies but also technical realities. For instance, TurAF transport aircraft were not equipped with adequate self-defense systems.[73] With regard to precision air-to-ground strikes, only the U.S., British, French, and Spanish units possessed the required equipment at the time.[74] In contrast, Dutch or Turkish fighter-bombers, for instance, employed nonprecision munitions on area targets that carried minimal risk of collateral damage.[75] Yet these technical deficiencies were by no means unique to the TurAF or to smaller NATO air forces. For example, no German Tornados were capable of delivering the laser-guided bombs available throughout the 1990s, and only selected German transport aircraft were equipped with adequate self-protection suites.[76] While the TurAF has largely rectified these shortcomings during the last decade, particularly in the domain of precision strike, Ankara has continued to follow narrow rules of engagement when operating alongside Western allies.

The Bosnia conflict revealed another distinct characteristic of Turkey's intervention policy. As an American political scientist phrased it, "Different NATO allies were differently disposed towards the various parties in the conflict, the most visible examples of which were the amity of Germany towards Croatia, of Greece towards Serbia, and of Turkey towards the Bosnian Muslims."[77]

Four years later a TurAF fighter-bomber detachment was again part of a larger multinational coalition in NATO's air campaign for Kosovo. Turkey deployed eleven F-16Cs for Operation Allied Force.[78] TurAF pilots probably operated under national caveats similar to those during Operation Deliberate Force, with their primary task limited to the air-to-air role. Yet at least as important as the TurAF's fighter-bomber contribution was Turkey's aid in absorbing an even greater number of allied planes in theater. By the end of the third week of Operation Allied Force, Gen. Wesley Clark, Supreme Allied Commander Europe (SACEUR), requested three hundred more aircraft. After approving these additional aircraft, NATO asked both Hungary and Turkey to make bases available,[79] but the two countries seem to have granted basing permissions rather reluctantly. Only toward the end of NATO's air campaign did USAF operations out of Turkey and Marine F/A-18 operations out of Hungary begin.[80] More important than Turkey's military contribution were the resulting political significance and leverage—an aspect that became particularly apparent in the course of the Libya air operations. When acting within the framework of a Western or NATO operation, Turkey avoids using "excessive" force against a fellow Muslim nation under any circumstances.

From Desert Storm to Iraqi Freedom

Turkey, the only Muslim-majority member of NATO, did not directly contribute to the liberation of Kuwait in 1991. Yet it offered Incirlik Air Base for logistical purposes as well as for air raids into Iraq, and the air bases at Diyarbakır and Batman served as important hubs for combat search and rescue and special operations. Furthermore, the Turkish Army deployed approximately 100,000 troops along the Iraqi border, pinning down substantial Iraqi forces. In the wake of Operation Desert Storm, Incirlik Air Base in southern Turkey remained an important forward base for allied air operations, particularly to monitor the no-fly zone over northern Iraq.[81]

To protect the Iraqi Kurds from air strikes, the USAF, the Royal Air Force, and the French Air Force kept a wing-sized force at Incirlik Air Base. Operation Provide Comfort was superseded by Operation Northern Watch in January 1997. After the French had decided not to contribute to Operation Northern Watch and withdrawn their forces, the TurAF joined with the United States and Great Britain, and together they provided approximately forty-five combat and support aircraft for Northern Watch.[82]

Protecting Iraqi Kurds from air strikes was an unlikely item on the agenda of Turkish decision makers when they joined Operation Northern Watch. Instead, the operation probably served as a conduit for Turkey to exert its influence over Kurdish-dominated northern Iraq. The no-fly-zone operations over northern and southern Iraq finally proved to be precursors to an invasion of the country. During Operations Enduring Freedom and Iraqi Freedom, Ankara restricted U.S. operations out of Incirlik Air Base to logistical tasks, including troop and matériel transports to Afghanistan and Iraq; it refused to offer the base for combat missions.[83]

Combating the PKK

Turkey's restrained approach to operating alongside Western forces in deployed missions stands in stark contrast to its military campaign against the PKK. In the 1990s the PKK abandoned its small-unit attacks after realizing that the casualties that they inflicted were more than offset by heavy losses suffered at the hands of Turkish close air support. The situation became particularly tense in September 2007, after the PKK had resumed small-unit attacks involving up to two hundred militants. With the PKK intensifying its assaults, the Turkish parliament on October 17 authorized the government to launch a cross-border operation into northern Iraq.[84]

A large-scale Turkish incursion would have threatened to destabilize the relatively calm Kurdish-dominated north of Iraq while U.S. forces were still facing insurgency and civil war in other parts of the country. Only on November 5, 2007, did Washington approve limited cross-border military operations by Turkey. Besides airborne commando forces, TurAF F-16 and F-4 Phantom fighter-bombers, together with Turkish Army AH-1 Cobra and Super Cobra attack helicopters, provided the primary means of conducting operations. The TurAF launched the first of a series of bombing raids on December 16, 2007. Imagery provided by U.S. Predator unmanned aerial vehicles (UAVs), satellites, and U-2 reconnaissance aircraft proved crucial for targeting. The raids reportedly destroyed a large number of shelters and training facilities, yet despite the air strikes the PKK again infiltrated Turkey in the spring of 2008. With its camps and supply lines in northern Iraq no longer immune to Turkish air strikes, however, the PKK was forced to divert resources from waging its campaign in Turkey to protecting its assets in northern Iraq.[85] Although some evidence suggests that the PKK was no longer as strong militarily as it had been in the early 1990s, it continued to exact a steady death toll, specifically through mine attacks.[86]

In light of the Arab Spring, the conflict between PKK separatists and Turkish regular forces intensified. In the summer of 2011 the PKK increased its attacks and killed scores of soldiers.[87] A year later, in the summer of 2012, PKK militants killed more than a hundred members of the Turkish security forces.[88] Hence, honing their skills in counterinsurgency operations remained a top priority for the Turkish military—a topic that will be examined in the section on future ambitions and procurement programs.

Libya Air Operations

The Arab Spring confronted the AKP with difficult decisions. On February 1, 2011, Erdoğan became the first leader to publicly call for the resignation of Egypt's leader, Hosni Mubarak, but he pledged support for the Muammar Gaddafi regime a month later. Turkish-Libyan construction contracts worth $15 billion were at stake, and the AKP had maintained close relations with Gaddafi's regime.[89]

Turkey's position was thus ambivalent, to say the least, as regards the transition from Operation Odyssey Dawn, the American-led coalition operation that started on March 19, 2011, to NATO's Operation Unified Protector at the end of that month. Both American and British officials favored a transfer of responsibility for the Libya air campaign to NATO. The French for their part attempted to carry on within a coalition of the willing framework. In contrast, both Turkey and Germany, which had reservations regarding military action from the outset, hesitated to assign NATO full responsibility for Libya operations.[90] Given Turkey's reluctance to support a NATO operation, President Barack Obama called Prime Minister Erdoğan personally on the second evening of Operation Odyssey Dawn.[91] Dissent by the only Muslim-majority NATO member had to be avoided at all costs.

Beyond the issue of NATO taking full responsibility, tensions were mounting between Ankara and Paris. Specifically, Ankara accused French president Nicolas Sarkozy of pursuing French interests over those of the Libyan people. The French failure to invite Turkish officials to the crisis summit at the Elysée Palace on March 19, which marked the start of the Libya campaign, did not ease the situation. Franco-Turkish disagreements were underpinned by the French president's staunchly opposing Turkey's membership in the EU. To undermine Sarkozy's ambition to proceed with a coalition of the willing format, Ankara supported sole NATO control of Libya operations, quite in contrast to its previous position.[92]

On March 24, six days into Operation Odyssey Dawn, Secretary of State Hillary Clinton obtained a preliminary agreement during a telephone call with her counterparts in Turkey, France, and Britain, but the Turks still balked at reaching a final agreement. Aware of Arab public opinion and concerns over possible civilian deaths, the leadership did not feel at ease with the coalition's ground attacks. Yet despite the ongoing air strikes Turkey eventually gave in, paving the way for the operation's being handed over to NATO.[93]

The Libya debate commonly overlooks that no clear-cut transition took place between Operation Odyssey Dawn and Operation Unified Protector. Instead, the two operations ran in parallel for a while, with Operation Unified Protector increasingly assuming a broader array of responsibilities. The NATO effort began as an arms embargo operation on March 23, 2011. Two days later it was extended to include a no-fly-zone component. Finally, on March 31 Operation Unified Protector became the framework for all military operations in the context of the humanitarian crisis in Libya and as such included the "protection of civilians" mission.[94]

From the start Turkey participated in NATO's maritime patrols in the Mediterranean to enforce the arms embargo. Yet the air-to-ground attacks remained a major dilemma for Turkish decision makers. By supporting NATO control of Libya operations, the Turks apparently hoped to exert influence in order to limit and shorten the air campaign.[95] After several unsuccessful calls for a cease-fire, Erdoğan on May 3 called on Gaddafi to step down and leave Libya.[96]

For the no-fly-zone component of Operation Unified Protector, Ankara dispatched six F-16C fighter aircraft and two KC-135 tanker aircraft supported by approximately 130 personnel to Sigonella Air Base in Sicily. This deployment lasted from April 4 to November 2.[97] Turkey's military contribution was of a primarily defensive nature and in particular avoided assault sorties.[98] Reportedly, the two TurAF KC-135 tanker aircraft were exclusively detailed to support Turkish missions only. Thus, Ankara put a premium on not even indirectly supporting allied strike missions with AAR.

Despite or because of Turkey's restrained stance, which ostensibly sought to mitigate an "overly aggressive" air campaign, opinion polls revealed that Arab nations perceived Ankara as playing the most constructive role in the Arab Spring; France placed a distant second.[99] Libyan National Transitional Council (NTC) chief Mustafa Abdul Jalil also reflected this viewpoint when he received foreign leaders in Tripoli, after Gaddafi had been ousted. On September 16, one day after Sarkozy and British prime minister David Cameron's visit to the Libyan capital, Erdoğan became the third senior foreign leader whom Jalil met at the Tripoli airport.[100] After the Friday prayer thirty thousand Muslims reportedly welcomed Erdoğan.

Turkey and the Civil War in Syria

"An unidentified aerial target violated Syrian air space, coming from the west at a very low altitude and at high speed over territorial waters, so the Syrian anti-air defenses counteracted with anti-aircraft artillery," said a press statement by the official Syrian Arab News Agency on Friday, June 22, 2012.[101] According to Turkish officials, the RF-4E Phantom reconnaissance aircraft entered Syrian air space near the Syrian port of Latakia by mistake. Some speculate that the aircraft, which carried dedicated reconnaissance equipment, was watching for arms shipments. As of late June U.S. officials stated that it was still unclear what the mission of the Turkish reconnaissance aircraft had been and where it was relative to Syrian territory when it was shot down.[102]

Whatever the causes for the shootdown of the Phantom, the incident occurred during a period of increased tension between Syria and Turkey, sparked by the internal unrest in Syria. As of 2012 Turkey had supposedly emerged as a main conduit for weapons to the Syrian rebels, with funds coming from Saudi Arabia and Qatar. At the same time southern Turkey had been flooded with Syrian refugees, among them members of the Free Syrian Army.[103] In mid-2012 Turkey formally denied arming the rebels, but Erdoğan pledged all possible support to liberating Syria from dictatorship.[104]

Changing the rules of engagement after the shootdown, Erdoğan announced that military vehicles or aircraft approaching the Syrian-Turkish border with hostile intent would be assessed as threats and treated as targets. At the diplomatic level Ankara—citing Article 4 of NATO's founding treaty—called for consultations among NATO ambassadors in Brussels. NATO expressed strong support for Turkey's course of action,[105] but NATO officials did not put forward any concrete measures against Syria apart from the intention to closely monitor the situation. "It is my clear expectation that the situation won't continue to escalate," NATO Secretary General Anders Fogh Rasmussen stated. "What we have seen is a completely unacceptable act, and I would expect Syria to take all necessary steps to avoid such events in the future."[106]

Four days after the incident off the Syrian coast, Ankara, emboldened by NATO's declaration of support, raised the stakes by issuing warnings of retaliatory strikes.[107] At the same time the Turkish military deployed more tanks and other heavy military equipment to the Syrian border area. To counter the air threat, the Turkish military also deployed ground-based air defense units along the Syrian-Turkish border. These military deployments, as well as Turkey's diplomatic activities, were aimed at putting Syria on notice that its military could not operate in the border area with impunity. Toward the end of June 2012, the TurAF did indeed scramble jets on several occasions to respond to Syrian helicopters approaching the border, but no violation of Turkish air space was recorded.[108]

Turkey's warnings and military deployments, however, did not avert further incidents. On October 3, 2012, shelling from across the border killed five Turkish civilians and wounded several more in the Turkish border town of Akçakale. This marked the most serious incident of cross-border shelling so far. Turkey immediately retaliated by firing at targets inside Syria for the first time since the civil war in Syria began. Turkish-built T-155 Firtina self-propelled howitzers executed the retaliatory fire. Identifying targets across the border seems to have been a joint action, involving AN/TPQ-36 Firefinder radars and RF-4E Phantom reconnaissance aircraft.[109] The Turkish Parliament also passed a bill authorizing cross-border operations for a one-year period, prompting domestic accusations that Erdoğan's AKP was acting as Washington's henchman.[110]

Late on October 10, a week after the shelling of Akçakale, TurAF F-16Cs forced a Syrian airliner traveling from Moscow to Damascus to land at Ankara's Esenboğa Airport, where Turkish authorities conducted security checks. The aircraft, suspected of transferring arms, was allowed to take off again early on October 11.[111] In light of ongoing tension between Syria and Turkey, the forced landing received significant media attention. Yet this action did not represent a fundamental shift in policy. A decade previously, following its May 2000 withdrawal from southern Lebanon and the continuing skirmishes along the border, Israel—greatly concerned about an Iranian arms airlift to Hezbollah—had persuaded Turkey to prevent Iranian aircraft allegedly carrying weapons to Syria from using Turkish air space.[112] Turkish authorities had also intercepted arms transfers from North Korea that violated embargoes and inspected cargo flights to Lebanon and Sudan. In March 2011, for example, Turkey inspected an Iranian aircraft en route to Aleppo, Syria, and Turkish authorities seized embargoed military equipment.[113]

On November 21, 2012, the Turkish government formally requested that NATO deploy Patriot missiles, capable of theater ballistic missile defense (TBMD). In its request the government stressed that the equipment would never be used to enforce a no-fly zone or to support offensive actions. NATO believed that the deployment of the defensive systems would contribute to de-escalation and would demonstrate alliance solidarity and resolve,[114] while Russia and Iran took the opposite view and openly condemned it.[115] Despite the international controversy NATO foreign ministers approved the deployment of Patriot missiles for defensive purposes on December 4, 2012. Germany, the Netherlands, and the United States declared their intention to provide Patriot missile batteries.[116] In early 2013 each country deployed two Patriot missile batteries to Turkey.[117]

Future Ambitions and Procurement Programs

Limiting the discussion to TurAF acquisition programs would provide too narrow a focus to capture Turkey's aerospace ambitions. Therefore, this chapter also examines the acquisition of attack helicopters and the development of ballistic missiles. Turkish procurement officials face two major challenges. While Turkey's top decision makers have embarked on an ambitious path toward substantial autarchy in producing defense matériel, procurement officials must strike a sensible balance between foreign products and indigenously designed and produced equipment. In addition to this drive toward autonomy, Turkey's military has struggled to adequately balance priorities between matériel primarily geared to counterinsurgency and equipment for regular warfare.

Defense Funding

In stark contrast to the general trend within a majority of NATO countries, Turkey's defense budget has been rising. Not only the country's economic growth but also Turkey's combat against the PKK and the threat posed by the Syrian civil war contributed to the budget increase. Between 2012 and 2013 the Ministry of Defense's budget increased from 18.2 billion Turkish lira (TRY) to 20.3 billion TRY (approximately $11.25 billion). This figure does not include undisclosed extrabudgetary resources, including a fund created for arms procurement.[118]

Most observers believe this trend will continue and predict a 20 percent increase in defense funding up to 2015. Since defense spending depends strongly on Turkey's overall economic growth, one must guard against an overly optimistic outlook. Turkey's economy has been known to grow erratically, and significant economic challenges persist. For example, in the aftermath of Turkey's post-2000 economic slump, a mismatch between Turkey's fiscal reality and its defense ambitions became obvious, with effects that included cancellation of several key programs. Since the AKP's rise to power, however, Turkey has experienced sustained economic growth up to the time of writing.[119]

Although specific figures of the TurAF's budget share are not publicly available, it can be assumed that the army receives the largest budget share of the services. Unlike other Western militaries, the Turkish armed forces have a clear hierarchy that stifles interservice feuds over funds. With the Turkish Army considered the senior service, the chief of the general staff is generally selected from the army officer corps,[120] and he has a vital say with regard to acquisition of defense matériel. He and the prime minister, the minister of defense, and the chief of Turkey's Undersecretariat for Defense Industries make up the Defense Industry Executive Committee, the ultimate decision-making body for Turkish arms procurement.[121]

Given the status of the TurAF as a junior service, its continuing rise to become one of the premier NATO air forces is all the more impressive. Since Italy has reduced its order for the Lockheed Martin F-35A Lightning II JSF from 131 to 90 aircraft in 2012, Turkey is likely to become the largest non-U.S. NATO purchaser of the advanced, stealth-capable fighter-bomber.[122]

Foreign Arms Supply

Between 2000 and 2010 the United States and Germany each supplied approximately 30 percent of Turkey's defense imports, followed by Israel with an 11 percent share of foreign acquisitions by value.[123] Given the significantly damaged relationship between the two countries, Israel ceased to deliver arms to Turkey. Among the European nations, Italy has recently emerged as a leading supplier of arms to Turkey. In addition to good political relations between Rome and Ankara, this results from Italy's willingness to transfer technology to Turkish companies[124]—a factor that has become a key to doing defense business with Turkey, as will be discussed later in the chapter.

Traditionally, Turkey has purchased combat aircraft of U.S. origin, such as the McDonnell Douglas F-4 Phantom and the Lockheed Martin F-16 Fighting Falcon. The purchase of the JSF will continue this tradition. On February 23, 2012, Minister of Defense Ismet Yilmaz confirmed Turkey's plan to purchase one hundred F-35As. In his statement, Yilmaz explicitly referred to ongoing negotiations with U.S. officials regarding transfer of technology—a vital issue in Turkey's acquisition strategy. "We continue talks with the US for Turkey to obtain local software source codes for electronic warfare, as well as for integrating new arms and ammunition independently on F-35s," Yilmaz commented.[125] Yet, according to a Turkish defense analyst, the likelihood that Turkey would receive software source codes that the United States does not even share with some of its closest allies was minimal.[126] Nevertheless, Ankara remained committed to the project. Turkish Aerospace Industries (TAI), Turkey's state-owned aerospace company, had already opened a composites manufacturing facility in Ankara in November 2008, securing a significant Turkish work share in the multinational F-35 project.[127]

To mitigate dependence on nonaccessible software source codes, Turkey launched the Özgür ("independent" or "free" in Turkish) project. Its goal is to develop an indigenous avionics suite solution, including software to be integrated on TurAF F-16 Block 30 fighter-bombers. The nationally developed solution is supposed to allow Turkey to autonomously integrate locally developed weapons.[128] Limited to the oldest F-16s in the TurAF's inventory, the exact extent of indigenously accessible software source codes cannot be assessed. Reportedly, a U.S.-Turkish software source code transfer underpinning the Özgür project might have been related to the NATO/U.S. basing of the AN/TPY-2 early warning radar in Kürecik, which is part of NATO's collective missile shield.

The issue of dependence on foreign arms supply manifested itself especially strongly as relations between Turkey and Israel worsened. After the two countries embarked on a strategic partnership in the mid-1990s, Israeli companies won contracts to upgrade TurAF F-4E and F-5 fighter jets.[129] Israel also filled a niche by providing Turkey with aerospace-related matériel, such as Popeye-I and Popeye-II medium-range air-to-surface missiles and Harpy antiradar drones. Before cutting all military ties with Israel on September 2, 2011, Turkey had taken delivery of ten Heron medium-altitude long-endurance (MALE) UAVs from Israel Aerospace Industries and Elbit Systems in 2010.[130]

Given the stalemate in the relationship between the two countries, the Israeli Ministry of Defense canceled the delivery of advanced reconnaissance pods for the TurAF's RF-4E Phantoms in December 2011.[131] Subsequently, in early 2012, the ministry also blocked sales of Israeli components to Boeing because the components in question were to be fitted into AEW&C aircraft destined for the TurAF.[132] Withholding these components might have further delayed the Peace Eagle program under which Boeing built four 737-derived AEW&C aircraft for the TurAF.[133]

Drive toward Self-Reliance

The United States ceased military assistance to Turkey and imposed an arms embargo in the wake of Turkey's 1974 invasion of Cyprus. More recently, in early 2008, Turkey attempted to acquire two MQ-9 Reaper and four MQ-1 Predator MALE UAVs—vital assets to bolster Turkish operations against PKK militants. By mid-2012 the Pentagon's Defense Security Cooperation Agency had still not undertaken concrete steps to proceed with the deal and had not asked for Senate approval. Reportedly, some U.S. senators were reluctant to sell this key technology to any countries other than the United States' closest allies, such as the United Kingdom.[134]

Given Turkey's history of at times facing significant obstacles to acquiring key technologies, the AKP's pledge during the 2011 election campaign to make the country self-sufficient in defense by 2023 was timely.[135] The reelection of the AKP for a third consecutive term gave a new impetus to Turkey's drive toward self-reliance—a path that three successive AKP governments have followed since 2002. The chief of Turkey's Undersecretariat for Defense Industries and Turkey's top procurement official, Murad Bayar, accordingly anticipated a substantial increase in locally designed and developed weapon systems which Turkey used to import. By 2011 the indigenous defense industry had become capable of meeting more than half of the Turkish armed forces' acquisition requirements. Key goals over the next fifteen years are to develop and manufacture indigenous main battle tanks, UAVs, satellites, trainer aircraft, and helicopters, and Turkey is seeking partners to manufacture fighter jets and submarines.[136]

Despite this move toward autarchy, Turkey still depends substantially on foreign suppliers.[137] According to Murad Bayar, Turkey needs to import approximately 35 percent of so-called critical military technologies, specifically engines.[138] Although Turkey might not realize all of its ambitions in the foreseeable future and dependence on foreign sources might persist longer than the country wishes, concrete evidence indicates that Turkey's thrust toward autonomy is bearing fruit. In 2011, for instance, Turkish defense exports reached $1.1 billion; prior to 2010 the export figure had been less than $700 million. Other Islamic countries constitute key markets for Turkey's defense industry.[139] On March 27, 2012, Ankara released a five-year plan for the defense industry that reiterated Turkey's drive toward independence and toward increased foreign sales of defense matériel.[140]

Turkey also considers bilateral and multilateral cooperation as a means to strengthen its defense industrial base. Accordingly, the Undersecretariat for Defense Industries released a requirement that foreign companies seeking Turkish deals guarantee that at least 50 percent of the work be performed locally by Turkish companies.[141] Italy, in particular, has met this requirement, as the country is willing to share technology generously with Turkish companies. In 2007 the Italians won a major deal estimated at $2.7 billion. Under two separate contracts signed in 2008 and 2010, the Italian-British AgustaWestland, which is part of Italy's Finmeccanica, would jointly produce attack helicopters with TAI. In the meantime TAI has successfully tested two T-129 gunships, Turkey's version of the A-129 Mangusta. As of the time of writing, the initial order had increased from fifty-one to sixty helicopters.[142] The T-129 is to be equipped with an indigenous antitank missile, the Umtas. With a range of eight kilometers, it has infrared imaging and laser-seeker homing options.[143] Originally, in 2000, Bell Helicopter Textron, manufacturer of the U.S. Marine Corps's AH-1Z and AH-1W Super Cobras, was poised to win the attack helicopter contract, yet disputes over price and—most notably—technology transfer derailed the deal.[144]

According to Giuseppe Orsi, AgustaWestland's chief executive officer, Turkey will become an exporter of helicopter gunships after completion of the program: "Turkey definitely will earn high-tech export capabilities."[145] Pakistan, also heavily involved in counterinsurgency operations, has shown an interest in the T-129, which was designed to meet mission profile requirements almost fully identical to those of Pakistan. Yet the U.S.-built engines are a source of concern for Pakistan, which fears potential sanctions.[146]

As with the T-129 project, Turkey set out to become a regional in-service support hub for potential A400M customers in the Middle East. Turkey itself has placed orders for ten A400M heavy-lift aircraft, and TAI is a key supplier to Airbus Military's facility in Spain.[147]

Gaining access to advanced aerospace technology lies at the heart of Turkey's ambition to develop and build a modern combat aircraft in parallel to the acquisition of a hundred JSFs. Turkish officials who seek to reduce the country's dependence on Washington consider most of the TurAF fighter fleet open to U.S. influence, with the exception of its older F-4 aircraft, which were modernized by Israel, and its oldest F-16s, updated in Turkey. "Turkey wants part of its fighter aircraft fleet to remain outside the technological and other influence by the United States," a Turkish defense analyst confirmed.[148]

On December 14, 2010, then minister of defense Vecdi Gönül publicly announced a plan to develop an indigenous fighter aircraft by the Turkish Republic's hundredth anniversary in 2023 (first flight). In this effort Turkey would partner with a friendly country other than the United States. At the time Gönül considered South Korea a potential partner in this endeavor.[149] Since Turkey had already drawn extensively upon South Korean expertise, the Far Eastern country did indeed appear to be a viable partner. For instance, Turkey's T-155 Firtina self-propelled howitzer is a Turkish derivative of South Korea's K-9 Thunder and is built under license in Turkey. Turkey has also been developing its first indigenous main battle tank, the Altay, with the support of South Korea's Hyundai Rotem.[150] Yet talks on the codevelopment of a fighter aircraft produced no results, with Seoul and Ankara reportedly unable to agree on terms for cooperation.[151] The two countries' different levels of expertise in the aerospace dimension might have presented a major obstacle to an equal partnership.[152] Attempts at bilateral collaboration between Brazil and Turkey also failed to yield any concrete results, despite the support of the two heads of state.[153]

Turkish officials also considered buying a squadron of Eurofighter Typhoons to complement the future F-35 fleet with a non-U.S. combat aircraft.[154] Yet these plans came to an abrupt halt in December 2010, when then minister of defense Gönül ruled out the Eurofighter Typhoon for unspecified reasons.[155] At the time of writing, Ankara was seeking assistance from Saab Gripen in the conceptual design work for its national combat aircraft.[156] In May 2013 TAI for the first time displayed three conceptual designs for the indigenous combat aircraft, the TF-X fighter. All three concepts featured a design with a low radar cross section and an internal weapons bay.[157]

At the same time Turkey has launched a program to develop an indigenous jet trainer,[158] and the locally developed Hürkuş-A turboprop basic trainer aircraft made its maiden flight on August 29, 2013. The Hürkuş is planned to be produced in three variants: basic trainer, advanced trainer, and close air support aircraft. Though a Turkish design, the aircraft relies on a set of foreign-sourced key subsystems, most notably its Pratt & Whitney Canada turboprop engine.[159] Engine selection is also a critical issue for Turkey's indigenous fighter aircraft project. In late 2013 Turkey's top procurement official, Murad Bayar, said that Turkey would choose between European and U.S. engines; the latter were believed to better meet the program's specifications.[160]

Turkey's planned acquisition of two sets of fighter aircraft, one U.S.-sourced and one indigenous, has a precursor in the acquisition of targeting pods. In January 2010 Lockheed Martin announced a deal for the delivery of an estimated sixty advanced U.S. targeting and navigation pods—a balanced mix of the AN/AAQ-33 Sniper advanced targeting pod (ATP) and the AN/AAQ-13 low-altitude navigation and targeting infrared for night (LANTIRN) with enhanced range (ER). These pods complement or supplant the TurAF's basic LANTIRN pods. Simultaneously, the Turkish arms manufacturer Aselsan has been developing a targeting pod for integration on TurAF F-16 and F-4 fighter-bombers.[161]

Turkey has made significant progress in the development and buildup of an indigenous deep-strike capability. On June 4, 2011, the Defense Industries Research and Development Institute (SAGE), the missile specialist subsidiary operating under Turkey's state scientific research institute Tübitak, unveiled the first indigenous air-launched cruise missile, dubbed Hassas Güdümlü Stand-off Mühimattı ("standoff missile," or SOM, in Turkish). Two months later, on August 9, the missile made its maiden flight over the Black Sea, covering a distance of more than a hundred nautical miles and guided by a Global Positioning System/Inertial Navigation System (GPS/INS). The SOM is reported to be capable of a variety of programmable ingress and attack profiles. Besides GPS/INS, midcourse guidance is supported by terrain reference updates and image-based midcourse navigation provided by the missile's imaging infrared seeker. Thus, the missile can navigate without GPS if the latter is denied or degraded. Moreover, the missile has a two-way data link for in-flight retasking. According to Tübitak SAGE, Turkish engineers developed the SOM, including its software, and *Jane's Defence Weekly* stated that with the exception of a French microturbo engine, most of the missile's elements were of Turkish design.[162] Although the SOM's proportion of foreign components cannot be assessed precisely, the cruise missile nevertheless appears to represent a milestone on Turkey's path toward greater autonomy since it requires mastery of a plethora of advanced aerospace technologies. Concurrently with the development of the SOM, Turkish engineers forged ahead with the development of an indigenously designed joint direct attack munition (JDAM) equivalent, the Hassas Güdüm Kiti (HGK), and a precision glide bomb, the Kanatlı Güdüm Kiti (KGK), with a range of up to sixty-five nautical miles.[163]

Interestingly, the development of the SOM, the HGK, and the KGK seems to have taken place in parallel to the acquisition of advanced U.S. air-launched cruise missiles, such as the AGM-84K standoff land attack missile (SLAM)-ER and the AGM-154 joint standoff weapon (JSOW). Raytheon stated that Turkey was the first international customer for the JSOW.[164] Thus the same logic applies as in the case of targeting pods: while Turkey purchases state-of-the-art technology from the United States, securing an advantage in its neighborhood, the country simultaneously undertakes efforts to complement foreign technology with indigenously designed equipment.

This arsenal of air-launched cruise missiles together with satellite imagery will provide Turkey with a significant capability for standoff deep strike. As early as 2004 the Turkish government identified space as a priority for scientific and technological progress.[165] At almost the same time, the Turkish armed forces declared space to be their emerging fourth service, with an emphasis on intelligence gathering, communications, and early warning.[166] In early 2012 *Defense News* highlighted a Turkish government road map outlining the country's space ambitions. The road map reportedly predicted seventeen Turkish satellites in orbit by 2020: three electro-optical reconnaissance and observation satellites, two synthetic aperture radar (SAR) satellites for reconnaissance and observation, one infrared satellite for early warning, five communications satellites, and six regional positioning satellites.[167] In a speech at a March 2013 air power conference in Istanbul, however, Undersecretary for Defense Industries Murad Bayar referred only to reconnaissance and observation satellites as well as to communications satellites, leaving room for speculation regarding indigenous space-based navigation and early warning capabilities.[168]

On December 18, 2012, Turkey's Göktürk-2, an electro-optical reconnaissance and observation satellite, was launched from a Chinese space station. The satellite consists of 80 percent domestically developed technology, and its software was developed entirely in Turkey.[169] At the same time, Ankara's aspiration is to develop an indigenous capability to launch satellites, at first into low earth orbit. Turkey's space ambitions are supposed to culminate in a fully operational space command by 2023.[170]

Addressing Requirements for Asymmetric Warfare

Given the significant number of casualties that Turkey has suffered in its fight against the PKK, a number of Turkish defense officials and analysts accord the highest priority to improving Turkey's ability to conduct counterinsurgency operations. These circles heavily criticize conventional programs that cannot contribute directly to combating PKK militants. Accordingly, they classify programs such as the acquisition of AEW&C or long-range air defense systems as falling outside Turkey's strategic needs.[171] Almost confirming this logic, Turkey's top defense procurement body deferred in mid-2012 a decision on the long-range air defense system and instead prioritized the early development of an indigenous armed MALE UAV.[172] In contrast, Syria's civil war and the threat it posed to Turkey have—according to some defense analysts—revealed the need to boost conventional warfare capabilities.[173]

Recent developments have highlighted in an almost unprecedented manner Turkey's requirements to strike an appropriate balance between asymmetric and regular warfare. Helicopter gunships and UAVs are principal weapons for the counterinsurgency mission, and Turkish security forces fighting the PKK in southeastern Turkey are in dire need of a robust number of T-129 gunships. In October 2012 the Turkish Army's attack helicopter fleet of six AH-1W Super Cobras, purchased from the United States in the early 1990s, and around twenty older Cobras was augmented with three former U.S. Marine Corps Super Cobras as a stopgap solution to support a sustained counterinsurgency campaign.[174]

As noted previously, Turkey used to depend on imports from Israel for MALE UAVs, and attempts to acquire advanced MALE UAVs from the United States have stalled. As of mid-2012 U.S. officials had signaled to their Turkish counterparts that Congress was likely to block the sale.[175] As a consequence Turkey intensified its indigenous MALE UAV program. At a meeting on July 17, 2012, Turkey's Undersecretariat for Defense Industries announced the planned development of an armed MALE UAV and initiated contract negotiations with TAI to develop a long-range, armed version of the existing Anka ("phoenix" in Turkish) UAV concept.[176] Underlining Ankara's wish to operate truly independent MALE UAV systems, national data links have been developed for aerial assets, including UAVs.[177] Nevertheless, the Anka project was—as of the time of writing—dependent on German engine technology, highlighting still existing shortcomings of Turkey's emerging defense industrial base.[178]

In a parallel effort the state-owned Turkish company Roketsan launched a program to develop and manufacture a 2.75-inch semi-active, laser-guided rocket with a range of eight kilometers. Dubbed Cirit ("javelin" in Turkish), the rocket is designed to destroy lightly armored targets.[179] The Cirit is intended to become a main armament for both the T-129 gunship and the armed version of the Anka MALE UAV.[180] These two systems, combined with the indigenously designed laser-guided rocket, are likely to significantly boost the Turkish armed forces' counterinsurgency capability.

Likewise, if Turkey realizes its ambitions in space, the satellite constellation will provide a space-based architecture not only for regular warfare but also for counterinsurgency operations. Specifically, a national satellite communications link can facilitate over-the-horizon guidance of the Anka MALE UAV, which would be necessary for seeking and destroying PKK camps beyond Turkey's border. At the time of writing, the Anka UAV was controlled by means of a line-of-sight data link.[181]

Essential Weapon Systems in an Unstable Environment

In July 2012 Iran launched surface-to-surface missiles (SSMs) at a mock-up air base in the desert with an explicit intent to send a deterrent message. The majority of the missiles fired during the Great Prophet 7 missile exercise landed within two kilometers of the center of the mock-up.[182] Syria also has SSMs in its arsenal—mostly of Soviet/Russian provenance.[183] Reportedly, the Syrian regime attempted to acquire Iskander 9K720 (NATO code name SS-26 Stone) SSMs some years ago. Fortunately for Turkey, these attempts have not borne fruit so far as the missile is very accurate and would pose a significant threat to Turkey's southern airfields.

Iran's 2012 missile exercise and Syria's attempts to acquire highly accurate SSMs unambiguously illustrate Turkey's unstable environment. Turkey's southern air bases, particularly Incirlik Air Base—a hub widely used by Turkey's NATO allies—are within range of regional theater ballistic missiles. Given Turkey's geographic position, the proliferation of more accurate SSMs is more of a danger than the proliferation of SSMs with an extended range.

Turkey's response to the threat potential is both defensive and deterrent/retaliatory. With regard to the latter, Turkey launched its own ballistic missile program. In late 2012 press reports stated that Turkey had successfully developed an SSM in the two-hundred-kilometer range class and that the missile had entered the army inventory. "Now, the next target is 500 kilometers," Nihat Ergün, the country's science, industry, and technology minister, said. "We have the technology to develop this missile. It finds the target making use of the GPS technology and ground maps."[184] Earlier in 2012 press reports alluded to the development of a Turkish ballistic missile with a range of twenty-five hundred kilometers in the medium term. At the time missile technology experts doubted Turkey's capacity to swiftly develop missiles in both the five-hundred-kilometer and twenty-five-hundred-kilometer range classes.[185]

Besides technological feasibility, Turkey's SSM program also raised doubts regarding the possibility of violating international arms control regimes on missile range and payload. A Middle East expert argued that Turkey's SSM ambitions were akin to those of rogue states: "Why would the Turks need these missiles? Where will they use them? Against which threats? It is also intriguing that Turkey, which seeks a modern air force with deterrent firepower, goes along the path many rogue states with no modern air force capabilities have gone."[186]

Given Turkey's unpredictable and unstable environment, an accurate long-range ballistic missile might significantly enhance the Turkish armed forces' conventional deterrence. In 2007 an expert on Turkey identified such a conventional missile capability as a possible response to Iran's nuclear program—an alternative to Turkey's developing its own nuclear device or expanding its cooperation on missile defense with the United States and Israel.[187] It is worth noting that South Korea, which has supported Turkey's defense industrial base, particularly in the domain of land systems, has also been pursuing ambitious cruise and ballistic missile programs.[188] Thus, criticism that Turkey's ballistic missile ambitions would lead the country down the path to becoming a rogue state is misplaced.

Another controversial program, at the time of writing supported by only a minority of Turkish defense analysts, is the acquisition of a long-range air and missile defense system as Turkey's defensive response to the proliferation of SSMs in its neighborhood.[189] In particular, NATO's 2013 Patriot deployment to Turkey during Syria's civil war caused Turkish commentators to argue that a national capability was no longer required; NATO had effectively filled the void.[190]

In 2007 Turkey's Undersecretariat for Defense Industries issued a request for information to potential bidders for the acquisition of the Turkish Long-Range Air and Missile Defense System (T-LORAMIDS).[191] Four systems were shortlisted, with bids coming from the United States, Europe, Russia, and China. Raytheon and Lockheed Martin offered the Patriot system based on a mix of Patriot Advanced Capability (PAC)-2/PAC-3 missiles, European missile maker Eurosam offered the SAMP/T based on the Aster 30 missile, China Precision Machinery Import Export Corporation (CPMIEC) offered an export version of its HQ-9 system (FD-2000), and Rosoboronexport from Russia offered an upgraded version of its S-300 long-range systems, the Antey 2500.[192] With a final decision deferred, defense analysts surmised in late 2012 that the ambitious $4 billion program might be postponed indefinitely.[193] Originally conceived as an off-the-shelf acquisition, the Defense Industry Executive Committee, chaired by Prime Minister Erdoğan, restructured the T-LORAMIDS program in January 2013. While the contenders' bids would remain valid, coproduction, including an enhancement of the systems and missiles through codevelopment, became an added focus.[194] Thus, Erdoğan's decision was fully in line with Turkey's thrust toward self-sufficiency. One Western military source put it succinctly: "Turkey wants ownership of the missiles and their technology. It does not want any restrictions to be imposed on the missile's use."[195]

While Eurosam reacted by offering a joint venture with a Turkish company, the U.S. bidder was keen to advertise the level of work share it was offering to Turkey.[196] Yet the latter offer did not guarantee transfer of critical technology.

On September 26, 2013, the Defense Industry Executive Committee selected the Chinese FD-2000 and decided to start contract talks with China's CPMIEC to jointly produce the missiles and their systems in Turkey,[197] creating consternation with Turkey's NATO partners. In light of CPMIEC's being under U.S. sanctions for violations of the Iran, North Korea, and Syria Nonproliferation Act, U.S. State Department spokeswoman Jennifer Psaki told reporters on September 30, "The main concern here was that the Turkish government was having contract discussions with a US-sanctioned company for a missile defense system that was not operable with NATO systems."[198] A day before Psaki's statement, China's state-run Xinhua news agency published an editorial noting, "There is no conflict of geopolitical interests, [so] China is willing to share its sophisticated missile technology [with Turkey]."[199] China's willingness to offer generous technology transfers coupled with an attractive price ($3.44 billion for twelve firing units)[200] and local work share was—according to Murad Bayar—a determining factor. He also remarked that T-LORAMIDS would be fully integrated into the Turkish and NATO air defense systems.[201] Integration of the FD-2000 into a NATO architecture was—at the time of writing—likely to remain a bone of contention.

Turkey's long-range air and missile defense system program originally had been conceived as operating independently from NATO's collective missile shield. As part of the latter program, the alliance had deployed an X-band radar in Turkey for early detection of missiles launched in the region.[202] Although Turkey's national system and NATO's missile defense shield aim to defeat ballistic missiles of different range classes, some degree of integration between the two systems would nevertheless be required for T-LORAMIDS to operate more effectively.[203] Throughout the evaluation process, the United States and some of its European partners staunchly opposed a potential integration of Chinese or Russian systems into the NATO missile shield, yet commercial motivations might have spurred Western concerns.[204] As regards T-LORAMIDS's antiaircraft role, integration into the alliance's network-based air defense architecture would be required for the system to work efficiently. However, NATO paid for approximately half of Turkey's air defense radars, which are an integral part of the NATO Air Defense Ground Environment, and NATO consent might be required for T-LORAMIDS's integration. In the wake of the September 26 decision, Bayar interestingly remarked that the system's primary mission would be air defense, with ballistic missile defense considered secondary, and he added that if contract negotiations with CPMIEC failed, Ankara would begin talks with the second comer, Eurosam.[205]

T-LORAMIDS was conceived as the upper tier of a triple-layered SAM network. The medium (T-MALAMIDS) and lower tier (T-LALAMIDS) systems were—at the time of writing—developed by two Turkish companies. Aselsan, acting as prime contractor, was responsible for the development of missile seekers, sensors, radars, and command and control systems, whereas Roketsan was responsible for developing the missile.[206] After rejecting foreign tenders, Turkey's Undersecretariat for Defense Industries signed contracts with Aselsan and Roketsan in 2011. The first test-firing of the lower-tier system occurred against the backdrop of Turkey's selection of the Chinese FD-2000 system in September 2013.[207]

After the downing of the RF-4E on June 22, 2012, analysts concurred that the TurAF Phantom had fallen victim to an attempt to test Syrian air defenses.[208] Whether this is true or not, Syria did significantly bolster its air defenses after an Israeli air raid in September 2007 destroyed a nuclear reactor that Syria was building covertly. According to Israeli estimates, Syria spent $3 billion to renew its air defense capabilities. In particular, it acquired Buk-M2 (SA-17 Grizzly) medium-range and Pantsir-S1 (SA-22 Greyhound) short-range air defense systems from Russia. This development forced the Israeli Air Force to adjust its flight patterns in northern Israel and to expect that it would have to direct more effort toward neutralizing Syrian air defenses in any future war with Syria. Still, the threat was not classified as existential.[209] Truly capable long-range air defense systems—so-called double-digit SAMs, such as the Russian S-300—were still missing from the equation as of the time of writing.

Turkey recognizes the threat posed by modern air defense systems in its region. Therefore, the country puts a premium on developing its electronic warfare capability.[210] In a similar vein Turkey has considered plans to provide the TurAF with an airborne standoff jammer capability, but it seems unlikely that such a capability will be fielded in the medium term. "This program has been on the procurement agenda in the last 10 years, and we are still probably a couple of years away from even a contract, leave aside deliveries," a Turkish industry source stated in 2012.[211] Apparently, converted business jets or smaller airliners may serve as potential platforms.[212]

With the AGM-88 high-speed antiradiation missile (HARM) in its arsenal, the TurAF possesses a combat-proven SEAD capability.[213] Moreover, the JSF will allow the TurAF to conduct hard kills against advanced air defense systems. Therefore, the need to acquire a standoff jammer is not urgent, unless Turkey intends to build such a capability outside the sphere of U.S. influence.

Conclusion

In the last decade and beyond, Prime Minister Erdoğan's AKP has raised Turkey's profile in the international arena and has unambiguously determined the paradigms for the development of Turkish air power. Despite this relative stability, one should remain cautious about making firm forecasts. Given the unpredictability of the Middle East, Turkey faces a fluid environment and may itself experience rapid changes. In March 2013 jailed PKK leader Öcalan unexpectedly offered a cease-fire—a development that can potentially unhinge long-held paradigms.[214] As a consequence Turkey's defense acquisition plans could begin to emphasize conventional platforms over dedicated counterinsurgency platforms.[215] The same month, on the initiative of President Obama, Israeli prime minister Benjamin Netanyahu extended his apologies to Erdoğan for the loss of life during the May 2010 flotilla incident.[216] Although this step might lead to normalization between the two countries, a strategic relationship like that in the 1990s is unlikely. Nevertheless, Israel's Elta in early 2013 was finally authorized to deliver $100 million worth of electronic equipment for the TurAF's four AEW&C aircraft.[217] Beginning in late May 2013, Ankara's leadership was confronted with domestic unrest.[218]

A 2008 study by the Rand Corporation concluded, "In the future, Turkey is likely to be a less predictable and more difficult ally. While it will continue to want good ties with the United States, Turkey is likely to be drawn more heavily into the Middle East. . . . The tension between Turkey's Western identity and its Middle Eastern orientation is likely to grow."[219] As of the time of writing, this estimate still holds true. In the meantime, the Arab Spring has accentuated Ankara's dilemma.

Increasingly taking Arab opinion into consideration, the AKP has pursued an independent foreign policy that at times has stood in stark contrast to Western interests. The restructuring of international relations in the wake of the Cold War led Turkey to rediscover the Middle East, a region it had historically been an integral part of. As one scholar succinctly put it, "Especially under the Ottomans, Turkey was the dominant power in the Middle East; its republican period—with its emphasis on noninvolvement in Middle Eastern affairs—was an anomaly. Turkey's current activism is a return to a more traditional pattern."[220]

This should, however, not obscure the reality that Ankara still views its relationships with the United States and Europe as important. During the Syrian uprising in mid-2012, Washington and Ankara increased intelligence cooperation. Taking Turkey's concerns into account, U.S. secretary of state Hillary Clinton stated, "We share Turkey's determination that Syria must not become a haven for PKK terrorists, whether now or after the departure of the Assad regime."[221] Likewise, and despite a seeming lack of interest among the population, Erdoğan has continued to pursue membership in the EU.

The Arab Spring also highlighted the drawbacks of a one-sided orientation toward the Middle East. Having forged close ties with Bashar al-Assad's regime in the last decade, the current cataclysm has unexpectedly turned Damascus and Ankara's relations upside down. Thus, Ankara's bilateral relations with individual Middle Eastern countries remain anything but stable.

At the crossroads between East and West, Ankara has also explored a third option in recent years by establishing defense industrial relations with other emerging powers, particularly South Korea. Although this relationship has benefited Turkey in the area of ground systems, it has not borne fruit in the development of a fighter aircraft; the two countries could not agree on terms for an equal partnership. The relations between Seoul and Ankara are not based on a truly strategic partnership but on a relationship of convenience, driven largely by mutual defense industrial interests. Yet the example reveals that Ankara has no reservations about diversifying its foreign policy options. In a similar vein Turkey invited the Chinese Air Force to participate in the 2010 Anatolian Eagle exercise and in September 2013 selected a Chinese long-range air and missile defense system despite Western opposition. Moreover, the Turkish Göktürk-2 satellite was launched into space from China.

Given Ankara's ambivalent relationship with the West and shifting relations with other Middle Eastern nations, Erdoğan's AKP has significantly accelerated Turkey's drive toward self-reliance in defense matters. In parallel, the TurAF has been developing into a full-spectrum air force capable of autonomously waging major combat operations. Over the last two decades, Turkey has made quantum leaps in all four basic air power capabilities: control of the air, situational awareness, strike, and maneuver.

As regards control of the air, the sheer size of its modern fighter-bomber fleet places the TurAF among the most powerful air forces in the region. However, Turkey still relies on its NATO partners for TBMD. Although Erdoğan's January 2013 decision to codevelop and manufacture an advanced TBMD system with an external partner might strengthen Turkey's industrial and technological base in the longer run, it does not meet immediate operational needs. Thus, balancing these operational needs versus indigenously mastering aerospace technology has become a particular challenge for Ankara's decision makers. Ankara has adopted a dual-track strategy for development of the TurAF's future combat aircraft fleets, as well as for other aerospace domains. Whereas the TurAF's F-35 fleet will be cutting edge, an indigenously codeveloped fighter fleet is likely to be less advanced but will offer Turkey assured access at all times. Yet the national fighter aircraft project involves significant technological risk.

In the domain of intelligence, surveillance, and reconnaissance (ISR), the TurAF is acquiring a state-of-the-art AEW&C capability. With four specialized aircraft in its inventory, the TurAF is capable of maintaining AEW&C orbits for a significant time span.

To obtain an accurate ground picture for targeting, the TurAF depended heavily on U.S.-generated ISR during its winter 2007–8 raids into northern Iraq. Furthermore, the rift between Turkey and Israel had detrimental repercussions for the TurAF, and Washington also proved reluctant to supply Ankara with its latest MALE UAV technology. No longer able to rely on Israeli and U.S. supplies, Ankara forged ahead with indigenous ISR programs. If Ankara successfully follows through on its ambitious, high-priority MALE UAV– and satellite-based projects, the Turkish armed forces will become capable of executing a complex sensor-to-shooter loop autonomously. At a March 2013 air power conference in Istanbul, Lt. Gen. Abidin Ünal, commander of the TurAF First Air Force Command, singled out both UAVs and satellites as two important key areas.[222]

With regard to strike Turkey has been developing a wide range of precision-guided weapons designed for both counterinsurgency and regular warfare. As in the case of fighter aircraft, these indigenous weapons complement U.S.-sourced matériel. Particularly controversial are Ankara's plans to advance its long-range ballistic missile programs, but given Turkey's unpredictable and unstable environment, an accurate long-range ballistic missile might constitute Ankara's deterrent to the proliferation of SSMs in its vicinity.

Over the last two decades, the tanker fleet, consisting of seven KC-135R Stratotankers, has significantly improved the TurAF's maneuver capability. The acquisition of ten A400M airlifters will ensure a solid renewal of the TurAF's existing air transport capacities. Given Turkey's primarily regional ambitions and its proximity to hotspots, Ankara has no need to set up an air mobility fleet like those of major European players to perform strategic airlift.

Ankara's broad ambitions in all dimensions of air and space operations will undoubtedly bolster the country's technological and industrial base. Thus, Turkey is likely to emerge gradually from its technological dependence on the West and to assume the role of a more equal partner. If Turkey succeeds in implementing its plans for indigenous development of aerospace capabilities, the resulting assets will unambiguously reinforce Turkey's position as a regional and sovereign power in its own right. Yet, since many programs involve uncharted territory, significant technological risk remains, and—for the foreseeable future—the Turkish technological and industrial base will continue to need foreign assistance in developing complex major weapon systems.

Up to the time of writing, Ankara had failed to find a strong non-U.S. or non-European partner for the development of its national fighter aircraft. Although collaboration with Saab Gripen in the conceptual design seemed solid, the engine question—as of late 2013—remained unresolved. Nevertheless, Turkey's Murad Bayar was hinting at a U.S. engine—a solution that is not likely to result in substantial jet engine technology transfers. Cooperation with France's aerospace industry would potentially have allowed Turkey to gain access to all key components required for the development of a modern fighter-bomber. Yet France's explicit opposition to Turkey's membership in the EU, particularly strong under the presidency of Nicolas Sarkozy, meant that Franco-Turkish cooperation was not an option. Why Defense Minister Gönül ruled out the Eurofighter Typhoon as a non-U.S. complement to the JSF is not known. As part of a Eurofighter Typhoon package, the Europeans offered generous transfers of jet engine technology to South Korea, which also aims at developing and building an indigenous fighter aircraft.[223] These unresolved issues have curtailed Ankara's drive to curb foreign influence and diminished its role as a genuine and alternative supplier of major weapon systems to the Middle East and to other Muslim-majority countries. Against this backdrop, the AKP's pledge during the 2011 election campaign to make Turkey self-sufficient by 2023, the Turkish Republic's centennial, was probably too ambitious.

Turkey's employment of air power also reflects the AKP's grand-strategic ambitions. Yet the AKP's rise to power in 2002 did not bring about a complete shift in the TurAF's participation in Western air campaigns. Instead, a set of relatively enduring paradigms has emerged. These paradigms include narrow national rules of engagement, a restrained use of force, and calculated risk. Ankara's approach seems to have garnered positive public opinion among Arab nations, particularly during the Arab Spring.

This limited involvement in Western-led operations also mutes domestic and Arab criticism of Turkey as a "stooge" of the United States—a particularly uncomfortable accusation for a Muslim-dominated country. This sort of accusation has been and is likely to remain inescapable in Turkish politics, preventing any Turkish government from aligning itself too closely with the West and prompting Turkey to use only restrained force when operating in the framework of a Western coalition or alliance. In accordance with this logic, the TurAF—with the largest F-16 fleet of any non-U.S. NATO member—does not participate in European F-16 cooperation, which seeks to enhance the combat readiness of several European F-16 operators.[224]

Narrow rules of engagement in Western air campaigns stand in stark contrast to Turkey's campaign against the PKK. That campaign aims at preserving the country's territorial integrity and as such is largely backed by public consensus. In the context of the Syria crisis, Erdoğan had—up to the time of writing—not invoked Article 5 of the NATO treaty, calling for collective defense. Instead, he stated in early October 2012 that the Turkish Republic was capable of defending its citizens and borders and that no one should attempt to test Ankara's determination in this regard. This assertion further underscored the AKP's ambition to cover a large military spectrum autonomously[225]—an ambition that, since the AKP's rise to power, Turkey continues to realize.

FOUR

British Air Power

Allowing the UK to Punch above Its Weight

Peter W. Gray

The direct relevance of air power must be discussed in the wider context of a nation's foreign, economic, and security policies. To do otherwise would risk having the debate deteriorate into a monologue on technology, platforms, and interservice rivalries over funding. Air power has developed over the last century—and particularly the last twenty-five years—during times of major change. But a consistent theme has been that a country must match its policies with its willingness to finance them. Over the past two decades, and in reality since the end of the Cold War, a recurring theme in British foreign policy has been the notion that the country consistently punches (or boxes) above its weight. What has made this theme so enduring over this period is immediately both simple and complex. At the simple end of the spectrum, the sporting metaphor suggests that Britain is still proud of its identity but that the old power is just that—aging, in decline, financially straitened, and nostalgic for its former grandeur. In short, Britain's size, expenditure, and potential for real contributions are no longer world class. But its role as one of the five permanent members of the United Nations Security Council, determination to play a strong leadership role in the North Atlantic Treaty Organization (NATO), ambivalence about the European Common Security and Defence Policy, and enduring desire to be seen as the United States' ally of choice all conspire to ensure that Britain will consistently aspire to a larger role than its per capita income would suggest as appropriate.[1]

The appealing nature of the "punching above weight" notion has ensured its proliferation, especially by the United States with regard to various allies; the idea has gone far beyond Douglas Hurd's simple statement at Chatham House in 1993. It now applies not only to Britain but to various other members of NATO and neighboring states, including some of those featured in the second section of this volume.[2] As with all simple quotations and concepts, it is worth noting the wider political context in which the "punching above weight" statements were originally made and the exact text. Specifically, at Chatham House Douglas Hurd acknowledged that NATO was one of the "principal props which had allowed Britain to punch above its weight in the world."[3] A similar theme had been expounded in 1990 by Sir Geoffrey Howe (then deputy prime minister), who insisted that the ability to punch above national weight could be exercised only if the United Kingdom participated as an essential part of a team. These references to NATO and to wider coalitions emphasize the importance of such relationships for small and medium-sized nations.

This does not necessarily imply that the notion of "punching above weight" is formally embedded in the United Kingdom's national security and defense policy or in successive Strategic Defence Reviews. But the importance of partnerships and alliances and the flexibility to act in coalitions of choice do receive formal emphasis in these documents.[4] Of the priorities formally documented in, for example, the 2010 Strategic Defence and Security Review (SDSR), the first, and presumably highest, is "our pre-eminent defence and security relationship with the US."[5] Although it is outside the scope of this chapter to conduct a review of the so-called special relationship between the United Kingdom and the United States, two issues must be acknowledged. The first is that the United Kingdom itself perceives this relationship to be alive and well.[6] But, second, this relationship is not unique; Britain's relationships with France, the European Union, and NATO are all important, if not accorded the epithet "special." The same is particularly true for the United States, which has many special relationships, including with Germany and the other nations discussed in this volume.

It is significant that the United Kingdom has chosen, over recent years, to express security and defense policy as a relatively coherent whole rather than as separate entities. This applies to relationships, special or otherwise, with the United States and other countries as well as to the formulation of policy through the National Security Council.[7] National air power debates must therefore be seen in this much wider context. It is neither practical nor relevant to consider air power merely in its relationship to land or maritime power. Furthermore, it is inappropriate to consider these debates in terms of the Royal Air Force (RAF) as the sole contributor to the national air power capability. Accounting for context, however, is not as simple as academic logic would imply. The realities of declining budgets and shrinking military services, the demands of elements of the defense industry, and unfortunately, the tribal nature of the armed forces at various levels (including the level of people who have retired from active duty) combine to make parochialism an inevitable factor in the debates.[8] In reviewing the national air power debates in general, and the key choices that the United Kingdom will have to make over future years, this chapter will seek to discriminate between the rhetoric and jingoism and the real challenges facing small and medium-sized powers in the development, funding, and deployment of future air power capabilities.

This chapter will first briefly review the historical context. Even though air power is of relatively recent origin, it has a dense and detailed history. The historical context will therefore concentrate on the rapid transition from the Cold War to the Gulf War and onward. This narrative must inevitably address the tensions caused by the clamor for peace dividends at a time when the world was becoming less stable and, particularly for air power (plus in later years space and cyber power), the need for more demanding and more expensive technology. The chapter will then scrutinize the current debates before going on to examine strategic choices and likely future developments.

The Historical Context

It is appropriate to start this historical review of UK air power with the end of the Cold War. The period from 1991 to now essentially comprises a seemingly never-ending series of defense cuts, although these cuts were sometimes disguised as nominal increases or fundamental reviews.[9] The cuts and reviews were carried out against a backdrop of continuous operations, which were often concurrent. For example, established commitments, such as the policing of the no-fly zones over Iraq, were carried out in parallel with operations over the former Yugoslavia or Afghanistan. It can be argued that standing forces—and air power in particular—exist in order to be used. This, however, presupposes that the standing forces are properly staffed and equipped and, importantly, can be sustained over a long period. Unfortunately, since the end of the Cold War, UK defense reviews, couched in the language of assumptions and guidelines, have been vehicles for wishful thinking rather than reliable indicators of what will happen. Nevertheless, actual funding has been predicated on the assumptions in these reviews, whether merely honored in the breach or not. Whereas the direct costs of contingency operations have been met by the Treasury, the broader, or implied, costs have to be borne by the Ministry of Defence (MOD).

The move from cold, or static, war to a mobile, expeditionary operational footing signaled a number of key changes in the practical nature of conflict and its funding. The first of these is the seemingly obvious reality of increasing weapons expenditure. Dropping bombs, firing missiles, and expending various types of ordnance results in a need to replace the used weapons. But the evolving nature of various recent conflicts has meant that a direct, like-for-like series of replacements is not appropriate.

Defense planners have also had to consider the twin issues of effectiveness and accuracy. In operations such as the 1991 Gulf War (Operation Granby in the United Kingdom), weapons that had been designed to attack Warsaw Pact airfields, such as the JP-233, placed crews in too much jeopardy to be used in any conflict short of all-out war.[10] Similarly, dumb bombs proved relatively ineffective against hardened bunkers. Furthermore, the demands of international law and the real-time, Cable News Network (CNN)–style coverage of conflicts meant that an unprecedented degree of discrimination and proportionality was essential in target clearance, selection, and attack. Air operations over the former Yugoslavia (Operations Deliberate Force and Allied Force) were particularly illustrative in these respects. The practical result was that the bombs dropped had, first of all, to be replaced with some alternate form of ordnance for the RAF to maintain its capability. Beyond that the new weaponry had to be precise, capable of penetrating hardened targets, and capable of being delivered in a way that guaranteed an absolute minimum of collateral damage. If necessary, the RAF would have to achieve these goals at the expense of crew safety.

As if the cost of reequipping an arsenal of dumb bombs were not enough in itself, the new and more capable generation of weapons brought its own financial challenges in terms of raw costs of the new equipment and modifications to the host aircraft. Following air operations over Libya, the House of Commons Select Committee on Defence formally questioned the appropriateness of using highly accurate and costly weapons and criticized the MOD for being unable to track the costs incurred on operations.[11]

The quest for maximums in accuracy, proportionality, and discrimination can be built only on excellent situational awareness. This has become increasingly apparent during the post–Cold War period. Again, the changing nature of conflict, from attacks on high densities of fielded forces to combat against insurgents and terrorists, has increased the need for accuracy and fine-grained discrimination. The price of failure to achieve maximums in these three areas—deaths of innocent people, psychological benefit to the enemy, censure by the ever-present media—is considerable. It is also vitally important, especially in long-drawn-out operations, to retain the moral high ground, for the sake of both the allied forces and their supporters. But so is the cost of acquiring, supporting, operating, and staffing (and subsequently decommissioning) platforms such as Sentinel, Reaper, and Rivet Joint. Although it is superficially easy to argue that these platforms do not contribute to the kinetic war, they have actually proved essential to its prosecution.

Air power tends to focus on the direct, or kinetic, aspects of warfare. But the fundamental roles of air power also include tasks with apparently less direct effect on the conflict at hand. It is therefore important to acknowledge the need for mobility of all forces. The air bridge for the Falkland Islands from 1982 onward gave some taste of the pressures that result from sustaining operations at a distance from normal NATO basing. The Gulf War and the subsequent maintenance of the bases required for policing the no-fly zones over Iraq, the Iraq War (Operation Telic) beginning in 2003, the two interventions in the former Yugoslavia, and missions in Afghanistan and Libya—in addition to relief operations worldwide—have all placed the enablers of war under exceptional strain. The air-to-air refueling force has been under continuous pressure, not only supporting UK aircraft but also on many occasions providing probe-and-drogue refueling to U.S. Navy and Marine assets (as opposed to the U.S. Air Force's boom operations). Similarly, the C-130 and C-17 fleets purchased following the 1998 Strategic Defence Review have all seen constant use and been under considerable strain. The VC-10 and C-130K fleets were already aging and have subsequently proved expensive to maintain. It is significant that the relatively new C-130J fleet has aged prematurely as a result of continual operations.[12]

A similar story can be told with regard to the helicopter fleet. Spanning all three services, this fleet is a truly joint enterprise that has suffered from constant use. The pressures on the capability are evident and have duly been reported by the House of Commons Select Committee on Defence: "Nevertheless, helicopter capability is being seriously undermined by the shortage of helicopters, particularly medium-lift support helicopters, capable of being deployed in support of operations overseas. We believe that the size of the fleet is an issue, and are convinced that the lack of helicopters is having adverse consequences for operations today and, in the longer term, will severely impede the ability of the UK Armed Forces to deploy."[13] The committee was again concerned about drawdowns in fleet sizes owing to cost-saving measures, delays in equipment procurement, and the resulting "capability deficit." It also expressed concern over "manpower" (albeit that female air and ground crews are deployed extensively), commenting that "the frequency with which personnel are being deployed to high-intensity operations is having an effect on retention."[14]

All three services in the United Kingdom have been subject to a series of personnel cuts over the post–Cold War period. The RAF has diminished from more than eighty-nine thousand to roughly thirty-six thousand, with the army and Royal Navy suffering in a similar fashion. The use of contractors has increased considerably, thereby reducing the size of the uniformed "tail," but outsourcing is not always a cheap option in the long term and has the effect of reducing recuperation time for personnel newly returned from operational appointments.

One of the key issues over this period has been that mounting recent detached, or expeditionary-style, operations takes at least three times the personnel once needed to staff static bases guarding against the Warsaw Pact. With one-third of the force preparing, one-third deployed, and one-third recovering, mounting enduring operations is necessarily expensive. In all three services, personnel in "low-density, high-value" trades and professions, such as key medical staff, intelligence specialists, and those who maintain high-technology equipment, experience considerable pressure; air forces employ a high proportion of these specialists.

Several factors have exacerbated the pressure on personnel. First is the changing, variable nature of the conflicts undertaken. In the 1991 Gulf War—a surge operation—it was evident that a large proportion of, for example, the Tornado force would be employed. That force was then required for longer-term roulement operations, as well as other commitments, such as operations over Yugoslavia. The second factor is the skills needed for different theaters, such as language specialists. The third is the continual pressure on personnel engaged in the enduring aspects of sustained expeditionary operations, which place considerable demands on air and ground crews involved in transport, helicopter, and air-to-air refueling missions. Many of these specialists have alternative career options open in the civilian aviation world.

The penultimate issue worthy of consideration in a historical review is command and control of air power. The Gulf War, the Iraq War, and the various expeditionary conflicts were a far cry from the static NATO system of countersurprise or formal alert states that was vigorously exercised during the Cold War. Instead, in these later conflicts air power was predominantly controlled by joint force air component commanders (JFACCs) through combined air operations centers (CAOCs) specifically set up for the operation at hand. A key factor was that contributing nations were directly represented on the centers' staffs and had authority to agree to or veto national contributions—the red card system.

The coalition of the willing CAOC, which depended primarily on U.S. processes and equipment, rapidly evolved into a beast different from its NATO equivalent. Operations outside the NATO remit had little room for confusion or bureaucratic strife. By contrast, where spheres of influence met, and operations had to be conducted within a NATO context, there was a greater possibility that command and control would be officially exercised by officers whose countries' assets were not represented in the order of battle. Equally, nations that made significant contributions might not be represented on the staff, leading to potential conflict between the formal command chain and the commanders of national contingents. In addition, there was always a risk—which actually materialized during Operation Ellamy (NATO Operation Unified Protector)—that non-NATO members might take unilateral action outside the formal command chain.[15] The Libya operation also highlighted the absence of a workable mechanism (including the sharing of intelligence) for incorporating non-NATO participants, such as Sweden.[16] In practical terms Libya also revealed the extent to which most nations had become dependent on U.S. command and control structures and facilities.[17]

Finally, the Western approach to planning during the Cold War relied heavily on NATO's procedures and basic doctrine. The likely courses of action in the event of East-West confrontation were well thought through and, within the constraints of available assets, well rehearsed. Deep intellectual analyses fell into the desirable, rather than the essential, category. However, pockets of original thinking existed within staff colleges, academe, and the military itself. From the RAF perspective, this intellectual dimension was well represented by the directors of defense studies, beginning with then group captain Tony Mason.[18]

The armed services also produced formal publications on air power—such as Air Publication (AP) 1300, *The RAF War Manual*—but this manual was withdrawn in the early 1970s to be replaced by NATO material.[19] The director of defense studies, Group Captain Andrew Valance, published a short volume of air power doctrine essays in 1990.[20] To some extent this book followed the lead set by the British Army after the Bagnall reforms, the formation of the Higher Command and Staff Course, and increased thinking about the operational level of war.[21] The collected essays were followed by the first edition of AP 3000, *British Air Power Doctrine*, in 1990, the second in 1993, and the third in 1999. The third edition included "fundamental principles" inherent in all doctrinal work, as refined by experience in the Gulf War and in air operations over Yugoslavia. It also followed the publication of the 1998 Strategic Defence Review. The fourth edition of AP 3000 was published in 2009, still as a single service publication. Its successor, a joint publication, was published as Joint Doctrine Publication 0-30.[22] Importantly, both the Royal Navy's BR 1806 (*British Marine Doctrine*) and AP 3000 represented attempts to catch up to the army, whose doctrine manuals had played a significant role in justifying much of what appeared in the defense reviews, which the other two services were ill equipped to counter.

The 2009 edition of AP 3000 had a new title—*British Air and Space Power Doctrine*—and sought "to set air and space power in the context of the Comprehensive Approach, which aims to achieve militarily and politically favorable outcomes in complex crises by using all available levers of power in a cross-governmental and inter-agency approach."[23] From an air power theorist's point of view, a significant change in this volume was the move to define four key roles in air power as control of the air, attack, air mobility, and intelligence and situational awareness. In a key departure from the third edition, it omitted the fourth role of air power: strategic effect. The revised doctrine includes a tacit acknowledgment that air power could have a strategic effect but does not identify creating this effect as a role in itself.[24] The text did not explain the reason for this change, but in informal conversation the reasons given were the route to jointness and the difficulty of explaining the concept to those who are not airmen.

Of course formal doctrine is only part of the fabric of thinking on air power, and it is worth noting that the United Kingdom has also generated a number of specialist publications. These include the *Royal Air Force Air Power Review*, a formally accredited, peer-reviewed journal that is issued three or four times a year. This journal has been further supplemented by edited volumes based on the Chief of the Air Staff's Air Power Workshop and on papers delivered at conferences.[25]

The establishment of the RAF Centre for Air Power Studies (RAFCAPS) further enhanced linkages between the service and academe. Formal links in this direction have traditionally taken the form of full- and part-time fellowships to study at King's College London in war studies, Cambridge in international relations, and Aberdeen in international politics, usually at the master's degree level. More recently the fellowships have been extended to include doctoral-level placements, with the overall aim of building a critical mass of qualified air power thinkers. It is relatively straightforward to discuss concepts such as the physical or moral components of fighting power in doctrinal terms; arguably, the various schemes to promote thinking on the subject of air power form an invaluable contribution to the intellectual component of fighting power in the United Kingdom.[26]

The Current Debate

The previous discussion suggests that the components of fighting power (moral, physical, and conceptual) in British defence doctrine, which date back to the writings of Maj. Gen. J. F. C. Fuller, could be updated to include the theoretical aspect as an explicit and separate component.

This argument could be extended to formalize some of the wider thinking on the so-called comprehensive approach described in the fourth edition of AP 3000. This would incorporate in formal doctrine the other components, most of which set the context for doctrinal thinking. This process could include specific consideration of the political, economic, social, technological, legal, and environmental arenas. If nothing else, an extension of the thinking around the components would provide a framework for analysis of the current debate surrounding UK air power.

The political component of power is potentially wide ranging but could usefully include the political parties' manifesto pledges on defense; relationships with Europe, allies, and international institutions; and links with foreign policy, security policy, and so on. The economic component should account for international and European trends, as well as ramifications of fighting power for UK and wider European defense industries. The social component could, for example, capture the current controversies regarding the role of women in the armed services, especially in direct, frontline combat roles, and the rights of same-sex partners of military members. It could also usefully cover the emotionally charged debate over whether the military represents the people and should incorporate representation from all sectors of the community or whether separate (higher) standards should be used to recruit and hire personnel. Regarding the technological component, air power and advanced technology are inseparable, as is evident in the incorporation of space into AP 3000 (even though space is arguably germane to all environments) and in the growing importance of cyber security.

The increasing need for vastly improved standards of target discrimination and proportionality in the employment of air power stems in large part from public scrutiny of the application of the international Law of Armed Conflict. Ensuring that proposed weapon systems comply with current, and presumably future, standards is now a regular part of weapon procurement. The wider perspective on legal standards is likely to include the debate about whether the right to intervene on humanitarian grounds includes a specific duty to defend populations at risk. The legal component also includes issues surrounding the trend toward warfare becoming more remote; remotely operated aerial vehicles, cyber, and space will be dealt with later in the chapter.

A further element of the legal component is the armed forces covenant and the extent to which it is a sort of gentleman's agreement rather than a legally binding addition to terms of service. An announcement of current policy confirmed movement toward enshrining the covenant's principles in law but also admitted, "In the current financial climate we are not able to do as much to honor that obligation, nor to do it as quickly, as we would like. But we can make clear the road on which are embarked."[27] The United Kingdom is traditionally reticent on this matter.[28] The key development from an air power perspective has been the broadening of the armed forces covenant to include the Royal Navy and the RAF.

The environmental component is traditionally the last to be considered in many similar analyses, and typically, the greater importance accorded to the earlier topics means that time has run out once the environment comes up for debate. Yet this component includes many issues, from the legal need to clear combat areas of dangerous detritus to the challenges of returning badly polluted brownfield sites to preacquisition conditions when contraction of the services has led to the property's no longer being required.

A consistent element in the preceding brief survey is what could be loosely described as the financial component of fighting power. The management of defense expenditure, as part of the wider gamut of government spending, is a complex issue in all nations. For the United Kingdom, this issue has been complicated by the manner in which operations are funded. In theory funding should be quite simple. Normal defense spending goes through the standard spending reviews, and the national purse is effectively doled out to the various departments. The Treasury pays directly for ongoing operations, but what about enduring operations, such as policing the no-fly zones over Iraq or in Afghanistan? Should the MOD simply budget for these routinely? Direct payments by the Treasury are supplemented by the extensive use of urgent operational requirements (UORs), which have amounted to more than £3.6 billion for Iraq and Afghanistan; some 85 percent of this total has been spent on force protection equipment, including Reaper unmanned aerial vehicles (UAVs), electronic countermeasures equipment, and defensive aid suites for aircraft.[29] Cynics in the Treasury wonder how much of this spending should have been absorbed into normal defense planning and how much represents the MOD having its cake and eating it too. More important, UORs cover the purchase of matériel but not its long-term sustainability, necessary updates, or absorption into the core program.

This financial predicament is undeniable and applies to most countries. The underlying questions, however, vary from state to state. A fundamental question when setting defense budgets is, what will the allocations actually purchase? In other words, how does military expenditure enhance or protect national interests? This question is particularly relevant to air power because the debate over future conflict and the United Kingdom's likely role therein highlights which of the military services is likely to play the primary role and which the supporting role. In simple terms, if a future war is based on an insurgency-type scenario, it is probable that boots on the ground will be most important and that air power will play a supporting role. In operational terms, however, commanders and practitioners are well aware of the benefits that a balanced and capable force, featuring both kinetic and nonkinetic air power, brings. As indicated previously with regard to force protection, expenditure on UORs shows the importance of the intelligence, surveillance, target acquisition, and reconnaissance (ISTAR) assets that air power provides.

In scenarios in which training indigenous forces receives highest priority, the indigenous force will eventually require air power. Intervening countries can bring ground troops up to speed in a counterinsurgency much faster than they can build a genuine air power capability. The open, but often unacknowledged, question for the longer term therefore concerns where Country X (say, Mali or Afghanistan) will obtain its air power capability after troops withdraw.

In an alternative scenario the international community is reluctant—for financial, political, or other reasons—to commit ground troops in a given operation. For example, in Libya it was clear from the outset that non-Islamic troops would not be allowed in theater. In this scenario, although air power cannot do it alone, it does provide the most feasible war-fighting option for politicians and senior commanders. In essence, the impermanence of air power in these situations is not merely essential but actually a great virtue. The policing of no-fly zones over Iraq similarly offered a flexible tool that allowed the coalition to vary the pressure on the Saddam Hussein regime without the need for a costly—in terms of lives and matériel—ground presence. The same can be said for the victory over Milošević in Operation Allied Force, after which even known detractors had to admit the utility of air power.[30]

The third possible warfare scenario involves state-on-state conflict. It is tempting to say that there are no conceivable scenarios in which this type of war is likely, especially if one invokes the cowardly time scale of "in the foreseeable future." Given the time that the United Kingdom needed to gain air parity with Nazi Germany in the 1930s with the relatively simple technology of the era, the challenges inherent in the twenty-first century are comparably huge, especially for the defense industry. But the possibility of state-on-state conflicts cannot be ruled out, even if they take place in the Far East. How involved the United Kingdom will wish to be in a conflict in India, China, Taiwan, or Korea remains to be seen, but the possibility must be considered given the lead times needed to produce the necessary equipment. The opening premise—of the United Kingdom being inclined to punch above its weight—suggests that the UK would likely take a back seat in terms of scale but not intent. In a state-on-state conflict, air power would probably dominate any UK contribution, albeit possibly aligned with some special forces operations.

It could be argued that these are merely sterile debates worthy only of the common rooms in academe. But when the conversations, or more important, their practical implications, move from academia into the corridors of power, their importance becomes clear. At the heart of the issue, military planners shift their focus from the united front that the services present in theater to single service parochialism over funding. This shift is all the more bitter because the stakes become increasingly high as resources decline. The traditional methods of reduction through salami slicing have become less tenable; these days roles, capabilities, and whole areas of defense are likely to be cut. The demise of the Harrier force and the Nimrod maritime patrol aircraft are of considerable significance for both the RAF and the Royal Navy. The army risks having its budget and personnel reduced to the point where key elements of fighting power (such as heavy armor) become unsustainable. The emphasis derived from operations in Iraq and Afghanistan, which have placed great importance on boots on the ground, if followed to its natural conclusion, threatens to diminish the overall army to little more than an expensive gendarmerie. It is therefore small wonder that the contemporary debate on air power centers ultimately on resources.

Strategic Choice and Debate for the Future

Operational Art

As the United Kingdom emerges from the era of Afghanistan and Iraq, it may well be time to take stock outside the financial arena. It has already been suggested that the components of fighting power could be expanded. It is also arguably worth examining what is meant by "operational art." This term covers the full spectrum of military capabilities, including air, space, and cyber, as well as land and maritime. The coordination and integration of all of these is of paramount importance to the conduct of operations. It is a fundamentally flawed argument to consider any one of these elements in isolation.

At the simplest level of definition, the operational level of warfare sits between tactics and strategy. John Kiszely, for example, has been content to rely on standard doctrinal definitions in which the operational level is that "at which campaigns and major operations are planned, conducted and sustained to accomplish strategic objectives within theatres or areas of operations."[31] According to Kiszely, "the operational level is determined by where operational art is practised."[32] Another retired general, David Zabecki, has used a more graphic means to illustrate the linkage between tactics and strategy.[33] In doing so he has fallen back on military teaching, in this case at the U.S. Army Command and Staff College, which used the medieval morning star as a metaphor to describe the levels of warfare; the handle wielding the weapon represented strategy and the spiked ball, which inflicts the blow, represented tactics. The chain connecting the two elements was operational art.[34] As a third alternative, the operational level of war can be defined as in line with a theater of operations and, as such, geographically contained.

Several problems arise from these three conventional depictions of the operational level of war. The first is the implication that operations is merely an intermediate level between tactics and strategy. Although neither Kiszely nor Zabecki in any way implies that the operational level is not as important as the other two, their writings leave a lingering impression that it sits between the well-understood, almost comfortable zone of the tactical arena and the ephemeral world of strategy. This perception is reflected in the wider literature, particularly by Edward Luttwak, who has highlighted what he describes as "a major eccentricity in the modern Anglo-Saxon experience of war" in which officers engaged in conducting warfare not only do "not *speak* the word [operational], but rather that they do not *think* or practice war in operational terms" (emphasis in the original).[35] Similarly, Shimon Naveh has opined that the "Western failure to coin a term to cover the operational field indicates, first and foremost, the lack of *cognition* regarding that field" (emphasis added).[36] Both authors here argue that the operational level of war has raised significant conceptual difficulties in the minds of practitioners. This confusion has been compounded over the last quarter century, a time when operations have been conducted in the media glare and under intense scrutiny from immediate command chains and the political level. Technology has effectively removed the geographically remote nature of the "theater" concept. Modern usage of the term has also eroded the concept through the implication that "on operations" actually—and often more accurately—meant "on tactics."

Whether one looks at the conflicts in Iraq and Afghanistan or the various operations other than war (to use a phrase that is now out of vogue), it is clear that Cold War thinking on the subject of operational art needs to evolve. For air power in particular, a geographically limited theater of operations makes no sense for aircraft basing (Tornados flying from the United Kingdom to Libya, for example) or reachback. Similarly, the old Soviet notion of the large size and scale of forces is inappropriate; modern weapon systems, with their accuracy of delivery, are capable of exerting considerable effect, and many are genuine force multipliers. The old metric of the number of aircraft assigned to each target has been replaced by the number of targets to each platform. This alone has serious consequences for the future of British air power, as it not only influences target selection but also has a direct bearing on aircraft acquisition, training, and deployment. More capable aircraft are essential to continuing relevance.

Furthermore, the nature of modern conflict requires the dovetailing of military power with the other levers at the disposal of nations, coalitions, or alliances. These may include the provision of aid, diplomatic pressure, threats and use of sanctions, and economic pressure targeted against the ruling clique. Each of these levers was employed in the Kosovo campaign to varying degrees.[37] In recent conflicts the practice of true operational art could be said to revolve around managing the interfaces between levers to optimal advantage. In some cases countries have missed this opportunity and applied the various levers of power in isolated stovepipes. Active management of the interfaces between internal and external players enhances the scope for true operational success.

The intertwined issues of conflict, security, and warfare in the twenty-first century create "wicked" problems, not "tame" ones that lend themselves to simple or linear solutions.[38] Process may be useful in helping to solve tame problems but in itself is inadequate to address genuinely wicked problems, which can be solved only with high-level leadership and intellectual capacity. A mechanical approach to campaign planning or reliance on doctrinal processes is doomed to failure, or at best mediocrity. This approach has real implications for the education and selection of future commanders and for development of familiarity among interagency players.

The Maritime Patrol Aircraft Debate

The 2010 SDSR instituted a series of "radical reforms" and "tough, but necessary decisions."[39] The reduction in the fast-jet force to two types—the Typhoon and the Tornado—was accompanied by the decision "not [to] bring into service the Nimrod MRA4 maritime patrol aircraft programme."[40] Notwithstanding the resulting turmoil for many air and ground crews and their families, the decision was highly significant in that it was effectively the first in defense review terms to remove a full capability from one of the services; previously cuts had been made by reducing numbers of aircraft or delaying their entry into service.

The antisubmarine capability would have to be taken from Royal Navy assets, including helicopters, submarines, and other surface vessels. In many ways the decision to end the MRA4 program was long overdue, as it, like a number of other programs, had become increasingly unaffordable. What had started as a £1.6 billion fixed-price contract for twenty-one aircraft had become a £4.5 billion project for only nine aircraft.[41] Although a considerable percentage of the aircraft was completely new, the name itself brought with it a degree of baggage following the crash of a Nimrod MR2 over Afghanistan in 2006, which resulted in the loss of fourteen lives and raised the question of why a maritime aircraft was operating over a landlocked country.[42] In fact, the Nimrod MR2 had proved to be a valuable asset in intelligence gathering in a wide range of scenarios. It could be argued that the aircraft's multiple uses had allowed it to remain in service well beyond the requirements of countering the submarine threat (until 2010).

One of the key tasks of the Nimrod or a successor platform is direct support for the submarine-borne nuclear deterrent. A common assumption within the RAF was that this mission alone would guarantee the Nimrod's survival both as a platform and as a capability. However, the SDSR noted that the services would have to depend on "other maritime assets" to provide the antisubmarine capability. Although the details of what is necessary to allow the deterrent to go to sea undetected are inevitably classified, it is highly likely that the Royal Navy's towed-array frigates, Merlin helicopters, and submarines will fulfill these roles. This compensation for the Nimrod's loss is by no means unreasonable or ineffective, but still, these assets come from an ever-shrinking pool and tasking them in support of the deterrent means they will be unavailable for other tasks. Notwithstanding Liberal Democrat aspirations to at least open the debate on the deterrent, the SDSR pledged to retain "Continuous at Sea Deterrence."[43] The "at-sea" element is interesting in that it is not beyond the bounds of possibility that missiles could be fired from the berth, negating the antisubmarine need completely.

The debate on ways to fill the antisubmarine warfare (ASW) capability gap in the future has raised several problems. The implication from the SDSR and subsequent statements is that the United Kingdom may have to rely on partner nations to cover the deficiency.[44] Given that the costs of a "whole aircraft" replacement have proved too high in the past, it is improbable that the MOD will consider a like-for-like replacement. Furthermore, as few other nations seek to acquire antisubmarine aircraft, it is equally unlikely that a collaborative venture will prove possible. Far more likely is a transfer of sensors, expertise, and command and control linkages to a variety of other platforms. Informally, the defense industry holds the view that if the political will and the necessary money are available, some of the sensors designed for Nimrod could be utilized in UAVs, with the operators acting remotely. Although UAVs are currently not designed to drop either sonar buoys or life rafts (in the long-range search and rescue role), the electronic capabilities could easily be transferred.

Carrier-Borne Air Power

The subjects of acquisition, employment, and replacement of aircraft carriers are emotionally charged in all defense communities, not only in the United Kingdom.[45] The subject of the acquisition of aircraft to operate from these platforms is equally contentious, not least because the demands of carrier aviation often call for concessions in aircraft design and capability. At its best carrier-borne air power offers a superb opportunity for jointness, with aircraft designed to be flown by personnel from all three services and, in some nations, from the marines as well. The use of army helicopters from HMS *Ocean* during operations over Libya, Spitfires from carriers in the Norway campaign during the Second World War, and Harriers during the Falklands War all serve as examples of interservice cooperation. But traditionally friction has arisen over everything from loaning aircrews to other services to doctrinal issues over aircraft employment. This friction has been evident in the military services of many nations over a long period.[46]

For the United Kingdom, the SDSR brought these issues into sharp focus with decisions on the acquisition of new carriers, their strike capability, and aircraft procurement. The review called for a move to a two-aircraft front line for the RAF, with the Typhoon and Tornado favored over the Harrier.[47] The rationale for this decision reflected the need to provide sustainable air support to operations over Afghanistan; the SDSR argued that the Harrier force would be unable to perform this mission and maintain the existing carrier-strike capability at the same time.[48] These arguments were validated when the Tornado force was called upon to support operations over Libya. Furthermore, operations in both Afghanistan and Libya showed the Tornado force to be not only more sustainable but also more capable than the Harrier in terms of avionics and the ordnance available.[49]

The demise of the Harrier force, however, had serious implications for the Fleet Air Arm, as it removed the organization's only fixed-wing asset at a stroke. The decision also threatened the end of vertical/short takeoff and landing (V/STOL) experience and capability. In addition, the SDSR announced a change in the aircraft that would operate from carrier decks: from the V/STOL version of the Joint Strike Fighter (F-35B) to the naval variant (F-35C). The carriers (Queen Elizabeth class) would be built with catapults and arrestor cables, rendering V/STOL capability and maintenance of aircrew expertise irrelevant.[50] This decision was reversed some two years later in what has been described as a "costly U-turn."[51] The reasons given for the reversal included problems with the development of the actual catapults and arrestor gear, development problems with the F-35C, and rising costs. Naturally enough, the reversal was heavily criticized by the House of Commons Select Committee on Defence.[52]

Beyond the regrettable cost to taxpayers, a further problem caused by the embarrassing cancellation of programs and reversal of decisions is that they deflect attention from the topics that should constitute the focus of the debate. The government justified its decision to proceed with a single carrier, with the second on "extended readiness," because it could not foresee "circumstances in which the UK would require the scale of strike capability previously planned."[53] The SDSR did not anticipate action in "large-scale air combat" but assumed that the carrier-borne aircraft were more likely to be used in "precision operations," possibly against "sophisticated air defence capabilities."[54] Affordability is clearly a large element of this logic.[55]

Cancellation costs would have been huge, given the terms of the business agreement with BAE Systems, under which the MOD "would be liable for payments of up to £230 million per annum for shipbuilding and support. The work provided by the carriers is integral to the delivery of the core workload assumed in this agreement. In its absence, the risk is that the Department would have a funding liability for which it would receive no outputs unless it could substitute alternative work."[56] According to the National Audit Office (NAO), the MOD therefore had to balance contractual liabilities against military need. The alternative would have been to "cancel the carriers before eliminating amphibious capabilities or making significant further reductions in destroyers or frigates. Although the Department also considered cancellation, which was feasible and offered significant medium-term savings, it concluded that this would have been unaffordable in the short term."[57]

It is clear from the NAO report on carrier strike that there was a high degree of emphasis during the SDSR on affordability and costs. The financial component was again at the forefront. It is also evident from the report that while the SDSR took industrial factors into account, no suitable analysis was available to justify the retention of a sovereign capability for building warships.[58] The decision to keep one carrier on extended readiness greatly reduced average sea-time availability, which would have to be made good by reliance on allies (primarily the United States).

As was clear from the First Sea Lord's evidence before the House of Commons Select Committee on Libya, the availability of a carrier undoubtedly increases policy makers' scope for action and involvement. A carrier's operational utility would not necessarily be constrained by the availability or lack of host nation support, as would the effectiveness of a purely land-based capability. A carrier-based task group should also be less vulnerable than ground forces to insurgent or terrorist attack,[59] although this would depend greatly on the carrier's location and the potential threat, including suicide attacks from fast patrol boats and so forth.

A carrier-borne capability offers a low footprint in sensitive areas but is necessarily limited in capability. The F-35 offers a genuinely high level of performance in attack and ISTAR against a wide variety of potential enemies. Together with the carriers, it certainly gives the United Kingdom the chance to punch above its weight, but it is not necessarily the answer to all prayers. As the NAO noted, "The design of the carriers is not optimised to embark the full range of capabilities or the manpower needed to carry out commando group scale amphibious operations and the carrier would have to be supplemented by additional ships for this work."[60] The report observed that the nearest analogy to the concept of operations envisioned was the U.S. Marine Corps. This viewpoint is obviously not reflected in the publicly available reports on thinking in the MOD but does offer a reasonable way forward in the debate.

But while the United Kingdom is procuring the air power element for the carrier capability, gaps remain elsewhere. As the potential cost of cancellation decreases, it is possible that the "sunk costs" will be consigned to history and the debate on whether to continue with the carrier program will remain contentious. Regrettably, the merits of the air power contribution to wider power projection will either again be secondary to affordability or be masked by emotional comments in the Letters columns of newspapers.

The Remoteness of Warfare

One of the greatest challenges facing all practitioners and proponents of air power is neither financial nor technological, although these factors inevitably have some part to play. Serious conceptual, ethical, and legal issues arise around modern warfare's becoming increasingly remote. It could be argued that since its inception air power has sought to increase the distance between foes, whether through increasingly effective air-to-air weaponry, strategic bombing, or intercontinental ballistic missiles. Almost perversely, the need for proportionality and discrimination has increased the technological demands for weaponry with digital ISTAR, cockpit screens depicting shadowy figures, and the ability to transmit these images back to headquarters, leading to a perception that aerial warfare is now more akin to an arcade game.[61] Only the world's media stand ready to depict the horrors faced by those on the receiving end with varying degrees of accuracy depending on the propaganda effect sought.

The world has seen an almost seamless continuity in the direction of air power since the 1991 Gulf War, but a subtle change in the strategic situation has largely gone unnoticed.[62] The convention built up over millennia that war fighting—and the use of lethal force in the furtherance of state objectives—is the sole preserve of military forces has been superseded by the actions of civilian agencies capable of using air, space, and cyber power. The air power element in this context consists largely of remotely piloted aircraft (RPAs).[63]

The conceptual and practical advantages of using RPAs can be summed up by the assertion that they can take over missions that are "dangerous and dirty." In other words, these vehicles can be used in areas where the operating environment is hazardous for conventional operations and still achieve precision and low collateral damage. RPAs with long loiter times and integral ISTAR capabilities enable operators to gather information over an extended period, fuse it, analyze it, and exploit targeting opportunities in fleeting windows of opportunity. This can involve sizable teams of operators working remotely rather than in the aircraft. More broadly, the use of air power generally, and of RPAs in particular, in areas such as the borderlands of Afghanistan and Pakistan allows reconnaissance (in all senses of ISTAR) and strikes to be carried out with no requirement for the costly deployment of land forces. This use may resonate with air power historians who recall RAF air policing of the Middle East during the interwar years, not least because the geographical areas are similar.[64] But the liaison between air power and political officers collecting tax revenues has been replaced by a more serious prosecution of the war on terror by the U.S. Central Intelligence Agency (CIA).[65]

While there is considerable room for ethical debate on this subject, it appears that the United States is content with its approach, at least at the official level.[66] The latest white paper by the Department of Justice effectively confirms that the standard rules of "national self-defense" apply and that Congress has authorized "the use of all necessary and appropriate military force against this enemy, and the existence of an armed conflict with Al Qa'ida under international law."[67] The critical aspect of this paper is that the Department of Justice focuses primarily on actions taken against U.S. citizens; lethal action against foreign nationals is a given. In any case, the United States may also be able to square the circle with domestic governments over whose territories these systems operate in.

If the United Kingdom is to maintain the moral high ground, this issue has wider implications. There is doubt in the United Kingdom regarding the concept of a war on terror and the definition of an armed conflict under international law. Furthermore, the Justice Department document specifically uses the term "military force," and other countries may not be willing to interpret this authorization as including civilian agencies, such as the CIA.

The practical aspects of applying the law in an operational arena extend beyond the debates over policing the no-fly zones, where the target clearance authorities could refuse permission for the prosecution of certain target sets on the grounds of, for example, proportionality or likelihood of collateral damage. The red card could be used. The matter became more complicated with the possible use of RAF air-to-air refueling assets during U.S. attacks on these targets. The issue is muddied even further by debate over whether the United States can use UK-derived intelligence in choosing its targets. There are also questions about multinational command and control arrangements in which allied personnel in digital positions can be called upon to make targeting decisions of dubious ethical or legal provenance. Reliance on straightforward rules of engagement may not offer sufficient guidance.

The same debates potentially apply to the use of RPAS, albeit with air-to-air refueling currently not a factor (but possibly becoming an issue in the future). There is, however, considerable potential for intelligence material to be absorbed into a black box, with no apparent control over its interpretation, usage, and exploitation. This possibility may be covered by classified protocols, but the ethical questions remain, especially in operations in which civilian organizations are de facto the supported component.

Remote warfare, conducted in either attack or defense, also embraces the cyber world. There have been numerous instances of cyber attacks, or alleged attacks, on various institutions.[68] At the strategic level these threats have serious implications for the complete range of computer systems, including those used for command and control. Air power depends fundamentally on such systems, both terrestrial and space based, including for command and control of manned aircraft and RPAS.

In many ways cyber attacks have the potential to mirror the use of armed force, with issues of collateral damage, proportionality, and so forth remaining relevant depending on the enemy system targeted. The placement of surface-to-air missile systems on hospital grounds has direct parallels in the areas of computers and electric power. Allied concerns over this possibility, as well as over sharing intelligence, are similar to those pertaining to the use of conventional forces or RPAS. This is especially true given the exceptionally high levels of classification in the cyber arena and the often difficult questions over interagency access.

A further question that extends beyond the legal opinions discussed previously covers the issue of the use of deterrent, or preemptive, air power against potential cyber foes. Press reporting suggests that the United States will apply a self-defense argument similar to that used for RPAs to allow preemptive cyber attacks.[69] The uncertainty surrounding this topic is exacerbated by the need to prove cause and effect linkages, intent, proportionality, and most important, the imminence of the threat, which is central to justifying preemptive action.

These debates may or may not be taking place in the corridors of power, in the National Security Council, and elsewhere. Security classification, although certainly reasonable, will prevent genuinely open debate. But there is always the embarrassing risk that what the United Kingdom (or another allied nation) wishes to keep secret could well be exposed under the U.S. Freedom of Information Act. In any event, a reasonable level of debate is essential for the air power community and the longer-term interests of all involved in the process.

Conclusion

This chapter has, by definition and design, represented a UK view of air power and its relevance, both in recent historical terms and for the future. It has deliberately restricted itself to a strategic level of argument because, short of a direct attack on national interests (however unlikely), the United Kingdom will engage in most wars, conflicts, and operations either from choice or to maintain national prestige. As indicated at the outset, the United Kingdom has tended to punch above its weight while stoutly maintaining that its defense expenditure remains at an appropriately high level. Examination of the context in which the sporting metaphor was first used shows that it is possible to hold views that, at first sight, may seem diametrically opposed. The United Kingdom, particularly in air power terms, is most likely to participate in any future conflict as part of a coalition or as a member of an alliance.

In this environment, air power arguably presents politicians, policy makers, and financiers with the greatest possible range of choices. In comparison to the costly and drawn-out commitment of ground troops, air power offers both actual combat capability and demonstration of political will. But even assuming a coalition of the willing—either one involving the United States or a strictly European partnership—UK participation in conflict must be relevant and effective. For this to occur, British air power must make a real and measurable contribution to the air tasking order or its equivalent. It must, ideally, be capable of performing the key roles or tasks in air power, including precision attack, and not just the inevitable token air-to-air deployments that have been a feature in many previous campaigns. Furthermore, British air power must be self-sustaining in transport, force protection, and air-to-air refueling. Key to all of these functions is a sound ISTAR capability, along with the means and agreements for intelligence sharing.

The United Kingdom is in a genuinely sound position to fill these roles for the foreseeable future. That said, however, it must be acknowledged that the last twenty-five years have been characterized by defense reviews and subsequent cuts in defense expenditure, not just in the United Kingdom, but among most of its allies. These cuts have led to reduction or elimination of key capabilities and to increased reliance on other services or nations. The change in warfare that the world has experienced over the same period, however, has brought a need to actually use the matériel and not merely to display it in the "shop window" of the Cold War standoff. The changing nature of modern warfare has forced increased expenditure in the form of ordnance actually fired, fuel consumed, and the premature retirement of whole fleets as a result of continued use, especially in hostile environments.

In addition, conflict short of all-out war has meant that tolerance of friendly casualties has decreased, leading to a change in tactics. Thus, there is now a greater need for proportionality and discrimination and a lower acceptability of collateral damage. These changes have occurred for a number of reasons, including domestic perceptions of air power, media scrutiny, and genuine concerns over separating not only friend from foe but also insurgents from neutral background populations. Within what is at best a finite defense budget, the United Kingdom has had to make a number of strategic spending choices, not all of which reflect narrow defense needs. Rather, the decision makers had to take into account the interests of society, economics, industry, and so forth. At the highest levels this situation should prompt UK policy makers to embrace a genuine analysis of the nature of future conflict. All too often, however, the debate more closely resembles a conversation with a financial spreadsheet.

Given the absence of defense matters from political election manifestos in the United Kingdom and the financial restraints on defense budgets evident in most, but not all, nations, it is essential that air power thinking continues to mature beyond the technological (and tactical) vocabulary loved by airmen and to embrace the broader, and deeper, context in which decisions are made and priorities set. There is undoubtedly a role in the future for an "airman-scholar" (not only the aircrew) who can contribute to this debate beyond the tribal rhetoric that has characterized much of the dialogue in the past. Despite the tight purse strings, air power in the United Kingdom is making sound progress toward raising meaningful questions.

This chapter argues for the necessity of examining the operational level of war and breaking the mold that sees "operational" merely as the middle level between the tactical dimension beloved by practitioners and the ephemeral strategic realm. The debate must also broaden from an exclusive focus on operations to an understanding of operational interfaces with the other key components of conflict resolution. Since these components include the political, economic, and diplomatic areas, it should come as no surprise that they are mirrored at the strategic level. Because air power's inherent diversity of employment provides policy makers with real choices, it is axiomatic that airmen also think along these lines.

The real world will continue to stress the importance of platforms and capabilities. Here the first issue is the seemingly obvious one: the two are different, but they have traditionally been confused or conflated. This has certainly been true with regard to the maritime patrol aircraft issue in the United Kingdom and will continue through the emotional debate over the carrier-strike capability and its weapons/

ISTAR platforms. Although it could be simplistically argued that a carrier is itself only a rather large platform, the debate must acknowledge that carriers also will provide prestige, project power, and contribute to future international operations. It is all too easy to see carriers only through the prism of the shipbuilding industry, political constituencies, and the prestige of a single service. UK policy makers must examine the capabilities that the platforms bring and the financial realities involved in canceling other acquisitions to make the full carrier capability affordable.

The final portion of this chapter has looked at the moral, legal, and ethical issues that arise from increasingly remote warfare. This extends far beyond the arcade-game type of conflict introduced in the 1991 Gulf War and reaches into an arena where state-sanctioned violence on the international stage is no longer just the preserve of the military. The growing role of RPAs in foreign policy not only requires a different mind-set when examining military-to-military arrangements but also prompts a series of debates about ethics, including questions related to sharing intelligence and the exploitation of air power assets and technology.

So, from the UK perspective, will air power remain relevant over the next two decades? The answer must be an unequivocal affirmative. Air power will continue to offer policy makers and planners an effective and relatively cost-effective option for dealing with real-world events and contingencies. It will continue to allow the United Kingdom to punch above its weight, not least because the self-supporting ability to project precision weaponry with a high degree of situational awareness will make the United Kingdom a coalition partner of choice. Though "punching above its weight" was originally uttered in a coalition context, the likelihood is that UK air power will continue to be welcome and effective in any coalition operations.

The unassailable maxim that control of the air remains vital in all possible contingencies is no trite phrase used merely to justify aircraft procurement or force structures. The events of 9/11, the planning for the London Olympics, and occasional Russian forays into UK air space combine to confirm the importance of air superiority. The lessons of the last twenty-five years suggest that these trends will continue and that any suggestions of "watersheds" or "crossroads" are merely theoretical constructs. Decision makers must shift their mind-set away from platforms and toward consideration of capabilities with bolt-on sensors and equipment. This may lead to a large suite of unmanned, or remotely operated, capabilities but represents a trend, not a fundamental change. Air power has traditionally been at the forefront of the United Kingdom's operational posture, and this leading role is likely to continue.

2

NORDIC AIR POWERS

The ubiquity, perspective and reach of aerospace platforms liberate them from the obligations to engage in sequential patterns of operations. Whereas ground forces have to achieve tactical breakthroughs in order to fulfill operational objectives which in turn leads to progress at the strategic level of war, in theory at least air power can undertake missions on all three levels from the very outset of a conflict. Furthermore, not only has the accuracy and lethality of modern weaponry endowed aerospace forces with unprecedented scope in terms of the spectrum of targets they can engage with a good prospect of success, but also such forces remain, for the time being at least, less vulnerable to destruction by terrestrial ones than the other way around.

DAVID GATES

FIVE

Norwegian Air Power

Staying Relevant in a New Era

Maj. Gen. Finn Kristian Hannestad

From Rumpler Taube to Joint Strike Fighter

Premier Lt. Hans Fleischer Dons was the first Norwegian to fly an airplane over Norwegian territory. The triggering event was not that the Finnish artist and sculptor Adolf Aarno had flown a Santos Dumont Demoiselle monoplane in Tampere, Finland, in April 1911 or that the Danish Naval Air Service had been founded later that year. Nor was it that a Swedish aviator, Lt. Olof "Olle" Dahlbeck, had undertaken the first flight in Sweden in February 1912. Rather, it was that Dahlbeck announced two months later that he was contemplating a similar flight in Norway. His intention was to fly over the main naval base, Horten, on Norway's independence day—May 17—and to drop a few oranges for good measure.

Dons and two other naval officers concluded that national pride was at stake and that they had to become airborne before the Swede. The problem was that they had no airplane, no money, and no pilot. Two of the officers stayed home to raise the necessary funds, and the thirty-year-old Dons went to Germany to buy a plane and take flying lessons. He estimated that he would need ten days of practice. He could handle a submarine in deep waters—how hard could it be to learn to fly?

Upon his arrival in Berlin, Dons selected a Rumpler Taube (Dove). Poor weather, long lines for flying lessons, disputes with the manufacturer about procurement, and the logistical difficulty of transporting a five-hundred-kilogram monoplane with a ten-meter wingspan to Horten caused delays, and a flight date of May 17 was no longer feasible. The naval officers asked Dahlbeck if he would kindly postpone his planned flight; the Swede admired their initiative and agreed.

The airplane arrived in Norway at the end of May. Dons returned on May 31, determined to get airborne despite having had only ten hours in the sky and without a pilot's license. He skipped the planned test flight, in part because he was impatient and in part to avoid the media—he feared bad publicity if the flight went badly. A submarine was placed in the Oslofjord for rescue purposes; the contingency plan was to lift the plane from underneath and bring it to the surface should it crash into the sea. Dons took off from Borre, near Horten, on June 1. He flew over the fjord to Øra, near Fredrikstad, navigating by church spires and railway tracks. The weather was perfect, although a few clouds obscured his view at times, and the landing was smooth. Dons received a hero's welcome and his exploit was celebrated by a growing crowd of locals who could hardly believe what he had achieved: he had covered forty-eight kilometers in thirty-five minutes. The airplane had fittingly been named *Start*, and Dahlbeck immediately sent a telegram: "Bloody well done."

One hundred years later, on June 1, 2012, the Royal Norwegian Air Force—formally established on November 10, 1944—marked the anniversary of Dons's exploit with an air show and exhibitions at the main square in Oslo. The weather was again favorable, more than 150,000 spectators showed up, and this time the media was present in force. The event showed that airplanes and air power still attract enthusiasm and excitement, from daredevils in white scarves struggling to reach a hundred kilometers per hour to modern fighters flying faster than the speed of sound.

This chapter briefly examines the current status of and some of the challenges facing the Norwegian Air Force, emphasizing a wide spectrum of tasks and capabilities rather than barrel rolls, roaring engines, and "pulling Gs." It demonstrates that the air force's decisions to field the C-130J transport aircraft and NH-90 helicopters, to purchase F-35 Joint Strike Fighters, and to modernize command and control are important to the future of Norwegian air power, but the heart of our air force still consists of dedicated, motivated, professional, and competent individuals at all levels of the organization.

The Norwegian Armed Forces—"Capable Force"

Any assessment of the Norwegian armed forces must take geography and distance into account. Norway's extensive coastline, facing both the North Atlantic Ocean and the Barents Sea, creates an enormous expanse of territorial waters and a vast economic zone, especially huge in comparison to our population of 5 million. Norway's prosperity is closely linked to the sea, with its extensive reserves of petroleum, natural gas, minerals, seafood, freshwater, and hydropower. Norway's territory includes many mountains and fjords, as well as inhospitable regions to the northeast and a short border with Russia. From an environmental perspective, the High North is vulnerable. The melting ice cap, potential new shipping lanes crisscrossing the Arctic region, and production of oil and gas in a harsh climate present challenges. Relatively speaking, the High North is a peaceful region but not easy to defend against attack from land, sea, or air. For better or worse Norway is tied to its geographic destiny and has structured its defense force accordingly.

The main features of Norwegian security policy have remained more or less constant over the years. The defense policy, as defined in our strategic concept, accords special priority to various tasks in three areas.[1]

First are national tasks that, as a general rule, must be undertaken unilaterally, without allied involvement. They include ensuring a solid basis for national political and military decision making through timely surveillance and intelligence, upholding Norwegian sovereignty and sovereign rights, exercising Norwegian authority in designated areas, and preventing and managing any incidents and crises that might arise in Norway and adjacent areas. Second come tasks carried out in cooperation with allies or partners: contributing to the collective defense of Norway and other North Atlantic Treaty Organization (NATO) members against threats, assaults, or attacks and taking part in multinational crisis management outside Norway, including peace support operations. Third, the armed forces must support other Norwegian authorities by contributing to international military cooperation, including arms control, disarmament, prevention of proliferation of weapons of mass destruction, and security sector reform. The armed forces must also aid in key societal tasks, such as protecting domestic security.

Norwegian Air Power Capabilities

The Royal Norwegian Air Force plays a critical role in military-political tasks—sometimes supported by, and at other times in support of, naval, special, and ground forces but always as part of the joint team. The air force defines all air power roles and missions in the joint context. The best way to view our air power capability is to see it as a system of systems: air power is one of several national instruments for foreign and defense policy; it is an integral part of the Norwegian armed forces; and it is itself a system of systems, with our personnel and competence at its core.

Air force personnel, and their skills, undeniably represent the most important resource of the Norwegian Air Force and of Norwegian air power. Professionalism in everything personnel do is the key to the air force's success. Air force personnel must be experts on the systems they operate, fully understand the strengths and weaknesses of air power, and have the ability to communicate this knowledge to fellow officers, the public, and policy makers. They must be able to relate technological capacities and capabilities to the overall mission at hand and constantly improve education and training procedures at the tactical, operational, and strategic levels. In essence, air force leadership must match personnel with core air power capabilities to produce air power competence. To provide a broad picture, I will outline four enduring core capabilities, none of which could prove effective without competent personnel.

Control of the Air

War and military operations are about decisions: decisions made, altered, rejected, or dodged. The decision-making process can be illustrated in different ways, but to most airmen John Boyd's observe-orient-decide-act (OODA) loop captures its essence. To act efficiently, we have to know what is happening; we have to *observe*. However, observation will have no value if we do not know what we are seeing or understand what it means; we have to be able to *orient* ourselves—to put what we observe into a larger context. We must next *decide* what to do on the basis of what we see and what we know. Finally, we *act*, and the loop continues over and over. The OODA loop—a model of reality and thus a simplification of a more complex process—applies at all levels of war. Pilots have their specific loop, as do the gunners on the ground and the mechanics in the hangars. The prime instrument for executing this loop is our air command and control system, which provides civilian authorities with timely and adequate information.

In addition to having strategic awareness, the Royal Norwegian Air Force must be able to plan, lead, and execute air operations at both the operational level (within a national joint framework) and the tactical level (as part of a multinational effort with allies). We must contribute at all levels of a multinational air operation, whether in peace, crisis, or armed conflict. This is a tall order, but I am confident that we have the human and fiscal resources to perform these tasks in accordance with NATO's command and control principles, processes, and procedures. We must maintain interoperability with our allies, physically through network-centric platforms and mentally through doctrine and operational procedures.

Giulio Douhet was one of the first to present airmen with what is now one of the oldest truisms of air power: to be beaten in the air means defeat and acceptance of whatever terms the enemy may be pleased to impose. Control of the air fundamentally enables air power's many contributions to tactical, operational, and strategic effects. Thus, control of the air is both a means to an end and an objective in its own right.

It is difficult to overstate the importance of a command and control network because everything else depends on it. Such a network is crucial to our operations, but even more important, the real-time situational awareness provided by the network is a strategic input for our national political decision makers and our NATO partners.

As a result, we need a network of sensors that can provide situational awareness in our area of responsibility, preferably 24/7. Norway has replaced the old NATO Air Defense Ground Environment (NADGE) with two control and reporting centers (CRCs): Sørreisa and Mågerø. The former has undergone an upgrade and is now a state-of-the-art facility, but the latter will be closed down in the near future. As part of the upcoming force restructuring, we will establish the National Air Operations Center (NAOC) at Reitan (near Bodø) for tactical command and tactical control, fully integrated and co-located with our national joint headquarters (HQ). The new NAOC represents a step toward meeting future demands for timely and effective command and control, as it will provide a solid air picture for Norway's area of interest.

Norway has been an important member of NATO's integrated air defense system for more than two generations, and we have every intention of sustaining that role. My biggest concern in this respect centers on obtaining new ground-based sensors. We plan to replace long-range radars within the next decade, ideally as part of a joint investment program. Part of the challenge facing the air force involves acquiring systems that can help us handle huge amounts of information. NATO's Air Command and Control System will be an important element of that capability. The first step is to implement NATO's system at CRC Sørreisa, which is primarily funded by the alliance, and the next step is to implement it at our national HQ using national means. The combination will provide us with a complete and modern capability.

We also work closely with the navy, exercising air command and control from operational centers on our new frigates. We exercise and cooperate with Sweden, Iceland, Portugal, and the three Baltic states.

Our personnel also take part in joint airborne warning and control system (AWACS) missions, including operations in Afghanistan, together with the United States, the United Kingdom, Turkey, France, Germany, and other NATO partners.

Our fighter squadrons constitute another essential component of ensuring control of the air. We have fifty-seven F-16s, all of which have undergone midlife updates. Although we marked their thirtieth anniversary in 2010, these fighter-bombers remain highly capable and operationally relevant. They can be scrambled on short notice to deter, defend, and respond to threats to Norwegian air space. Our pilots have considerable experience operating along the Norwegian coast and intercepting Russian combat aircraft. They also participate in regular NATO exercises and air campaigns, such as Operation Allied Force in 1999, the International Security Assistance Force (ISAF) contribution to Afghanistan, and Operations Odyssey Dawn and Unified Protector over Libya in 2011.

The F-16s will require further upgrades, including improved avionics, to stay fully interoperable with our coalition partners' fleets. Yet another challenge is to enable the transmission of video from an aircraft to other assets at sea or on land or directly to our national military HQ.

Airframes currently represent the main limitation to further upgrades, and the air force must perform a cost-benefit analysis to decide how many F-16s should be fully upgraded before we start operating large numbers of F-35s. We also must ensure that enough F-16 pilots have the necessary flying hours to maintain their combat-ready status.

Ground-based air defense missile systems complement fighter-bombers as the sharp end of ensuring air sovereignty. The Norwegian Advanced Surface-to-Air Missile System (NASAMS) II is probably the best system in its class. It is modern and exceptionally capable, and it is one of the few systems in the world that can counter incoming cruise missiles. The Norwegian Air Force is developing a new operational concept that involves four NASAMS combat groups. Today the main challenge is staffing rather than equipment. As we emphasize quality over quantity, we cannot forget that a certain critical mass is essential.

Intelligence, Surveillance, and Reconnaissance

Figuratively speaking, our ground-based and around-the-clock radars serve as our outdoor lights, illuminating our backyard. These sensors give us a rough idea of the situation both in and outside our borders. We often know a little about overall conditions, but sometimes we need to know everything about a specific incident or action. In those situations we must bring out our most powerful torches: our F-16s. With their speed and flexibility, these aircraft can quickly reach nearly any location of interest in Norway. Their modern sensors and data-link systems make our F-16s crucial sources of detailed information that can serve as the decision makers' most important eyes and ears.

The new F-35 offers a powerful intelligence, surveillance, and reconnaissance (ISR) capability. To put it bluntly, the most important capability of the F-35 is not necessarily intercepting other aircraft or destroying targets but gathering information and distributing it swiftly to other sensors, shooters, and decision makers in the network-centric systems. The aircraft's real strength is in its reliable and timely situational awareness, interoperability with other systems in our air force and in our partner nations' air forces, and firepower, which allows it to take effective action when needed. The F-35 is a quintessential enabler for all other operations—on land, at sea, and in the air. That stated, we need personnel who can collect, process, and analyze raw data to determine the relevant information.

Our maritime aircraft, P-3C Orion, plays a similar role when it comes to patrolling the seas. As already mentioned, the seas under Norwegian sovereignty are almost incomprehensibly vast: seven times bigger than Norway's landmass. Given the area we must safeguard, we need maritime aircraft that can work hand in hand with naval vessels. The air force's maritime patrol aircraft operate in the High North every week. In 2011 Norway contributed one P-3N Orion as part of Operation Ocean Shield, based in the Seychelles. This aircraft took part in a counterpiracy operation outside the Horn of Africa (the Somali basin)—a mission few foresaw a decade ago. The sensors of our P-3Ns are undergoing an upgrade to improve their information-gathering capability. However, because the United States is replacing its Orions, Norway will need alternative partners to provide simulator training and education, as well as spare parts, for its Orions.

The era of maritime Lynx helicopters will come to an end before our new NH-90 fleet is fully in place, so we are working at finding solutions to fill the gap. We plan to purchase fourteen of the new helicopters—eight for the coast guard and six for the frigates—and have already started training and educating staff to operate the NH-90. The new system will represent a considerable improvement over the Lynx, both technically and operationally. This cooperation with the navy also illustrates how air power encompasses far more than the air force.

Even though the satellite involved is not an air force asset, it is worth mentioning that Norway now operates a test program involving an AISSat-1 ship-tracking spacecraft. This seven-kilo Automatic Identification System (AIS) spacecraft enables Norway to monitor shipping in its vast territorial waters by picking up signals from larger vessels' AIS transponders. The spacecraft will on average provide full coverage of Norway's economic zone every one hundred minutes. The area of interest is larger than the Mediterranean, so taking the step into space seems both prudent and exciting.

Precision Engagement

During Operations Odyssey Dawn and Unified Protector over Libya in 2011, Norwegian F-16s flew about six hundred combat sorties—of which roughly 25 percent were for air interdiction and 75 percent for strike coordination and reconnaissance (SCAR)—and dropped 588 precision-guided bombs.[2] We conducted deliberate targeting in the form of combined air operations involving fighter aircraft from different nations and different bases. The preselected targets included command and control facilities, hardened aircraft shelters, ammunition storage facilities, landlines of communication, artillery, and various military vehicles. SCAR represented dynamic targeting, that is, determining targets of opportunity based on pilot observation and target acquisition from ISR assets in the area (kill boxes). The weapons of choice were always precision bombs, both laser and Global Positioning System (GPS) guided.

This mission presented several operational challenges: for example, distinguishing between pro- and anti-Gaddafi forces in the heat of combat and avoiding collateral damage when Libyan loyalists used human shields and parked equipment close to civilian infrastructure. The air force is acquiring and fielding small-diameter bombs (SDBs), which can reduce the risk of unintended damage in complex operations. Furthermore, although the Link 16 data link proved useful, the experience revealed communication issues that the air force needs to address. The Norwegian Air Force also became fully aware of NATO's dependence on the United States for command, control, communications, and intelligence and for air-to-air refueling.

Participation in the NATO intervention in Libya showed that the Norwegian Air Force could manage a rapid deployment. It also revealed the high level of competence and experience of all personnel involved and demonstrated that they were thoroughly prepared and trained to execute their various missions. Our pilots had a sufficient number of flying hours to execute missions effectively, and we received positive feedback on the relevance, quality, professionalism, and effectiveness of the Norwegian contribution.

Such successful performance derives from years of training and exercises, including war-like scenarios. Although it is important to have upgraded equipment to ensure precision and thereby strategic effect, the human element is ever more important. It is a great advantage that we are used to deploy and operate together with international partners. We have been active for many years in the European Participating Air Forces (EPAF) cooperative program for the F-16, which involves Norway, Denmark, the Netherlands, Belgium, and Portugal. The benefits of the EPAF became manifest during Operation Unified Protector.

National exercises (such as Nordavind at Banak) and international exercises (such as Red Flag at Nellis Air Force Base in Nevada) are of utmost importance in order to sustain deployment readiness. Over the last few years, we have also held joint exercises in the Nordic region with Swedish and Finnish squadrons almost every week. The Arctic Challenge Exercise 2013 was based on the cross-border training concept. During the exercise NATO and Partnership for Peace (PfP) nations deployed from northern air bases to practice relatively large-scale combined air operations, based in part on the experience from operations conducted in Libya in 2011.

National and international exercises widen our experience by providing the opportunity to operate in various areas and settings, practice with different aircraft, and gain insight into other nations' operational concepts. They extend the initial training and education that we give our pilots so that, by the time we are called upon to contribute to a military campaign, our airmen are familiar with the tasks and roles that they are expected to perform. In other words, we train as we fight.

Precision engagement means more than hitting the target; it includes the ability to bring about those effects that will ultimately accomplish the mission. Whereas engineering and weaponeering determine *how* to conduct air bombardment, targeting determines the *why*. To get "bombs on target," an air force needs good intelligence and information gathering. More than ever before, these factors are essential to our network-oriented systems in peacetime, crises, and armed conflict.

Precision engagement does not necessarily involve lethal weapons. Electronic warfare, for instance, is an integral part of modern air operations. Two of the three DA-20 Jet Falcons are our main assets for electronic warfare missions, which provide a service to all the armed forces. The air force has a highly competent squadron that works closely with Norway's electronic warfare center. Both Norway and NATO appreciate this important competency, which will become even more crucial as we prepare to receive the F-35.

Air Mobility

The air force also performs other kinds of missions. Search and rescue, medical transportation and evacuation, and transportation more generally are undoubtedly the air force's major contribution to society at large. Most air power theorists focus on air power's ability to destroy infrastructure, but air power's ability to provide services when infrastructure and supply are lacking, for whatever reason, is more important still.

Air mobility is the backbone of our overall national defense. The air force does not have huge numbers of personnel or aircraft dedicated to this mission, but this service is highly appreciated and has tremendous impact. Cargo and transport aircraft are in many ways the unsung heroes of air power. Air mobility is rarely considered the core of air power, although ground forces, from World War II to the present, would probably beg to differ. The army, and particularly the special forces, depend on the air force's ability to move soldiers, even under threat of fire. Air mobility is therefore a crucial facilitator; the army's readiness, reach, and flexibility rest on air power.

As the number of bases and garrisons has decreased, the demand for air mobility has increased. When forces are positioned at fewer forward locations, they usually have to travel long distances to reach the area of operations. Obviously, international operations have also made the ability to bring our men and women home rapidly—from the other side of the world if necessary—a priority.

Norway gained immensely valuable experience from participating in ISAF. The Norwegian Aeromedical Detachment (NAD) provided three Bell 412 helicopters for medevac and tactical transportation of international and Afghan ground forces. In addition, our four new C-130J Hercules contributed to operations in Afghanistan during the first half of 2013. The newer Hercules may look like the older versions, but they have a more powerful engine, better propellers, and more space for cargo. The avionics system is now digital and improved, which enables reduction of the crew to two pilots and one airman in charge of loading and unloading.

On behalf of the Ministry of Justice and Security, the air force also conducts search and rescue using twelve Sea King helicopters. The airframe is old, but the fleet has 98 percent operational readiness—proof positive of professional maintenance.

Together with ten other NATO countries, and with Sweden and Finland, Norway takes part in operating C-17s as part of the Heavy Airlift Wing based in Papa, Hungary. This aircraft offers a strategic airlift capability that we cannot provide alone; the C-17 is three times bigger than our C-130J Hercules, and we have used it, among other things, to transport our own helicopters to and from Afghanistan.

Vital Services Too Often Overlooked

In addition to the four basic roles—control of the air, ISR, precision engagement, and air mobility—several lesser-known air force activities also deserve mention. For example, one of the least appreciated branches in the air force, or in any force, is the logistics branch, which ensures that equipment works and that personnel have food, water, and shelter. Force protection is another example of a lesser-known activity. In modern air operations it is difficult to shoot down sophisticated fighters at thirty thousand feet, but all aircraft are vulnerable on the ground. Hence, our force protection teams are just as crucial as multimillion-dollar air-to-air missiles.

Force protection plays other roles as well. Between January 1 and September 30, 2012, the Norwegian Air Force delivered force protection for the Provincial Reconstruction Team in Maimanah, Afghanistan. Its main tasks included providing perimeter security, a quick-reaction team, airport security, and escort and patrol in the city of Maimanah and surrounding areas. This was the first time the air force had been responsible for this type of mission abroad, and again it was a positive experience that confirmed that our personnel could meet the challenges they confronted.

Looking to the Future

Air power professionals and the media have for a long time been preoccupied with the potential of unmanned aerial systems (UASs). Acquisition of the NATO Alliance Ground Surveillance (AGS) Global Hawk constitutes the most important milestone in Norway's approach to UASs. Norway's armed forces are already exploring the possibility of designing and allocating functional air space for future joint and combined training and exercises to identify the strengths and limitations of unmanned platforms. We are also studying the utility of unmanned platforms for cross-border training. Improvements in the technical capabilities of UASs are sought, but the moral, legal, and ethical aspects of their employment call for careful consideration.

Some speculate that UASs of various sorts can replace the P-3C, but the air force should carry out further research before reaching a conclusion on this matter. Our approach to "the new ocean" in the Arctic will be based on further analysis of how UASs can become an important element in Norway's overall ISR strategy. As we introduce the Raven into the Norwegian armed forces, we must examine organizational, logistic, and operational implications; at the time of writing, the Raven is not part of our integrated command and control system. In the future unmanned platforms may play an important role in air and sea surveillance, but currently they remain only a supplement to manned aerial vehicles. After all, homeowners do not throw out their stoves when they buy microwave ovens. Even as their kitchens become steadily more diversified and their utensils steadily more specialized, the need for the basics persists. The same rule applies to military power and aviation.

Air power is an important enabler and an important team player. Debates over whether air power can win wars alone are thus only as meaningful as arguments over what is most important: air, water, or food. Realizing that air power works best as a complement to land and naval power is especially important in Norway, given its geography and its politico-military objectives. We have based our force structure on mobile, modular systems in a network-centric system of systems and on the four basic capabilities highlighted in this chapter. We have a modern air force and a competent team of men and women, but we cannot afford to slow our momentum or accept the status quo. We have to stay relevant in the new security era.

In terms of investment the F-35 will dominate our defense force for years to come. The F-35 is a new generation of fighter-bomber with unprecedented ISR capability. But the new C-130J Super Hercules also contributes significantly to our capabilities, as do the new NH-90 maritime helicopters and our NASAMS II. Our next investment will be in the modernization of the maritime patrol aircraft and in new long-range radars, all under the air command and control of the NAOC. The center and the F-35 fleet will receive the bulk of public attention, but we must continue to consider the totality of operational capabilities for both joint and combined operations and give the highest priority to air personnel and air power competence. That competence extends far beyond operational and logistical skills; it also includes air-minded education with focus on expertise, ethics, and attitude. Only once we have developed our personnel and competence can we truly live up to our motto: "Air power at the right place, at the right time, and with the right effect."

SIX

Danish Air Power

From the Cold War to Contemporary Air Operations

Maj. Gen. Henrik Røboe Dam

"Air power"—in itself an intimidating, forceful, and convincing term—is easy to comprehend but often hard to define. The air power concept dates back to the early years of the twentieth century, when recent technological achievements by the Wright brothers allowed a remarkable revolution in warfare: the utilization of the third dimension. Fixed-wing aircraft delivered the decisive triad of air power characteristics—speed, range, and elevation—and air became the third domain that military forces needed to dominate.

With this new type of warfare, controlling the third dimension by gaining air superiority in time and space became a sine qua non for the exploitation of air power and a natural top priority in any campaign. During the First World War, airplanes were sent into combat and conducted many of the types of missions that we recognize from contemporary air power doctrine, but air power had not yet been conceptualized to a degree that allowed for full exploitation of its central characteristics.

Following the First World War, U.S. Army general William "Billy" Mitchell (1879–1936) was one of many theorists who attempted to conceptualize this new contribution to warfare. Mitchell defined air power simply as "the ability to do something in the air." By any standard this is a succinct and simplistic definition that should be regarded as a testimonial to the incredible flexibility of air power. Modern definitions are less brief than Mitchell's; for example, in 2011 the U.S. Air Force basic doctrine defined air power as the ability to project military power or influence through the control and exploitation of air, space, and cyberspace to achieve strategic, operational, or tactical objectives. Both definitions are equally correct, and one should view them as complementary perspectives. The military context for air power is most easily understood in terms of the current U.S. definition, but Mitchell's broad definition may better capture the flexibility and possibilities of air power, removing mental barriers to consideration of its full exploitation. In my capacity as the commander of Tactical Air Command Denmark, I intend to present a perspective on how this "something" is manifested in a military and comprehensive context framed by the Royal Danish Air Force (RDAF).

Although Mitchell's definition of air power is simplistic, a more accurate but still succinct definition will be hard to achieve if the goal of defining air power is to encompass the myriad effects that modern air forces can deliver. Briefly put, air is the environment in which an air force operates, and all aspects of power—soft, hard, and smart power—are what an air force brings. The RDAF provides Denmark with the ability to "do something in the air" as a state actor, both defensively and offensively. A continued focus on purposely adjusting this "something" will ensure the relevance of Danish air power as a credible military capability that enables Denmark to shape, deter, and respond to threats, both as a nation and as part of a coalition, and to maintain air superiority over sovereign territory.

Recognizing that future development is rooted in past endeavors, I have allowed myself to reminisce on a few significant events during my career. The rationale for this approach is fairly straightforward and logical: development of air power capabilities stems from the unfolding events of history in combination with predictions of future threats and—most important—the political preferences and aspirations emanating from these events. This perspective ensures the continuing relevance of Danish air power. Therefore, I first present a brief recapitulation of key events that affected the RDAF during the last three decades as an introduction to a description of current Danish air power, and then I offer a perspective on future directions.

The Defensive Comfort of the Cold War

My career dates back to the early 1980s, in the midst of the Cold War. Since then the world has undergone profound transformations in many significant ways, as has the use of air power. A number of so-called black swan events have altered the world political map to a point that seemed unlikely just twenty to twenty-five years ago, and even though some of those events may seem trivial today, reflecting on their significance can bring about insight.

In the early 1980s Denmark was one of several frontline states in the North Atlantic Treaty Organization's (NATO's) collective defense against the Warsaw Pact. Denmark's geostrategic location made it possible for the alliance to monitor sea lines of communication between the Baltic Sea and the Atlantic Ocean. In those days Danish defense planners were fortunate in the sense that they had a clearly defined enemy and knew the direction of the threat. The RDAF was introducing the F-16 Fighting Falcon into active service, and the Saab 35XD Draken served as the backbone of the RDAF. These aircraft carried out frequent intelligence collection flights and sovereignty missions in the Baltic Sea to reaffirm Denmark's posture and presence. Along with ground-based air defense, the main purpose of these missions was deterrence, and the primary modus operandi was defensive. The principle of mutual assured destruction kept the world in a tense equilibrium and required conventional and reactive Danish air power.

The Post–Cold War Era: Increased Uncertainty and Complexity

The ability to carry out surgical attacks without being restricted by enemy air defenses, enabling enemy centers of gravity to be targeted anywhere and at any time, came about as the Cold War ended. With stealth technology, air superiority could suddenly become tightly confined in time and space. Combined with precision-guided munitions, these attributes of air power proved valuable enablers in the coming conflicts, initially in Operation Desert Storm and later during the civil war in the former Federal Republic of Yugoslavia. The latter conflict afforded the RDAF a significant role in international efforts to defuse tensions between the belligerents. In 1992 the RDAF projected soft air power by deploying a C-130 for tactical air transport as an enabler of humanitarian relief to the besieged city of Sarajevo.

In 1998 and 1999 NATO conducted an air campaign to stop the repression of the Albanian population of Kosovo. As part of the campaign, the RDAF deployed F-16s to Grazzanise Air Base in Italy to perform the defensive task of flying combat air patrol missions over the Adriatic Sea, and in the ensuing NATO air campaign, the F-16s participated in the bombing of Serbian installations.

The traditional NATO perspective had always been defensive in nature and focused on exercising and training for operations within the borders of allied countries. Participating in a coalition during the intervention in the Balkans opened new prospects for Danish air power that entailed deployable forces and offensive operations. This fairly epoch-making employment of NATO forces indicated the beginning of a new security environment, and the need for a more expeditionary air force seemed pertinent. During the conflict the RDAF had managed tasks as different as bombing and humanitarian relief in a hostile environment. Based on these experiences, moving toward an expeditionary air force did not seem like a distant goal and would soon become a main effort for the RDAF.

A Decade Dominated by the Asymmetric Threat of International Terrorism

On September 11, 2001, the world witnessed international terrorism on an unprecedented scale. The events of that day raised questions as to whether cultural and religious identities would henceforth replace political ideology as the main source of conflict. Moreover, what would such a fundamental change in circumstances signify with regard to the development and use of air power?

It is still too soon to answer these fundamental questions in detail. However, to achieve the desired effects of military power projection in an asymmetric conflict, either defensive or offensive, the targeting process needed to be far more complex and was far more critical than it had been in earlier symmetric conflicts. Thus far asymmetric conflicts have illustrated a shift in emphasis toward air power, since the Western powers can achieve air superiority effortlessly against nonstate adversaries. Some would claim that the September 11 attacks disprove this statement, since air superiority implies nullification of air threats. But in the case of the 2001 attacks, the decisive factor was to a high degree the discourse at the time, which influenced the policy for the use of air power—a topic to which I will return shortly. In fact, achieving air superiority has not ensured progress in asymmetric campaigns, but nonetheless it remains vital for other air power roles—such as intelligence, surveillance, and reconnaissance (ISR)—which in turn enable progress in other domains.

Defensive Tasks in an Asymmetric Scenario

The U.S. Air Force (USAF) constituted the final bastion against the September 11 attacks and could have countered the attacks in the sense of preventing the terrorists from destroying their intended targets. The USAF reaction could be described as insufficient, but casting blame in hindsight is unjust. A decision to engage commercial airliners, with no precedent to draw on, would have been difficult to make. Defense planners never envisioned actually having to combat coordinated attacks carried out by commercial air transport. However, the fact remains that air power was the only means for dealing with this type of event, and as a result, Western nations now routinely exercise terrorist attack scenarios derived from September 11, 2001, as an integral part of operations. Denmark has rehearsed its response, and if an antagonist decides to challenge our air defenses in a highly asymmetric way, we and our allies will undoubtedly be better prepared than the United States was in 2001.

Offensive Tasks in an Asymmetric Scenario

The September 2001 attacks sparked the U.S. intervention in Afghanistan, and in late 2001 RDAF C-130s supported the employment of special operations forces. During the summer of 2002, RDAF F-16 fighters deployed to Manas Air Base, Kyrgyzstan, to provide firepower support for ground forces. By participating in operations in remote locations, the RDAF had taken a leap into serious expeditionary operations.

The decisive step toward an expeditionary air force came in December 2004, when the Ministry of Defense published a memorandum describing the politically consolidated implementation basis for the Danish Defence Agreement 2005–2009. This agreement entailed the final drastic change for the RDAF in its transformation from a garrison air force to an entirely expeditionary air force. The agreement dictated the restructuring of the RDAF into centralized capability centers designated as wings. This restructuring promoted a high degree of synergy and a modular concept that allowed tailoring of Danish air power to any mission.

Current Air Operations

Even though this transformation caused a complete restructuring of the RDAF and therefore affected all capabilities, the RDAF has maintained a presence in Afghanistan since 2001. The RDAF has frequently deployed C-130s for tactical air transport; sensor support has aided safe air traffic control at Kabul; and most recently, a tactical command and control center for control of the air space in the northern regions has proved the force's new expeditionary nature.

During the decade of fighting insurgency in Afghanistan, the RDAF has also applied its capabilities to different kinds of tasks. Denmark carries out a recurrent air policing task in Iceland and the Baltic States. Furthermore, the RDAF has supported the fight against piracy off the coast of Somalia, known as Operation Ocean Shield, by deploying a maritime patrol aircraft, as well as helicopters operating from Danish naval vessels. These Danish air power capabilities greatly increase the ability to conduct surveillance of the waters in question and to respond to pirate attacks before civilian lives are at risk.

Operating in asymmetric scenarios, such as the conflict in Afghanistan and the counterpiracy mission off the Horn of Africa, presents the air force with a role very different from its conventional role during the Cold War. Despite this the large majority of the capabilities utilized are the same, which testifies to the flexibility of Danish air power and the resourcefulness of the RDAF. The RDAF has adapted to its new role, but the underlying question remains: have we managed to preserve our ability to strike decisive blows in a more conventional conflict?

The Fall of Gaddafi

Implicit claims in the preceding sections about unpredictability in the development of the global security situation were confirmed in December 2010 as the Arab Awakening started to unfold in Tunisia. After ten years of fighting insurgents in Afghanistan, the RDAF found itself in Libya, taking part in a scenario in which air power confronted an offensive task against a state actor possessing a conventional layered air defense. The United Nations had announced adoption of Resolution 1973 on March 17, 2011, and a mere forty-eight hours later, Danish F-16s were reported as ready to perform missions. On March 20 at 1510 local time, four fully armed Danish F-16s took off from Sigonella Air Base on a combat mission to enforce Resolution 1973. In the case of Libya, the responsiveness of air power outpaced decision making among the twenty-eight NATO nations, which did not reach a consensus before air operations began. This meant that the initial air strikes were conducted in the framework of Operation Odyssey Dawn, led by the U.S. Seventeenth Air Force based at Ramstein Air Base, Germany. On March 31 NATO Operation Unified Protector effectively assumed the responsibility for executing a combined NATO operation. This did not reduce the capability and interoperability of the RDAF fighters, nor did it in any way hamper their effectiveness and ability to assume their share of the burden. It simply reaffirmed that we can truly "plug and play" with our coalition partners regardless of the setting.

Danish Air Power—Status Quo

Looking back on these historic events brings me to the point where it seems natural to summarize the current potential and limitations of the RDAF. Since disbanding its ground-based air defense system, the RDAF possesses four focused operational capabilities—fighters, fixed-wing transport, helicopters, and air surveillance and control—all of which are extremely efficient and fully interoperable with NATO forces. This has been proved in Kosovo, Afghanistan, and Libya as well as during extensive participation in exercises. This interoperability allows Denmark to share burdens with its allies, which will remain the preferred approach for the RDAF.

As mentioned at the beginning of the chapter, the effects of military power fall within the constructs of shape, deter, and respond, and air power traditionally offers four capabilities: control of the air, situational awareness, strike, and maneuver. In combination, this framework provides a template for assessing the collective capability of an air force.

A central part of Danish air power's ability to shape, deter, and respond derives from Denmark's membership in the NATO alliance, which partially alleviates the burden that delivering these effects entails. As was reconfirmed during the Lisbon summit of 2010, NATO's Strategic Concept continues to stem from the pledge of member nations to defend one another against attacks, including new threats to the safety of NATO citizens or vital interests of NATO citizens. This premise also applies to the future of the RDAF. Using the previously mentioned constructs as a template for assessment, Table 2 portrays the current state of the RDAF. As the table shows, the RDAF provides capabilities that cover the entire air power construct, although some areas require a coalition effort.

Comprehending New Threats

The threats that Denmark has faced during the last decade could be characterized mainly as asymmetric, but this is likely to change, even in the foreseeable future. The asymmetric threats will endure, but their nature will change as the traditional way of distinguishing between

Table 2. Current RDAF Capabilities

RDAF at Present	Control of the Air	Situational Awareness	Strike	Maneuver
Shape (influence the security environment by presence)	Platforms capable of ISR and weapons employment, in combination with a deployable tactical command center that includes sensor and link fusion and dissemination, provide a control and situational awareness package interoperable according to NATO standards.		Air power projection through the use of multirole platforms, primarily in the role of air policing, enables strike capability as a policy option.	Acting as a force multiplier, tactical airlift (fixed and rotary wing) functions as the linchpin for tactical mobility of ground forces, especially in locations with poor infrastructure.
Deter (display credible defensive force to potential aggressors)	A highly capable and sustainable peacetime air defense, consisting of fighters and ground control, safeguards sovereignty of Danish and NATO airspace.	Extensive radar coverage enables production of a recognized air picture, and similar extensive link coverage enables integration of multiple platforms for joint deterrence.	The ability of multirole fighters to operate independently at standoff ranges and with high precision in a rapid response to aggressor action provides a credible force.	Airlift enables the ability to tactically deploy, for example, special operations forces covertly, which directly enables the potential operational and strategic effects that special forces can achieve.
Respond (actively and reactively employ air power to reverse or control a significant security event)	A fully expeditionary fighter force and tactical command center, including staff functions for operational planning, enable the RDAF to take on missions for control of the air anywhere on the globe, with any NATO partner.	The ability to respond relies on the same capabilities as the ability to shape. This can occur because the platforms employed in total cover the entire spectrum of conflict.	Fighter aircraft in an offensive role, equipped with state-of-the-art munitions, enable the RDAF to strike at almost any conceivable target. This is pending support from electronic warfare capabilities provided by coalition partners.	Fixed- and rotary-wing platforms equipped with countermeasures enable airlift of troops and equipment in hostile scenarios.

symmetric and asymmetric threats becomes inadequate. An addendum to this distinction is the term "hybrid threat." As is often said, technology makes the world a smaller place. In the context of weapons, technology brings threats closer even though their origins remain unchanged. This development may be the root cause of the increased threat posed by conventional weapons. Factors such as the weapons' range, the speed at which they can be delivered, and their physical size relative to their destructive power reduce the probability of successfully warding off an attack.

State-of-the-art strategic weapons technology has so far remained exclusively in the hands of Western state actors and state actors that are interdependent with the West and have an interest in maintaining the status quo. Rogue states do not share this goal, and as advanced conventional weapons continue to proliferate, attacks become more likely and more imminent. The attacks would probably not come from the rogue state itself, given the fear of massive retaliation, but from asymmetric actors that support the rogue state's goals. This combination constitutes a hybrid threat and makes retaliation elusive and deterrence hard to achieve.

How can a nation deter or retaliate against an asymmetric enemy that possesses no territory but is supported by a symmetric enemy? This conundrum does not have a simple answer. A military response to this hybrid threat should therefore emphasize capabilities that reduce the chance of a successful attack through shaping the security environment to counter the asymmetric enemy and using deterrence to counter the symmetric enemy. Tactical ballistic missiles represent a relevant threat in this context. A ballistic missile defense (BMD) program provides a deterrent to this threat, but NATO must alleviate the burden here, since BMD covers an area so vast that no single country can establish a credible warning and engagement system.

Danish Air Power—*Quo Vadis*?

The future development of Danish air power must take the perspective described previously into account. The focal point for the development of air power capabilities will be present and predicted future threats in the third dimension that can be appropriately averted by air power, and air superiority will remain the highest priority. Currently, three main factors define the circumstances under which this development must take place. First, the RDAF, like Western armed forces in general, faces budget cuts, which necessarily limit its ambitions. Second, Denmark continues to be a member of NATO, and therefore the RDAF does not need to cover all areas of air power, given that it will operate as part of a coalition. Third, an expeditionary setting is the most likely context for future air power projection; thus, the RDAF must have the capability to operate in all types of environments. In light of these three factors, I provide some specific illustrations using the well-known distinction between symmetric and asymmetric scenarios, even though these lines may well become obscured in future scenarios, as indicated by the term "hybrid threats."

Asymmetric Scenarios

Situational awareness is indispensable in asymmetric scenarios. Afghanistan, as a representative example of such a scenario, presented the RDAF with an unprecedented demand for 24/7 airborne ISR to deal with nonstate actors through continuous counterinsurgency operations. ISR platforms enable situational awareness, which facilitates the ability to engage the proper targets and minimize collateral damage. The development of unmanned aerial systems (UASs) accelerated greatly in order to meet the high demand for long-endurance ISR, and UASs will continue to provide decisive situational awareness in future battles. Danish participation in the Alliance Ground Surveillance (AGS) system will increase the ISR capability of NATO as well as Danish air power. This initiative is fully in line with the principle of burden sharing and also enables expeditionary ISR.

Symmetric Scenarios

The ability to strike is essential in symmetric scenarios. The conflict in Libya, for example, reaffirmed air power as a sine qua non. Air power made it possible for the international community to rapidly project military power across borders by gaining air superiority, which, in conjunction with other means, enabled coercion of the enemy. The powerful effect achieved in a short time span resulted from interoperability and burden sharing. The results are highly visible, demonstrating that air power can target rogue states and their regimes instantly and with high efficiency.

The use of air power in Libya presented an illustrative example of the effectiveness of collaboration at combined and joint levels and of working on the basis of shared doctrines, standards, tactics, techniques, and procedures. Furthermore, the Libya operation showed how the value of four Danish fighters significantly increases when they complement a coalition operation. Admittedly, Gaddafi's forces did not possess the highly sophisticated weapons technology of Western actors, but nonetheless, he did have the advantage of being in the defensive role on his own soil. Future adversaries may have greater capability, which implies the need for a fifth-generation multirole combat aircraft.

Common Denominators

None of the recent scenarios, symmetric or asymmetric, has unfolded on NATO territory, and theaters so far have been characterized by poor infrastructure and medium to high risk for ground forces. Thus, there has been a high demand for transport, strategic as well as tactical, using both fixed- and rotary-wing platforms. In this role air power capabilities and air superiority again become indispensable, since they enable shifts in weight of effort by rapid movement of troops, equipment, and supplies, in addition to mitigating the risk of ground attacks on troop movements.

The key capabilities reinforce each other. As demonstrated in both Libya and Afghanistan and during other campaigns, systems made interoperable through standardization have become the prerequisite for burden sharing, which functions as a strategic mission enabler. Air power is most efficient when coordinated to achieve synergy and avoid duplication. Modern command and control systems form an enduring part of this capability, regardless of whether air power is projected across borders in a symmetric scenario or deployed to an asymmetric scenario with limited host nation support. A high level of situational awareness has proved a necessary precondition in any campaign to ensure effective command and control and at the same time avoid collateral damage.

Strike capability, coupled with the ability to coordinate the employment of air power by exercising command and control, ensures air superiority. Air superiority enables flexible maneuver of forces by airlift—a vital capability in any scenario, since it enables forces to adapt rapidly to unfolding events by adjusting the weight of effort and allowing forward basing of platforms.

I do not envision any future scenario in which Danish air power would be employed without orchestrating all four capabilities: control of the air, situational awareness, strike, and maneuver. This serves as a significant basis for planning and developing future Danish air power capability, but circumstances deny us the possibility of building credible capabilities in all four areas.

Weight of Effort: Flexible Key Capabilities

The preceding paragraphs reveal the need for the RDAF to decide where to concentrate the greatest effort, especially given the scarcity of economic resources, which will influence the development of capabilities. This brings me to a focus on synergy among key capabilities. For example, ISR and strike are two highly flexible and key capabilities in all scenarios. If strike platforms could enable situational awareness or if ISR platforms could enable strike capability, the resultant hybrid platforms could cover both imperatives in all scenarios. There is no doubt in my mind that strike platforms carry out the more difficult task of the two. If equipped with the appropriate sensors and electronic warfare package, such platforms could become fully capable of providing ISR as well. The reverse is much more difficult to achieve, given that current manned ISR platforms have characteristics that make them unsuitable for initial or responsive strike. Unmanned ISR platforms

25. Bell 412 multirole helicopter, Royal Norwegian Air Force, *Jon Anders Skau*

26. F-16, Royal Norwegian Air Force, *Lars Magne Hovtun*

27. F-35 Joint Strike Fighter, *Norwegian Armed Forces*

28. C-130J Hercules, *Norwegian Armed Forces*

29. Sørreisa Control and Reporting Centre, *Torstein Liene*

30. Norwegian Advanced Surface-to-Air Missile System II, *Sigurd Tonning-Olsen*

31. C-130J Hercules, Afghanistan, *Royal Danish Air Force*

32. C-130J Hercules airdrop, *Royal Danish Air Force*

33. Challenger, Greenland, *Royal Danish Air Force*

34. Eurocopter EH101, *Royal Danish Air Force*

35. F-16, *Royal Danish Air Force*

36. Lynx helicopter, *Royal Danish Air Force*

37. JAS 39 Gripen fighter jet, *Swedish Air Force*

38. Formation flight, *Swedish Air Force*

39. HKP 16 Swedish Blackhawk transport helicopter, ISAF, *Swedish Air Force*

40. JAS 39 Gripen air-to-air refueling, *Swedish Air Force*

41. HKP 15 transport helicopters, *Swedish Air Force*

42. JAS 39 Gripen fighter jet, *Swedish Air Force*

43. C-295M EADS CASA transport aircraft, *Finnish Air Force*

44. F/A-18 Hornet, Lapland, *Finnish Air Force*

45. F/A-18 Hornet air-to-air role, *Finnish Air Force*

46. F/A-18 Hornet air-to-ground role, *Finnish Air Force*

47. Hawk Mk 66, small, *Finnish Air Force*

48. Thales Ground Master 403, *Finnish Air Force*

alleviate this shortcoming partly by their long endurance and partly because no lives will be lost if they are shot down. However, this takes the pilot out of the equation, which makes it difficult, and in some scenarios practically impossible, to factor the political will and mandate into a decision to engage targets. With the next generation of fighters, we will witness a synergistic merging of strike and ISR; therefore, the RDAF may focus on acquiring an organic but limited ISR capability integrated into a strike platform.

Although strike platforms can display a high degree of flexibility, the majority of scenarios, especially asymmetric scenarios, require boots on the ground to achieve strategic success. This holds true for both expeditionary troops—i.e., coalition forces—and indigenous troops, but in the strategic perspective the indigenous troops are a crucial part of any campaign, regardless of the nationality of air power. Special operations forces present a way of achieving strategic effects with relatively few resources, whether engaging a symmetric, asymmetric, or hybrid threat. Drawing on lessons identified in recent conflicts, the RDAF has placed emphasis on developing the ability to conduct special air operations. This ability encompasses not just the distinct tactical maneuver capability necessary for employment of special operations forces. All air power characteristics—command and control, ISR, and strike support—play a vital part in special air operations. The personnel involved are rigorously trained to adapt to the special operations mind-set, which is crucial to maintaining the necessary flexibility and creativity that forms an integral part of the dynamic world of special operations, as well as the established relationships that are critical for mission success. The demand for special air operations will only increase in the future, and given our current highly credible capability, it is only natural for this to remain a focal point for the RDAF.

A key enabler for success in planning and carrying out special operations is establishing a high degree of situational awareness. Therefore, the earlier discussion of manned versus unmanned platforms does not preclude a focus on UASs, especially as UASs represent one of the technologies that the RDAF can also expect to encounter as a threat. New scenarios may arise that involve UASs as small as insects or high-altitude long-endurance strike platforms capable of supersonic autonomous operations, and existing defense capabilities may prove insufficient to counter this new challenge.

A central part of this new challenge will be interoperability among platforms and every aspect and entity of the cyber world. For example, UASs that function autonomously by neural network technology might independently be able to hack into and exploit information technology infrastructure. In essence, this type of technology could make any cyber-based system, military or civilian, vulnerable to enemy exploitation. The possibility that an enemy will target civilian systems is worth noting, since the level of security applied to these systems lies outside the control of the armed forces. If vital infrastructure systems are attacked and become inoperative from the attack, the only option is to employ direct weaponry to meet these future challenges and threats.

This type of scenario creates a need for the RDAF to acquire new capabilities that can credibly counter these threats, starting with deterrence. Today the only RDAF platform that can combat UASs is the F-16, but as UAS technology becomes more sophisticated, the requirements for fighter aircraft increase. The fighter will remain a main contributor to Danish air power, and as technology develops, the RDAF will be able to do more with less. Currently, Denmark sees no obvious one-to-one replacement for the fighter aircraft, and thus flexibility is vital for a credible defensive and offensive capability.

Eventually, fifth-generation fighters will be developed to counter UASs; in addition, UASs will be paired with these fighters. This will bridge the dimensional gap between present UAS warfare and the expected future uses of these unmanned systems.

Conclusion

Danish air power will continue to contribute significantly to the goal of maintaining a peaceful world. We will achieve this goal through continuously updating and developing the air force's capabilities. The RDAF currently possesses the relevant operational systems, an effective and adaptive organization, and personnel with professional mastery of air power. Ultimately, the development of our capabilities must reflect the complex reality of the present security environment and ensure that the air force remains economically viable and relevant to Denmark. It is crucial that the RDAF concentrate on acquiring and sustaining robust, flexible, conspicuous, and interoperable platforms that can be continuously updated to remain relevant in the employment of soft, hard, and smart air power. For this reason we will continue to increase cooperation with the other Danish armed services and to work within the framework of an alliance or coalition.

Efficient collaboration, both internal and external, rests upon mutual respect. Ideally, this leads to a win-win situation, since the whole is greater than the sum of its parts. To achieve efficiency, the RDAF must present unquestionable professionalism, fostered by combining state-of-the-art equipment, high training standards, and the will to put forth the extra decisive effort that makes a difference. This emphasis on professionalism will ensure that the RDAF can provide military solutions that not only satisfy but in most cases exceed the expectations of our counterparts. This is the core of the RDAF's vision. In the next twenty years, Denmark will maintain and increase the effect of the "ability to do something in the air"; the strategic choice is "how much"?

SEVEN

Swedish Air Power

Delivering Independently, Joint, and Combined

Maj. Gen. Micael Bydén

Sweden celebrated the one hundredth anniversary of its first military flight on February 3, 2012, but the Swedish Air Force did not come into existence as an independent service until 1926. Despite its relatively short history, the Swedish Air Force and its personnel have contributed both to Swedish defense and to several international missions. The Swedish Air Force bears the stamp of the buildup during the Second World War and the Cold War era. During that time the air force focused on conducting air defense and reconnaissance missions and on ensuring a high level of readiness to conduct strike missions. In the global context the Swedish Air Force contributed a voluntary air squadron (the F 19 Wing) to assist Finland against the Soviet Union in 1940 and took part in the United Nations (UN) missions during the Congo crisis in the 1960s and several other missions up to this day. Most recently, it has conducted helicopter operations in Kosovo, outside Somalia, and in Afghanistan; supported an air base unit in Congo; performed tactical airlift in Afghanistan; and flown fighter missions over Libya. Swedish Air Force ground units have also contributed in several missions around the world.

This chapter describes the Swedish Air Force from the author's personal point of view. It covers the air force's origins, its current capabilities, and its plans for the future. The chapter begins with the missions and tasks of the Swedish Air Force, moves on to focus on recent and current operations, and ends with some thoughts on leadership.

Mission and Tasks

The mission of the Swedish Air Force—and of the nation's armed forces as a whole—is to support Swedish security and foreign policy and help to maintain peace and independence in accordance with four major tasks: helping to maintain territorial integrity, participating in various crisis response operations, defending Sweden against armed aggression, and safeguarding civilians and securing vital public functions. This means that the air force must be able to counter an advanced opponent through the whole spectrum of conflict and continuously maintain high readiness for various missions, which in turn means training and equipping the necessary standing units and ensuring their availability. The air force must be prepared to conduct operations independently or as part of a coalition, primarily in Sweden and the near abroad, but also in distant locations when appropriate.

The basic characteristics of air power—speed, reach, and maneuverability—form the foundation for the strengths of air power—responsiveness, flexibility, and versatility. Through its broad scope and ability to exploit the third dimension, air power enables all other actors, including the army, navy, and civilians, to succeed in their respective domains. The Swedish Air Force adapts its systems and methods to gain the benefits of these factors. As an advanced and strategic asset, air power demands long-term solutions, continuity, redundancy, and well-trained personnel.

The Swedish Air Force must be able to participate in all kinds of missions and conflicts, in either a supporting role or a leading one. This implies that all of its training, actions, and missions must, directly or indirectly, increase the air force's ability to control Swedish air space in order to safeguard civilians, critical infrastructure, and ground units. The air force must also strive to achieve information superiority and the ability to conduct missions wherever and whenever it is needed.

Operations

Maintaining territorial integrity, which includes conducting air-space surveillance and keeping fighters on quick readiness alert, is a task that continues twenty-four hours a day, seven days a week. This is the air force's highest priority, perhaps easily forgotten and sometimes taken for granted.

Sweden has taken part in the International Security and Assistance Force (ISAF) in Afghanistan since the mission began. Currently, Sweden provides a helicopter unit, based at Camp Marmal, Mazar-i-Sharif, in the northern region. In April 2011 the Swedish Air Force made a long-term commitment by supplying a unit for tactical medical evacuation with two Super Pumas, which were replaced with UH-60M Black Hawk helicopters in the spring of 2013. From May to September 2012, and previously in the summers of 2009 and 2010, the air force also deployed one C-130 for tactical transport in the framework of ISAF. In addition, during the spring and summer of 2013, the air force conducted maritime patrol missions with helicopters from the Swedish Navy ship HMS *Carlskrona* outside Somalia, as previously conducted in 2010. Sweden also takes part in the North Atlantic Treaty Organization's (NATO's) Strategic Airlift Capability program through the combined C-17 Heavy Airlift Wing based at Papa Air Base, Hungary. In fact, Sweden has signed up as the second-largest contributor of any participant in the program and has made a long-term commitment spanning thirty years.

Operation Unified Protector (OUP) over Libya in 2011 represented a major recent effort by the Swedish Air Force: the first time since the 1960s that Sweden had deployed fighters abroad. From April to October the air force deployed roughly a hundred airmen and eight (later reduced to five) Gripen fighters to Sicily; in the spring Sweden also dedicated one C-130 to air-to-air refueling (AAR). Sweden contributed to OUP mainly by performing tactical air reconnaissance but also by flying defensive counterair missions in order to implement UN Resolution 1973, with a primary focus on protection of civilians. During OUP the Swedish Air Force flew roughly 580 missions over Libya and produced nearly 2,300 reconnaissance exploitation reports.

But Afghanistan and Libya do not account for all of the air force's recent operational activities. During the last ten years, the Swedish Air Force has also supported the UN Organization Mission in the Democratic Republic of Congo by establishing an aerial port of debarkation in the Congo (2003–4) and flown helicopter reconnaissance missions in Kosovo to support the UN's Kosovo Force (2006–7). The Swedish Air Force learned many valuable lessons from these operations. The successful results also show that during the last decade the air force made the right choices in transformation, modifications, interoperability, and participation in international exercises, such as Red Flag.

Looking Back

To navigate properly into the future, one must know one's origins. The Swedish Air Force was founded on July 1, 1926, when Sweden merged the flying units of its army and navy. Because of escalating international tension during the 1930s, the air force was reorganized and expanded to seven wings. When World War II broke out in 1939, Sweden initiated further expansion; this substantial growth in the air force continued until the end of the war. Although Sweden never entered the war, the country considered a large air force necessary to ward off the threat of invasion and to resist pressure from military threats. By 1945 the Swedish Air Force had approximately eight hundred aircraft, organized in nineteen wings or training centers. However, not all the aircraft in the inventory were modern, and the difficulties of importing state-of-the-art fighters during the war spurred domestic aircraft production.

The expansion of the Swedish Air Force continued during the early part of the Cold War, and in the late 1950s the Swedish order of battle included roughly a thousand modern jet fighters and fighter-bombers, most of Swedish design. In fact, Sweden had the fifth-largest air force in the world at the time. The overarching doctrine of nonalignment resulted in an emphasis on a relatively strong defense and a goal of becoming as independent as possible regarding weapon systems. This meant a strong air force that could develop without relying on external partners, including in the area of doctrine.

During the Cold War the possibility of an invasion by the Soviet Union shaped the direction and structure of the air force. The Swedish Air Operations Doctrine, although not formally expressed as such, included the goal of establishing relatively centralized command to ensure the ability to mass power when and where needed. It placed high priority on developing an air defense system that would encompass air surveillance, tactical control, fighters, and surface-to-air missile (SAM) systems to counter Soviet bombers and airborne invasion. Air-to-air aspects of offensive air operations had a lower priority.

The tasks of the fighter-bomber force changed somewhat during the Cold War. Military decision makers never lost sight of the possibility of an invasion over the Baltic Sea, but in the 1940s and 1950s, the tasks envisioned for the air force typically ranged from close air support (CAS) to attacking bases on the other side of the Baltic Sea. From the mid-1960s on, the Swedish Air Force focused almost entirely on repelling an invasion by sea, with a secondary mission of air interdiction in case of a ground invasion in the far north. The trainer aircraft designed during the 1960s—the Saab 105, or SK 60—was designated as a light attack aircraft for CAS and became operational during the 1970s and 1980s. In light of the nuclear threat, the air force developed a large-scale and highly dispersed base system, including roads, that was designed to get the fighters airborne as fast as possible and staffed by a large conscript force.[1]

The doctrine of nonalignment persisted to the end of the Cold War era. At that time Sweden, which had a large military component, could have been described as a society prepared for war. The country could mobilize approximately 850,000 soldiers, more than 10 percent of the population. In 1992 the Swedish Air Force still had twenty operational fighter squadrons equipped with Viggen and Draken fighters.

During the last twenty years, many aspects of Sweden's foreign policy have gradually changed. As a member of the UN and the European Union (EU), and as an active partner to NATO, Sweden is now building national and international security together with other nations. A declaration of solidarity has replaced the policy of neutrality. In the words of the Swedish foreign minister in the 2012 Statement of Government Policy to Parliament, "Sweden will not remain passive if another EU member state or a Nordic country suffers a disaster or an attack. We expect these countries to act in the same way if Sweden is similarly affected. We must be in a position to both give and receive support, civilian and military."[2]

Present

Today the Swedish Air Force has the following operational units:

Fighter squadrons	4
Transport squadron	1
Airborne early warning and control (AEW&C) unit	1
Signals intelligence (SIGINT) unit	1
Helicopter battalion	1
Air surveillance and control battalion	1
Air base battalions	2

The Swedish Air Force operates approximately a hundred fighters, all of them JAS 39 Gripen; from 2013 on, the air force will use only the C/D versions. In addition, the air force has eight C-130 cargo aircraft, two airborne surveillance and control (ASC) 890 AEW&C aircraft, two Saab 340s for transport duties, and five Gulfstream aircraft of different makes for transport of dignitaries and SIGINT. The air force also operates a number of different helicopter models to support both the army and the navy. The number of helicopters is increasing from roughly thirty to fifty with the delivery of the NH-90 and Black Hawk models. In addition the air force uses two squadrons of the Saab 105 as fixed-wing trainers.

These units and aircraft are normally stationed at four main bases, but if needed, they can operate from several other bases, including bare bases and even roads. The two main fighter wings, with two operational Gripen squadrons and several helicopters each, are stationed in the far north and south of Sweden: F 21 Wing in Luleå and F 17 Wing in Ronneby. All helicopter operations are organized in a joint helicopter wing based at Malmen. The Gripen Operational Test and Evaluation Unit, the Airborne SIGINT Unit, the AEW&C Unit, and the Basic Flying Training School are also located at Malmen. The F 7 Wing at Såtenäs hosts the air force's C-130s and two Gripen squadrons for conversion training and combat readiness training of both Swedish and international students. Most of the air force's schools are part of and located at the Air Combat School in Uppsala. The Air Component Command, as a part of the Joint Forces Command, is located at the Armed Forces Headquarters (HQ) in Stockholm.

Aircraft and units are important, but people are the heart of the air force. Currently, the Swedish armed forces are conducting a major transformation of personnel affairs, abandoning conscription for an all-volunteer force with professional soldiers and re-establishing a noncommissioned officer (NCO) corps. The Swedish Air Force seeks to retain approximately four thousand continuously serving personnel and seven hundred temporary personnel, more or less equally divided among officers, NCOs, enlisted, and civilians. However, at the time of writing there were still vacancies for professional soldiers.

The Swedish Air Force has a broad spectrum of capabilities for its size. In spite of the reductions of the last decades and its current limited size, the air force is still capable of carrying out air, land, and maritime operations with a high level of interoperability. It can also conduct personnel recovery, AEW&C, and a variety of transport, SIGINT, and intelligence, surveillance, and reconnaissance missions.

The Swedish Air Force is self-sustaining, which connotes the ability to develop, operate, and maintain its own systems and platforms. Furthermore, the air force can ensure continuity by educating and training all of its personnel and can support other air forces. The air force accompanies export of the Gripen to Hungary, the Czech Republic, South Africa, and Thailand with training and support for the purchasing nations' aircrews and maintenance personnel. This training and support is provided both in Sweden and abroad. The Gripen User Group serves as a framework for excellent cooperation and long-term partnership.

The Swedish Air Force has always emphasized cost efficiency. Maintaining a ratio of fewer than forty employees per fighter, not to mention all other platforms and systems in operation, speaks for itself. Controlling costs and limiting the number of personnel also requires retaining highly professional officers and soldiers and keeping a technological advantage. Both aircraft and personnel must be capable of performing swing roles. This, in turn, affects leadership, as discussed later in this chapter.

Being a small or medium-sized air force capable of conducting a broad spectrum of capabilities does have some drawbacks. For example, the restricted number of personnel and equipment obviously limits the endurance and protective redundancy of the Swedish Air Force, at least in comparison with some larger air forces.

Looking to the Future

For various reasons the defense budgets of many countries are likely to decrease over the remainder of the decade. Furthermore, the United States is reducing its military presence in Europe. This situation provides clear incentives for further reform of European defense policies and forces.

Despite the current limited military threat against Sweden, the country still confronts some concerns that affect the development of the Swedish Air Force. The areas surrounding Sweden are complex from a strategic perspective. The air force must monitor an increasing military presence from both Russia and other actors. Russia has instituted an ongoing military reform that to some extent replicates the earlier Western transformation; at the same time nuclear weapons will probably remain important. The effects of this transition are still difficult to assess. The Barents region and the Baltic Sea will always be of great strategic importance for Russia, and the High North is becoming of increased strategic interest to many actors. The Baltic Sea region is already characterized by high and increasing commercial traffic and extensive regional cooperation.

From a Swedish perspective a future threat could come from nation-states or from different interest groups or individuals who would use various methods for attacking from the land, sea, or air. These aggressors differ in the capability of their weapons. Sweden hypothesizes that aggressors with less-capable systems will compensate for deficiencies by using multiple asymmetric angles of attack. One example is the cyber domain. Computer network attacks have become an area of concern to all countries; Sweden and its armed forces are no exception.

Until 2025 several countries in northern Europe will expand their ability in the air through purchase or development of new fighters, missiles, and other systems. Many of the fighters possess stealth capability. Missile development will also continue, and Sweden can assume that during the next decade several advanced SAMs and long-range high-precision surface-to-surface missiles will become operational in the region.

Development Strategy

The Swedish Air Force has throughout its history combined technologically advanced systems with individual skills and professionalism. This approach also will serve as the foundation for success in the future. The air force will avoid costly technical solutions and instead use technology to support increased capability. The next generation of aircraft will evolve based on today's digital systems and platforms, with continuous, coherent development of updated methods for networks, decision support, and communications, including increased use of robust information technology. The objective is a flexible air power asset that can adapt to specific missions using the means necessary to achieve an appropriate and coordinated effect and that can ensure a quick response, wide reach, and a high level of protection.

The air force will need competence, continuing development, and flexibility to adapt to different challenges in different times. This will enable the air force to adjust its defensive capability to match developments in the surrounding world and guarantee freedom of action in support of security and foreign policy. To meet the demands of the future, Swedish Air Force units must be flexible; all operational units must be ready to shift between different levels of conflict, missions, and regions. The air force should focus on making this flexibility possible in the near future.

Three criteria can be highlighted as a foundation for success in employing air power: numerical superiority, tactical superiority, and technical superiority. The Swedish Air Force should aim to achieve at least two of those three. Its development strategy rests upon the recognition that superiority in numbers cannot be the norm for the Swedish Air Force, which implies that it must emphasize development in tactics and technology. Tactical superiority combined with technically advanced systems can create local superiority.

The air force's development strategy also derives from four basic mission categories. The first, control of the air, is the foundation for employing air power and sets the conditions for all other activities on the ground, at sea, and in the air. Control of the air is a key factor of success in every military operation. In combat, obtaining air superiority and maintaining territorial integrity are the main objectives of any air force. The Swedish Air Force must keep its ability to enforce control of the air despite potential competitors' increased air power capabilities. Examples of recent activities that the air force instituted to reach its goals are development of the heat-seeking IRIS-T missile and the long-range, active, radar-guided Meteor missile, as well as the further improvement of the Gripen fighter.

The second category, air mobility, facilitates moving units and equipment regionally and globally. Air transport cannot replace transportation on land or at sea, but in certain situations it offers the only possible means to deploy or resupply at the right time or to reach remote areas. When it comes to strategic airlift, international cooperation continues in the Heavy Airlift Wing, which flies C-17s from Papa Air Base, Hungary. The Swedish Air Force is currently conducting studies concerning upgrading or replacing the current C-130 fleet. Early in 2013 the UH-60 Black Hawk became operational in the Swedish Air Force. Development of the NH-90 system will proceed.

Third, situational awareness and decision making form the basis for reconnaissance and surveillance to detect, locate, and track targets. The air force will maintain the ability to conduct airborne early warning as well as conventional surveillance over Swedish territory and the surrounding regions. Understanding opponents' intentions is essential in aiding leaders to make the right decisions. The air force must have the ability to conduct deep analysis of the intelligence gathered in order to reveal adversary intentions and support effective decision making. The "find, fix, track, target, engage, assess" approach will become the standard for upcoming development. The air force radars, combined with AEW&C, the Gripen reconnaissance pod, and other sensors, serve as examples of this constantly evolving capability.

Fourth and finally, precision engagement on land and sea signifies the capability to engage targets at sea or on the ground with high precision in various weather conditions and at long distances—the true trademark of air power. The Swedish Air Force's capability for precision engagement of ground targets will increase. The GBU-39 small-diameter bomb, for example, allows a more calibrated effect on ground targets. Advances in technology must aim at reducing the limitations created by weather and light conditions even further. Sweden must also maintain the advanced capability to engage targets at sea in the years to come.

The Swedish Air Force must progress using balanced development in all the areas mentioned previously. Development efforts must be directed toward technical and tactical superiority in several key areas simultaneously. In terms of operational capability, the air force must continue to build toward a structure of operational, modular, and versatile units that need only a limited interval between the time when an order is issued and when operations begin. The modular units and their capabilities will confer flexibility so that units can better adjust to the needs of each specific mission. The units must be able to carry out missions alone, with other Swedish units, or with coalition partners. Enabling functions—such as command and control, logistics, force protection, and intelligence—must be adapted to fulfill the needs of the mission. The air force must support its own units but might also provide limited support for coalition air forces in Sweden as well as abroad.

Presence, or the ability to enter the area of operations, is another criterion for the success of air force missions. It can include transportation to the area of operations, basing, and the ability to operate in a contested and hostile environment. Presence depends on the number of air bases and their geographic location, together with the range and availability of the fighter aircraft. All factors must be balanced in order to reach a high level of presence in the area.

The importance of protection is increasing, not only because Sweden has reduced the number of units in the air force, but also because potential opponents' capabilities are developing. To ensure survivability, the air force must develop in several areas. The airborne units will be protected by sophisticated missile warning systems and agile armament. Dispersed basing, hard shelters, ground-based air defense, and tactical concepts will contribute to protection of fighters, personnel, and equipment on the ground.

The ability to deliver desired effects with limited assets is crucial for operational efficiency in the Swedish Air Force. The squadrons, both fixed wing and rotary wing, will continue to build broad capacity and extend their ability to act in several types of missions simultaneously, functioning as an omni-role force. International cooperation can help to reduce the costs of production and development while at the same time increasing operational output. During an operation, efficiency can be enhanced through shared basing with other nations. Peacetime productivity must always evolve without interfering with combat readiness.

Interoperability is the key to cooperation. Since the 1990s the Swedish Air Force has improved its ability to work alongside other nations. This was demonstrated by Sweden's commitment to various exercises (such as Red Flag) and to missions in Congo, Afghanistan, Libya, and the Gulf of Aden. Interoperability represents the way ahead, and the air force will continue training in this area. The Swedish Air Force has procured command and control systems and purchased Link 16 to increase its capacity to work alongside other nations on missions both inside and outside Sweden.

Gripen

As described previously, balanced development is important for the Swedish Air Force. This also applies to the evolution of the Gripen fighter system. The A/B versions are being taken out of active service in 2013 and are to some extent being modified in response to the political decision to purchase a hundred Gripen C/D. Each version of the Gripen has increased the aircraft's availability, endurance, deployability, survivability, interoperability, and effective armament. This development path and balanced design will continue with the E version.

During the early spring of 2012, the Swedish armed forces sent a proposal to the government regarding the development of the Gripen system in order to ensure a commitment to funding the fighter into the 2030s. The Armed Forces HQ devoted significant effort to analyzing requirements and needs and concluded that an upgraded version of the Gripen presented the best solution for Sweden. Recently, the Swedish government agreed to the purchase of sixty Gripen E fighters. The upgraded version will include a slightly bigger airframe, a more powerful engine, and more advanced sensors. Bilateral negotiations are currently ongoing with Switzerland as a partner nation.

Key features of the next-generation Gripen include increased range and endurance, which make the aircraft less dependent on AAR and improve sensor and area coverage. The new version also features a larger payload and greater flexibility, including ten weapon stations, greater maximum takeoff weight, and full support for future smart weapons. In addition, it has new operational capabilities, such as omnirole, minimized radar cross section (though below the level of stealth), supercruise capability, and increased situational awareness. Finally, the platforms offer greater cost efficiency, with a low life-cycle cost and high growth potential.

Reflections on Leadership

Technology is important, but an air force is fundamentally about people. The ongoing transformation of the Swedish armed forces from a military service consisting mainly of conscripts to one made up only of professional soldiers and the reestablishment of an NCO corps could, from the air force perspective, be called a revolution in personnel affairs and will continue to demand considerable effort the coming years. It is crucial that the air force maintain its focus on recruiting and training high-quality personnel and make full use of their knowledge and abilities by ensuring their active involvement in the air force's missions.

In my view the "first-line leadership" and the trust between higher ranking officers and airmen are fundamental. Trust forms the basis for the success of dynamic command and indeed for all leadership in the air force. Trust, and therefore leadership, must be based upon openness, results, and responsibility—conditions sustained only through continuous work. Especially important in establishing trust are the commanders' integrity, their ability to serve as role models, and their skills in communicating clearly. Within their own areas, all first-line commanders are responsible for stimulating participation and making efficient use of their personnel's skills. Leading with questions stimulates dialogue and participation, which in turn build trust and create a better basis for decisions. Commanders are responsible for making decisions and carry the responsibility for the results.

Individual discipline is more important than formal discipline. Those of us in leading roles must always remain humble, both in completion of our tasks and in interaction with our comrades. We should not analyze problems in order to identify scapegoats but to find solutions. It is the outcome that is important, not necessarily who made or invented something. Initiative is paramount to achieve the desired results.

Centralized command is an important principle underlying air power. The Swedish Air Force uses the term "dynamic command" to describe centralized command with a mission command philosophy. This approach is essential to utilizing the responsiveness, flexibility, and versatility of air power and makes it possible to choose which level of command should have decision-making authority in each particular instance.

Conclusion

My views on leadership and on the air force's development strategy, as presented in this chapter, highlight some key focus areas that demand special attention over the coming years if the Swedish Air Force is to realize its goals. National readiness and ongoing operations will always have top priority. Safety in the air and on the ground is the foundation for operations, training, and exercises as well as for development. This can be summed up as follows: Mission First—Safety Always!

My current focus areas are threefold: personnel and recruitment, in both the short and long terms; improved national defense capabilities and planning, with an emphasis on base operations and command and control; and long-term system (aircraft) development. The Swedish Air Force must aim to remain a well-organized, professional, and robust service that offers high availability and usability for both national and international missions.

Current operations and national defense planning drive the air force's development. Important enablers are interoperability and cooperation, including pooling and sharing of resources. Together with the rest of the Swedish armed forces and other means of power, the air force will contribute by shaping, or trying to influence, its operating environment to favor Sweden's interests and by deterring behavior that might be inimical to those interests—and, if that approach fails, by responding as necessary anywhere along the spectrum of action. In summary the Swedish Air Force will help to sustain security at home and abroad by delivering air power independently and in joint and combined operations.

EIGHT

Finnish Air Power

In Defense of the Homeland

Maj. Gen. Lauri Tapio Puranen

Air Strategy

Air power is not religion, yet nations must have faith in it to make the substantial investments that quality air power requires. That faith must be based on proven results and credible, scientifically supported analysis of air power's future significance. Both the recent and earlier history of combat contain ample proof of its efficiency and decisive role. In operations it repeatedly provides the decisive kinetic effects or firepower and the most reliably predictable capabilities in the modern battle space.

Air power is not the only game in town. Airmen usually understand the limits of air power as well as the importance of superior professionalism in joint warfare, and they recognize the unique strengths of other service branches. No airman would suggest to colleagues in sister services that military capability be founded on air assets only. Partly owing to its unaffordable and elitist "corporate image," air power will continue to face exaggerated peer scrutiny, sometimes accompanied by unjustified criticism. Air power must continually earn its place among a nation's military assets.

Air power has no substitute in Western defenses. Success in warfare between industrialized nations is unthinkable if the opponent enjoys air superiority. Only air power can provide a credible defense against modern air threats and a conventional deterrent and retaliatory capability against other long-range strike threats. In less symmetric scenarios surface-based kinetic means can offer an alternative option, albeit one with less versatility and limited range. But when an enemy nation throws strike packages and standoff precision projectiles at a country's high-value assets and infrastructure, the target country needs superior-quality air power to protect itself and to reverse the odds. Without it, land and sea operations stand little or no chance of success. Although all this has been true for a long time and can be taken as a starting point when planning and preparing for the next two decades, changes are in progress or in sight.

The air strategic environment of northern Europe appears to be reshaping again with a steeper change gradient than the region witnessed during the relatively stable years of the late 1990s and the first decade of the twenty-first century. Russia has initiated a military transformation program, with priority given to new air power assets and capabilities and with deliveries of new combat aircraft taking place. All four Nordic air forces have moved into a phase of strategic planning regarding the future direction of the capabilities provided by current combat aircraft fleets. Plans and acquisitions are at different stages in these countries, but all of them see multirole air forces equipped with manned combat aircraft as the core air power solution for the foreseeable future.

However, the future seems to demand that the Nordic nations review the capabilities that their military forces must provide. Most, if not all, current missions will remain relevant, but air forces can and should expect to deliver more versatility. Technology offers possibilities and creates requirements as new capabilities—such as supercruising stealth airframes with fused, all-aspect active and passive sensors—emerge in our environment.

Gaining and maintaining air superiority while denying it to the adversary will remain decisive. But the significance of many new technologies remains to be proven in air combat. Experience obtained in operations has demonstrated a changing role for long-range stand-off precision strike in major theater warfare that will require in-depth analysis. It is hard to imagine achieving operational success against an enemy that can find a nation's key assets and hit them with pinpoint accuracy from a sanctuary, unless the defender has either a similar or a superior capability or can deny the enemy the successful use of its long-range strike assets. Short-range strike weapons will stay relevant in many scenarios and missions, not least because of their affordability, but for credible defense a nation must be able to retaliate at a longer range.

Even with a capability to deter and strike back, the Nordic nations need missile defense. Ballistic and cruise missile defense capabilities are built in the framework of air and space power. Ballistic, quasi-ballistic, and cruise missiles armed with conventional warheads pose a threat to many air power assets; thus, missile defense seems to have become increasingly important in force protection and surviving to fight.

Joint intelligence, surveillance, target acquisition, and reconnaissance (ISTAR) assets and capabilities are also increasingly associated with air and space power. The Nordic air forces will have to adapt to a permanent and growing responsibility for serving as the eyes and ears of their respective nations' defenses. Air power's ability to gather, process, and distribute data—especially sensor data—lies at the center of joint network-enabled operations. Air ISTAR systems must be robust and reliable and must integrate effectively with air and space command and control (C2) as well as with joint targeting structures.

Yet acquiring and operating the key capabilities that are indispensable for tomorrow's air power will become increasingly expensive. The future significance of Nordic air power will depend largely on the nations' ability to resolve budgetary challenges, to balance their capabilities, and to build fruitful cooperation. The Nordic countries are exhibiting a new desire to find common ground for pooling and sharing capabilities among them. Although no quick wins are in sight for the air forces, they should seize the opportunity to explore the possibilities with an open mind. The Nordic nations have already demonstrated new, mutually beneficial cooperation in the field of training. Their ability to operate together in combined air operations has made substantial strides within the framework of regular over-the-border exercises.

Role, Mission, and Tasks

Current legislation contains a clear, well-defined, and prioritized task set for the Finnish defense forces: (1) provide for the military defense of Finland; (2) support other public authorities; and (3) participate in international crisis management. This task set constitutes the framework in which future Finnish air power should be analyzed and in which future planning, construction, and reshaping will take place.

Defense of the homeland remains important to Finns, not least because of centuries-old geostrategic challenges that—in the eyes of the majority of citizens—have not changed. Throughout the country's history, Finland's ability to defend herself has several times determined the country's fate. Finns want credible, self-sufficient national defense and do not like to depend on other nations or alliances for key military capabilities. Therefore, defending Finland against the use of military force outweighs the other two tasks by a healthy margin. It is also the only task of the three in which air power can claim to be indispensable.

Thus, Finnish air power must prove its value and expertise in the field of symmetric warfare against superior numbers and provide a strong and credible demonstration of air power's role in dissuasion and deterrence. Air power should find its justification and role in delivering not merely more, but unique, credibility in prevention and not merely more, but unique, effects in combat for each euro spent when compared with competing arms. Air force planners and decision makers should also ask whether air power has the potential to do more than governments have come to expect from it in the past.

Among the defense forces the Finnish Air Force is tasked with performing traditional standing air surveillance and air policing duties and has occupied an equally traditional, albeit important, "ecological niche" in joint warfare owing to its having been limited to air-to-air operations only. To fulfill its tasks, the Finnish Air Force operates a fleet of sixty-two F/A-18 Hornet C/D strike fighters, the first of which were introduced into service in 1995. While the Finnish Hornets retain full swing-role capability, they were originally evaluated and selected to perform in the air-to-air arena. Now this defensive counterair role is about to be complemented with air-to-ground tasks. An ongoing upgrade to the Hornet fleet will introduce into service a modern family of precision-guided weapons, including a state-of-the-art long-range strike capability. This will radically expand the potential missions of the air force. The air force's new role in the field of kinetic effects is being developed as a part of normal operational planning.

Finland's concept of homeland security emphasizes a comprehensive, whole-of-government approach. This approach avoids duplication of expensive assets and makes unique capabilities under the control of different government branches available to the ministry that most needs them. In this context air power assets are offered to support, for example, domestic no-fly-zone surveillance and enforcement operations, search and rescue, and special transport. The actual use of military force in support of police operations, including armed response to renegade situations in which hijacked aircraft are used as weapons, is always subject to a decision by the police or the Ministry of the Interior.

The Finnish Army NHIndustries NH-90 helicopters carry out many of the support missions. The army ordered a fleet of twenty NH-90s in 2001, and the first helicopters entered service in 2008. Transport and utility aircraft are operated by the air force's Supporting Air Operations Squadron. These aircraft include two EADS CASA C-295M tactical airlifters, six Pilatus PC-12 NG liaison turboprops, and three Gates Learjet 35 A/S target towing, maritime surveillance, aerial photography, and personnel transport aircraft. Air sampling for radioactive and other hazardous substances is performed by the Training Air Wing using its BAE Hawk jet trainers equipped with air sampling pods.

The Finnish Air Force has not yet taken part in international crisis management operations. The air force began to create the capability to do so several years ago and now has a North Atlantic Treaty Organization (NATO)–certified F/A-18 Hornet unit that will participate in the NATO Response Force (NRF) 2014 rotation. The preparation and training associated with the NRF increase interoperability and create the opportunity to benchmark best practices and performance levels in many areas, thus contributing directly to the Finnish Air Force's main mission of national defense.

No responsible decision maker in Finland would seriously contest the need to have an air force. But the size, role, tasks, and especially the cost of the air force of the 2030s will be profoundly debated within the defense forces and, most probably, throughout the state leadership before the government decides on the air force structure after the Hornet. The debate has already begun to emerge in the course of normal strategic planning, even though the decision is likely to lie almost ten years in the future.

Emerging Assets and the New Force Structure

Before considering new combat aircraft, the Finnish Air Force will complete a makeover of its combat air base system, renew its ground-based air surveillance and joint air defense C2 systems, and introduce new capabilities via a second Hornet midlife upgrade. The air force will do all this concurrently with a reorganization and downsizing program that will close down two air bases and one sector operations center, fuse three air force schools into one and three fighter squadrons into two, and cut the number of personnel by 15 percent and the air force wartime reserve strength from forty thousand to twenty-five thousand.

By 2015 the new air force structure will consist of two fighter wings, a transport and research wing, the Air Force Academy, and Air Force Command Finland, the air force commander's headquarters. A more centralized command concept will abolish the current geographic area responsibilities of today's three air commands and introduce a new air operations center while reducing the role of the remaining two sector operations centers to control and reporting. Will leaner be meaner? The Finnish Air Force will certainly make a serious effort to that end by shortening chains of command, increasing mobility for survivability, and creating permanent savings through better focused operating costs.

The Finnish concept of dispersed fighter operations calls for a large number of air bases to which the fighter force will be dispersed in small units. This prevents its destruction on ground by a surprise attack and guarantees that at least some runways will survive enemy strikes, thereby enabling interceptor takeoffs. Many of the base runways are in fact strips of national highways especially designed for flight operations and surrounded by some simple base infrastructure. These bases are activated at mobilization and are manned mostly by reservists. As can be expected, this Finnish bare base concept requires a huge amount of base matériel and equipment, as well as tens of thousands of trained airmen. Once activated, the bases become a relatively static asset and therefore vulnerable. Relocating base troops and equipment is labor intensive, which makes operational base maneuvers slow and difficult.

The reorganization has given impetus to a healthy and welcome change. The new combat air base concept combines modern force protection and surviving-to-fight tactics with more mobile base troops and equipment. Most of the current runway strips will be kept ready for use, but a smaller number will be active at any one time. The air force will have fewer base troops, but they will be better equipped, and a significant proportion of them will be able to move swiftly to a new bare base and activate it so that it becomes combat ready.

More mobility and less vulnerability are also emerging in the field of air surveillance. The new, mobile Thales Ground Master GM-403 surveillance radar is entering service and removes the need for peacetime operating personnel at Finland's medium-range radar stations. During a crisis the radar can move and evade air strikes and missile attacks, greatly improving the combat survivability of the country's previously fixed medium- and long-range radar surveillance.

The army and the navy develop and operate Finland's ground-based and sea-based air defense capabilities, respectively, but the air force has the responsibility for advising and coordinating acquisition projects to guarantee coherent and complementary joint air warfare assets and to take advantage of economies of scale when possible. An example of the resulting synergy is the army's brand new Norwegian Advanced

Surface-to-Air Missile System (NASAMS) II medium-range air defense system, which fires the same joint advanced medium-range air-to-air missiles (AMRAAMS) the air force F/A-18s fire and which can be deployed to protect air bases. The air surveillance–capable sensors of all services contribute to a joint air picture that forms a core element of the Finnish joint ISTAR structure. Finally, a joint air defense C2 system will replace legacy systems and further enhance the air force's ability to perform the centralized control of joint air defense fires, which is a joint task of the air force.

A major priority for the Finnish Air Force during the present decade is making the most of its near-future multisensor tracking, new air C2, and joint Link 16 capabilities, as well as the new networked joint services. In some cases reliable and capable but inherently single-service systems will be replaced with perhaps less agile but more joint and interoperable successors. The air force must master and tailor labor-intensive network and data-link management to optimize structures and procedures nationally while ensuring full interoperability with international partners. Here participation in multinational interoperability demonstrations and exercises is, and will remain, invaluable.

The second midlife upgrade to the Finnish F/A-18 fleet will impel the air force to relearn the forgotten art of air-to-ground operations. The acquisition and integration of the joint direct attack munition (JDAM), the AGM-154 joint standoff weapon (JSOW), and the AGM-158 joint air-to-surface standoff missile (JASSM), along with miscellaneous upgrades to avionics and air-to-air performance, will keep the Hornet competitive through the 2020s. The air force is already learning how to operate the new capabilities.

People: Recruitment, Education, Training, and Research

The enormous importance of motivating the right individuals to commit themselves to a career in the air force will not change. The motto of the Finnish Air Force, "Qualitas Potentia Nostra," underlines the significance of quality. Without high-quality personnel, there can be no high-quality performance, no matter how well equipped a service might be materially. An air force career is still attractive to a sufficiently large proportion of the nation's outstanding youth, but the shrinking demographics make it increasingly difficult for the armed services to compete with civilian employers in recruitment. The military's previously competitive education, service, and retirement benefits have become less unusual today, and the outstanding international education and career opportunities that globalization has opened to the younger generation often outweigh them. The Nordic nations must balance the quality of life and leadership style in the military services with the development of their societies and nurture expertise in recruitment. For the Finnish Air Force, this will mean greater investment in, for example, public events, air displays, and school road shows.

The opportunity to obtain a Bologna-compatible college degree for free, with living expenses and allowance paid, represents a good bargain for any young high school graduate. The active and athletic lifestyle associated with military academies constitutes a bonus in the eyes of many prospective officers. Military aviation still has a magical appeal. But to create the best possible air force, potential candidates must become inspired and receive the right information at the right time. Finland's mandatory military service is the basis for the recruitment of its uniformed personnel. Mandatory service forces all healthy young men to consider how to make the best out of their months in the military. Female volunteers are provided the same opportunity. Every year the mandatory service process gives the air force a good shot at attracting the best of each graduating class.

Unique to the Finnish Air Force is the annual Pilot Reserve Officer Course that combines conscript service and Phase I flight training into twelve months of pilot officer screening. About forty lucky individuals are selected out of the hundreds who apply, and normally a third of them later sign up for careers as air force pilot or army helicopter pilot officers. Once these young people have been recruited, the National Defense University, the Air Force Academy, and the Training Air Wing do their best to train and educate the cadets to become proficient lieutenants in three years' time. Common studies for all services start at the military academy and give the army, navy, and air force cadets the chance to get to know each other and to build lifelong cross-service friendships. Pilots, nonflying air force cadets, and army ground-based air defense cadets continue their studies together at the Air Force Academy and build a common air warfare spirit. All officers graduate with a bachelor's degree and pilots pin on their wings with a Phase III military pilot diploma in their hands.

In jet training Finland has a national solution with a potential lifespan extending into the 2030s. This solution was enabled by a recent purchase of eighteen BAE Hawk Mk66 jet trainers from Switzerland and a program to modernize them together with a batch of Finland's existing Hawk Mk51A aircraft. Advanced Phase III and IV training has made it possible to download selected parts of the Hornet syllabus to the Hawk, which is not only cheaper but also extends the operating life of the F/A-18 fleet. Pilot training could also represent a future area of cooperation in the Nordic region.

Realistic and diverse air power exercises are nearly impossible to arrange without multinational cooperation. Several high-quality exercises take place yearly in northern Europe, and participation in them will remain a fixed part of Finnish advanced pilot training. Much has also been achieved through regular live flying exercises among Norway, Sweden, and Finland. Regularly scheduled events are valuable, but detrimental routine should be avoided to ensure continued motivation. The Nordic air forces could explore avenues for broadening the scope of multinational flying exercises to include, for example, more operational planning, targeting and fires procedures, and electronic warfare. Air forces with new weapon systems and capabilities should be invited to join the regular participants.

A well-educated and trained force needs solid tactics, techniques, and procedures (TTPs). When changes occur in the operating environment, those TTPs must be assessed, sometimes through modeling and simulation. The air force must evaluate new systems before selecting among the candidates and must test new capabilities before introducing them into service. To this end the new force structure will fuse the Finnish Air Force's test and evaluation-oriented Flight Test Centre with the Air Combat Centre, a fighter weapons school responsible for research on and formulation of TTPs. This will bring a more operational flavor to flight testing and attract more resources to operational analysis and research. Newly trained operational test and evaluation pilots are already flying MLU 2 Hornets fresh from the modification line to enable type approval.

Future Capabilities

In the Nordic air strategic environment, and in view of current and prospective tasks and resources, the Finnish Air Force can realistically look forward to building and sustaining three main capabilities into the 2030s. First comes the ability to predict, detect, evade, and survive a surprise first strike by conventional long-range precision weapons and to retaliate with limited but qualitatively superior strike power. This capability aims to create an adaptive deterrence threshold to protect Finland against politico-military pressure and against the use of military force from a sanctuary.

Second, the air force must be able to deter and defend against air strikes aimed at Finland's infrastructure or defense assets and to maintain air superiority in the area of operations. Third, the air force must build the capability to damage an attacking force and its assets to an extent that prohibits the successful continuation of the attacker's operations and the completion of its primary mission. In addition, the air force will continue to operate a small number of light transport and liaison aircraft to support joint operations and the state leadership.

These capabilities translate into an integrated air defense system with a multirole-capable combat aircraft fleet supported by appropriate infrastructure, ISTAR, and C2. So, is this just a continuum of what we are already developing in this decade? Yes and no.

Quality personnel, competitive weapons and equipment, focused training, critical information and knowledge, and high situational awareness will no doubt retain their importance. But developments in politics, economics, and technology will bring about shifts from today's priorities. While the air force must continuously adapt to change, it must also make far-reaching decisions based on uncertain predictions of the probable future.

The Finnish Air Force must at least try to identify the game changers of the next decades and will need completely new capabilities to complement the traditional ones. Even small nations must learn missile defense and build a degree of space situational awareness. Cyber warfare will hit hard at networked capabilities and the protection of secure systems, and a purely defensive approach in cyberspace will not work. The mismatch between the rising costs of acquiring and operating defense matériel, on the one hand, and a state economy struggling with growing debts, on the other, is such that even if Finland musters the will to make large investments in air power, the air force might find itself owning equipment that it cannot afford to operate and end up with a hollow force.

For Finland a major decision will concern the replacement of the capabilities of the F/A-18 Hornet fleet by the early 2030s. The air force already knows that this issue should not—and for budgetary reasons cannot—be approached merely as a replacement project. Instead, it must be seen as an opportunity to review and possibly redefine many elements of conventional air warfare and its relation to the other armed services. Defense leadership must ask who should do what in the joint battle space of the 2030s and how many of their goals are most efficiently achieved by air power.

The Finnish Air Force can safely assume that it will need a powerful air-to-air fighter capable of achieving air superiority and denying it to the enemy all the way through the 2040s. This is already a very demanding requirement and limits the number of possible candidates. Equally safely, the air force can expect that the fighter platform must be able to carry several of the most advanced strike weapons and be engineered to enable their effective launch and support in the most heavily defended environments. A modern and modular structure enabling a long and affordable service life is paramount. The performance and interoperability of sensors and communication systems must support multinational networked joint operations.

But the Finnish Air Force must still solve many complex problems before the decision is made. What is the future significance of current stealth technology? What should be the role of unmanned platforms in a small air force? How should the air force balance numbers against performance? Should the fleet be a single type or mixed? What joint effects can the new fleet create? What is its role in joint ISTAR? Will it be expected to play an antisurface role? Can the fleet incorporate the ability to threaten and destroy moving ground units from standoff distances? The list goes on, but fortunately, we still have time to find the right answers.

Naturally, Finland closely monitors the equipment becoming available in the market and seeks to understand the choices made by other nations. From the political and industrial perspective, Finland probably enjoys more freedom of choice than many other nations; from an economic standpoint, it certainly does not.

Conclusion

The Finnish Air Force is, in essence, undergoing a transformation. In the midst of major organizational changes, we are building strong new capabilities. Our leadership wants air force personnel to see change as an opportunity and not a threat. With our new organizational structure and with our new capabilities now operational, we can fulfill our mission and confront the next decade with our minds at rest.

The relevance of air power is likely to persist. The key question is whether our nation's resources will enable us to sustain an air force that will meet the requirements of our operating environment into the 2030s and beyond.

3

REFLECTIONS

Where Do We Go from Here?

We must not start our thinking on war with the tools of war—with the airplanes, tanks, ships and those who crew them. These tools are important and have their place, but they cannot be our starting point, nor can we allow ourselves to see them as the essentials of war. Fighting is not the essence of war, nor even a desirable part of it. The real essence is doing what is necessary to make the enemy accept our objectives as his objectives. . . .

We have moved from the age of the horse and the sail through the age of the battleship and the tank to the age of the airplane. Like its illustrious ancestors, the airplane will have its day in the sun, and then it too shall be replaced.

JOHN A. WARDEN III

NINE

Approaching the End?

Martin van Creveld

A little more than a century since the first machines rose into the air and military air power first started playing an important role in warfare, where may air power be heading? Most observers, impressed by what they see as dazzling technological progress, seem to believe that the sky is the limit. This author, to the contrary, has several times argued that air power as traditionally understood is in deep trouble and that its days may be numbered.[1] The objective of the present essay is to briefly explain and update that claim, especially with respect to medium-sized and small states. By so doing the author also hopes to put the other chapters in the present volume into perspective.

Given how short the history of air power is, summarizing its development is relatively easy. Skipping over balloons, airships, and the like, heavier-than-air "flying machines," as they were known, first saw action during the Italian-Turkish War of 1911–12. As a result, for some time the Italian air service was the most progressive in the world. Observers, both professional and amateur, flocked to Libya to see how aerial warfare was waged. The most important types of missions flown were reconnaissance, liaison, and bombing. Pilots were supposed to use their teeth to arm hand grenades and then throw the grenades overboard, all the while controlling their craft with their other hand. However, the impact of air power was limited, both because the equipment was primitive and because the Italians probably never had more than twenty or so machines available in the gigantic theater of war at any one time.

During World War I the main belligerents produced well over 200,000 aircraft between them. Losses, owing either to accidents or to the fighting itself, sometimes amounted to one-third of the strength *per month*, making it hard for factories to keep up. The number of workers involved in aviation increased from a few thousand in 1914 to hundreds of thousands four years later.[2] In 1918 the Royal Air Force became the first independent service of its kind, to be followed by several others during the interwar period. By the time the war ended, many different types of missions were being routinely flown. Reconnaissance and liaison apart, they now included air-to-air combat, strafing with machine guns, interdiction of enemy lines of communication, and "strategic" bombing hundreds of miles behind the front. Participating in naval warfare, aircraft also launched torpedoes, laid mines, and hunted submarines. In 1919–20 the British in Iraq became the first to use air transport; the earliest experiments with paratroopers and gliders were conducted in Germany and the Union of Soviet Socialist Republics (USSR) during the 1930s. The period between 1939 and 1945 saw the birth of electronic warfare. By the latter year the list of missions was substantially complete.

Looking back, the role of air power in war probably peaked during World War II. The total number of aircraft produced by all belligerents combined was over three-quarters of a million—a figure so far beyond present-day horizons that it appears to be taken from some kind of fantasy world. There were times, such as during the invasion of Normandy in 1944, when no fewer than twelve thousand missions were flown on a single day. Budgets, requirements for energy and for raw materials, factories, the number of workers, ground facilities, and the size of the various air forces, corps, or whatever they were called, all underwent dramatic expansion. From the Germans in Poland in 1939 to the Allies in Western Europe in 1944–45, in all major campaigns the side that dominated the air practically always won. From the Poles in 1939 to the Germans in 1944–45, the side that did not have air superiority practically always lost. The largest and most important operations, such as the German invasion of the Soviet Union and the Allied invasions of southern and Western Europe, were always planned with considerations about the role of air power uppermost in mind. The same was even more true at sea. Here air power, whether ship or land based, quickly made battleships obsolete. Having done so, it went on to play a critical role in every form of naval warfare and amphibious operation. Indeed, not the least important reason for the quick defeat of the medium and small powers of the time, such as Poland, Norway, the Netherlands, and Yugoslavia, was that they simply could not afford the air power they needed to defend themselves. As a result, they were quickly overwhelmed.

At the end of the war, the ruins of Germany and Japan offered mute testimony to the ability of air power to lay waste entire countries. No wonder that during the late 1940s observers such as Winston Churchill held that "air mastery is today the supreme expression of military power" compared to which "fleets and armies . . . must accept subordinate rank."[3] In fact, naval and ground power never became secondary to air power. By far the most important reason why this did not happen was the introduction of nuclear weapons in 1945 and their subsequent proliferation. Nuclear weapons put those in charge of delivering them, primarily air forces and the air arms of a few select navies, in a position where they were literally able to bring an end to "civilization as we know it," as the saying went. For that very reason those air forces and those air arms never once openly fought one another on any scale and for any length of time. Combat between them, to the extent that it occurred at all, was limited to isolated incidents when a few of their pilots fought each other in disguise (as in Korea) and to fighting by proxy.[4] Nuclear weapons, in other words, restricted the use of air power to wars fought between, or against, medium-size and small powers that did not yet have them.

Whatever role air power continued to play had to unfold within this rather limited framework. Allied air forces certainly helped turn the Korean War into what it was, i.e., a stalemate; however, the precise impact of air power at various times in the conflict remains moot to the present day. Israeli air power played a decisive role in the Arab-Israeli Wars, which peaked in 1967. Twice the Israelis also used their air power to attack nuclear facilities in neighboring countries, thus preventing those nations from acquiring the bomb and possibly putting an end to the greatest advantage they themselves possessed. Air power was important, though probably not decisive, in the Indo-Pakistani Wars of 1965 and 1971. Only once, in 1982 at the Falklands, did air power clash with air power at sea. The role it played on that occasion was indeed decisive; however, the scale on which it was deployed was minuscule, and most of the aircraft in use were semi-obsolete. Finally, air power, now supplemented by space power in the form of satellites, played a critically important role in the 1991 Gulf War, in the first days or weeks of the 2001–2 U.S. war in Afghanistan, and in the first weeks of the 2003 U.S. invasion of Iraq, after which President Bush dramatically declared that "major combat operations" had ended.

As the reader will have noted, the last two wars were waged by the world's only superpower against extremely weak opponents. The same applied to the wars in Serbia (1999) and Libya (2011), although in the second of these the superpower limited its role to providing firepower, intelligence, and logistic support to its allies. In none of these cases were the small powers that came under attack able to put up more than token resistance in the air, and usually they could not do even that.

Yet if one takes into account not only interstate wars but also counterinsurgency campaigns—the great majority, as it turns out—the picture changes substantially. The difference was already evident during the first air war, that of 1911. As long as it was a question of fighting the Ottoman Army near the coast, the nascent Italian air force proved useful, particularly for reconnaissance and artillery spotting. However, as the regular units melted away into the desert and were replaced by Arab tribesmen employing guerrilla tactics, the situation changed. Aircraft still had a role to play; especially when it came to reconnaissance, the sheer size of the theater of war meant that there was no alternative.

Aircraft were also used to bomb "enemy" concentrations, but so often did the primitive munitions in use either miss their target or kill the wrong people that the Italians decided to replace them with leaflets. Ultimately, the campaign, which had been planned to last for just a few weeks, stretched out over no fewer than twenty-six years of intermittent warfare. Only in 1927 was the opposition finally subdued. Even so, the main fighting was done by a quarter million ground troops; aircraft played an important, but ultimately auxiliary, role.

Since then this story has been repeated almost endlessly. Time after time, air power played a critical role in conventional warfare. Usually it did so by first obtaining air superiority and then weakening the opposing forces by attacking them at the front, striking at lines of communication, and occasionally bombing their hinterland. However, when dealing with insurgency, guerrillas, and terrorism, air forces found that there were no enemy aircraft to shoot down or destroy on the ground, no fronts, no lines of communications, and no hinterlands whose destruction could make a difference. To note a few landmark cases only, though the Rif of Morocco had neither an air force nor antiaircraft defenses of any kind, it took 300,000 French and Spanish ground troops, complete with tanks and artillery, several years to subdue them. When the Palestinian Arabs rose against the British in 1936, the failure of the Royal Air Force, which was in charge of security, to deal with the revolt was so complete that London decided to shift responsibility to the army. Ultimately, an entire division under then major general Bernard Montgomery, complete with heavy weapons, was needed to accomplish the task.[5] After 1945, too, absolute command of the air did little to help the British in Palestine, Kenya, Cyprus, and Aden or the French in Algeria.[6]

The classic example of air power failure is, of course, Vietnam. As in every other conflict of this kind, the Viet Cong did not have air power, although, as time went on, North Vietnam did acquire a growing number of antiaircraft weapons to cope with the air capabilities that the Americans brought to bear. As in every other case, the "counterinsurgents," as they came to be known later on, thought they could capitalize on the enemy's lack of air power by using their own air power to reconnoiter, liaise, transport, strafe, and bomb the enemy with relative impunity. At first the machines deployed in Southeast Asia tended to be leftovers from Korea. Later on, the most modern and most advanced models available were added. Employing a combination of fixed-wing aircraft and helicopters, including an entire air-mobile division that was the first of its kind anywhere, the Americans sent nearly as many aircraft as there were Viet Cong. Not counting flights by the South Vietnamese Army, in 1963 the Americans flew no fewer than 300,000 missions, and even this was just the beginning.[7]

During the next ten years South Vietnam was turned into the most-bombed country in history. The Americans used every possible kind of aircraft, including some totally unsuitable F-102 Dagger interceptors. The United States did not even hesitate to resort to chemical warfare in the form of Agent Orange, which was designed to cause leaves to fall from trees and thus deny the enemy cover. Testifying to the magnitude of the effort, the Americans suffered staggering losses of equipment, ultimately amounting to over ten thousand fixed-wing and rotary-wing aircraft. Operations Linebacker I and II did succeed in halting the North Vietnamese attempts to invade South Vietnam with conventional forces, but this merely serves to illustrate the vast difference between the two kinds of war. In the end air power did not keep the Americans from defeat, nor their South Vietnamese protégés from destruction.

Behind the frequent failure to combat guerrillas from the air (and on the ground—but that is not our subject here) was the reality that many of the systems in use turned out to be too expensive, too fast, too indiscriminate, too big, too unwieldy, and too powerful for the purpose. As had already occurred with the Italians in 1911, too often these aircraft either hit no targets at all or else destroyed the wrong ones, doing more harm than good. Compared to what was to come later, the air power used by the Americans in Vietnam and the Soviets in Afghanistan during the 1980s was primitive. When the so-called revolution in military affairs swept the world around 1990 or so, it brought with it entire arrays of new weapons, including precision-guided munitions, various kinds of sensors and computers, and the sort of digital communications needed to link all of them together and enable some of them to function autonomously. However, as events in both Afghanistan and Iraq showed, when it came to dealing with insurgency, guerrillas, and terrorism, the systems in question were only marginally more effective than their predecessors had been, if indeed they were effective at all. Even as these lines are being written in February 2014, the fact that President Bashar al-Assad of Syria has air power (and is making rather barbarous use of it), whereas the insurgents who are putting his regime in danger do not, seems to point in the same direction.

As conventional warfare, hemmed in by nuclear limitations, slowly faded away and was largely replaced by various forms of insurgency, guerrilla warfare, and terrorism, air forces slowly started melting away. In 1944 American factories rolled out some three hundred military aircraft of all kinds per day. Nowadays the same country, although it is the most powerful and richest country in history, may count itself lucky if it can provide its armed services—all four of them combined—with a similar number per year.[8] Everywhere else the number of aircraft built is in the low dozens, if that. As a result, with hardly any exception orders of battle have been shrinking at an average rate of perhaps one-third per decade and a half. Some medium-sized and small countries simply gave up on maintaining an air force at all, but even those that did not were forced to slow new acquisitions to the point where the gap separating them from the major players has become huge. The only exception to the trend is Israel, and this is the case only because of massive American financial support.

Confronted with these facts, the proponents of air power will invariably claim that declining numbers have been more than compensated for by growing "capabilities." In their support they cite statistics. In World War II, they will argue, it took so and so many sorties to destroy a tactical target. Nowadays the same result can be achieved at, say, one-tenth of 1 percent of that number.[9] In fact the statistics are misleading, not seldom deliberately so. It is true that World War II bombers, flying at perhaps twenty thousand feet, could hit their targets almost exclusively by accident. However, comparing them with today's fighter-bombers is like comparing sledgehammers with ice picks. Smaller, more agile aircraft—such as the German Stuka and Focke-Wulf 190, the Soviet Sturmovik, the British Typhoon, and the American Mustang and P-40—could hit both stationary targets, such as bridges, and mobile ones, such as tanks or locomotives, quite as accurately as their successors. The real difference is that on pain of being shot down by the much more powerful antiaircraft defenses now existing, these successors have to fly much higher.

Meanwhile, serious wars against serious opposition capable of responding in kind have all but disappeared. With such wars rare, few aircraft are lost to enemy action. As a result, existing ones are kept flying and tend to last for decades, albeit at growing cost in terms of maintenance and repair. The best-known example of this phenomenon is the B-52. Production of the most advanced model, the B-52H with its turbofan engines, ended in 1964. However, the bomber, crewed by pilots young enough to be the grandchildren of the original ones, still remains operational. It is used to drop bombs now here, now there, but always on opponents so weak as to be practically defenseless.

In the meantime growing technical sophistication has led to escalating cost. In 1945 a P-51 Mustang fighter-bomber, in many ways the best produced by any country during World War II, could be had at a price of just under $51,000. Taking inflation into account that works out to $613,000 in 2009 dollars. However, in that year the real cost of an F-22 stood at $140 million, representing a 228-fold increase (19-fold, after inflation).[10] No wonder Secretary of Defense Robert Gates, specifically citing the difficulty of using high-performance aircraft in subconventional war, decided to bring the program to an end.[11] Whereas over fifteen thousand P-51s were built, the figure for the F-22 is just 187. The situation in respect to many other aircraft, both American and foreign, is hardly any better. Consider the F-35. Originally, it was designed as a (relatively) low-cost alternative to the F-22; by now it costs more than its older brother did.[12] The unit cost of some aircraft—notably the B-2, the Joint Surveillance Target Attack Radar System (of which only a handful were ever built), and the C-117 (a successful, though extremely expensive, program)—is even higher.

If the largest power with the largest air force has suffered, medium-sized and small powers did so even more. As research and development came to form a major part of the cost of every new program, a vicious cycle was created. The fewer aircraft produced, the higher the unit cost of each one. The higher the unit cost of each platform, the greater the temptation to cut production programs in order to prevent budgets from skyrocketing. Furthermore, the two problems are related. So expensive are some systems that even the few countries that acquire them in the first place cannot afford to lose any of them. Since these assets cannot be lost, there is always a temptation to use them with extreme caution, if at all. The best that medium-sized and small powers can hope for is to have a handful of high-performance aircraft surrounded by a slightly larger fleet of older ones, as is the case in Switzerland and Austria. Others will have to make do with forty-year-old crates more suitable for display in museums than for waging real-life warfare.

The literature often presents the combination of high performance with high cost as an indication of rapid technological progress. In fact, history shows that it is a typical sign of degeneration.[13] A good example of this is the development of ancient Greek warships. The Athenian triremes used in the Peloponnesian War had three banks of oars each. Later more banks were added until some Hellenistic vessels had ten or more.[14] So few, expensive, and cumbersome were these ships that they could never be used in battle; faced by smaller, but more numerous, opponents, they must have been helpless. Some are known to have ended up being captured in port by the Roman legions, which, needless to say, advanced by land. Similarly, by about 1525 full suits of armor had become so heavy, so elaborate, and so expensive that only a handful of knights could afford them. On campaign even those few had to be escorted by infantrymen whose function was in many ways like that of today's "strike packages," causing the armor to become even more expensive and even less useful. By 1550 the process of shortening, lightening, and simplifying armor began. Two hundred years later it had been all but completed, leaving cuirassiers as the only troops who still wore any armor at all.

Perhaps an even better example of the way things work is offered by naval history from about 1860 to 1945.[15] As steam engines took the place of sails, ships of the line, with their multiple rows of guns on both sides, were gradually transformed into modern battleships. As battleships developed and their guns grew more powerful, they became much larger and more expensive, while their numbers went into a steep decline. As the number of vessels decreased, fleet commanders surrounded them with all sorts of smaller ships to act as scouts and protect them against emerging threats, such as torpedoes, submarines, and finally, aircraft. As in the case of armored knights, the outcome was the creation of "strike packages." By 1939 the floating steel castles were at their last gasp. Over the next six years quite a few on both sides were actually sunk or damaged by aircraft, submarines, or manned torpedoes before they were able to raise steam and leave port. After 1945 they all but disappeared.

Whereas manned military aircraft, the traditional mainstay of every air force around the world, seem well on their way to becoming an extinct species, unmanned flying vehicles of every kind are proliferating as never before. This trend began during the last years of World War II, when the Germans developed, produced, and used the famous V-2 ballistic missile. During the 1950s various countries produced many more missiles until, toward the end of the decade, the first intercontinental ballistic missiles (ICBMs) capable of reaching any target from practically any other point were added. Other technical improvements, such as the switch from liquid to solid fuel and the introduction of more accurate navigation systems, also made their appearance. Right from the beginning it was feared that missiles would end up taking the place of aircraft, particularly bombers capable of operating far behind the enemy front. In fact it was the German Army, not the Luftwaffe, that developed the V-2 with precisely that objective in mind.[16] With the exception of the U.S. Air Force, which (as explained previously) still flies a few ancient crates of this kind, those fears have long been realized.

Next, it was the turn of cruise missiles. In some ways the development of the V-1, the first operational cruise missile, proceeded in the opposite direction from the V-2 effort. The V-2 was the German Army's answer to the Luftwaffe; the V-1 was the Luftwaffe's answer to the V-2. During the 1950 and 1960s few cruise missiles were built, the apparent reason being the complexity and unreliability of the guidance mechanisms. However, the introduction during the early 1970s of terrain contour matching navigation systems capable of much greater accuracy caused the picture to change. Since then the Global Positioning System has permitted even greater accuracy at low cost, enabling many countries to build the devices. Quite a few of those countries have decided to all but dispense with a modern air force. Increasingly, they base their defense on ballistic missiles and cruise missiles with or without nuclear warheads.

In late 1957 the USSR launched the first earth-orbiting satellite into outer space. Within a few years *Sputnik* was followed by other satellites, which could perform a whole array of military functions. Some of those functions, notably communication (introduced during the 1960s) and navigation (introduced during the late 1980s), were new. Most, however, were old, including surveillance, reconnaissance, target acquisition, and damage assessment. Compared to aircraft employed on the same missions, satellites had some disadvantages, mainly that they flew much higher—requiring the development of altogether new photographic and radar equipment—and could only pass over the same area once in some number of minutes without being able to loiter over them. Conversely, they had the advantage of staying in orbit much longer than any aircraft could—thus cutting cost—and of freedom to go anywhere without (so far) having to encounter enemy opposition. On the whole the advantages of satellites, as compared to military aircraft, must be great; otherwise it is hard to see why, even as the number of the latter declined, that of the former increased to the point that there are now hundreds of billions of dollars' worth of satellites circling the earth.

The last addition to the order of battle that must be discussed in this context is drones. Like cruise missiles, drones, known first as remotely piloted vehicles and then as unmanned airborne vehicles, go back to World War II. Also like cruise missiles, they started coming into their own during the late 1970s, when sophisticated miniaturized electronics were developed. As the 1982 Israeli invasion of Lebanon in particular demonstrated, at first their use was limited to reconnaissance and related functions. Later communication and electronic warfare were added. Some drones were designed to carry out suicide missions: homing in on the radar pulses of hostile antiaircraft defenses and destroying them. Others were armed with their own air-to-ground missiles, thus taking over functions previously entrusted to much larger, much more expensive fighter-bombers. Compared to those fighter-bombers, drones had many advantages, including lesser complexity; lesser cost in human life, as well as in production and employment; and greater ability to loiter over the battlefield, something that modern fighter-bombers, owing to their immense speed and relatively large turning circles, find it hard if not impossible to do. Above all, when it came to counterinsurgency warfare of every kind, they were much more useful than any manned aircraft. No wonder they have been proliferating almost like the proverbial rabbits.

Before 1945 wars were waged primarily by "great powers," which often "owned" territories measured in the hundreds of thousands of square miles that were located as far apart as, for example, the United States and Germany or Britain and Japan. The distance between the powers and their territories, from 1918 on, led to the creation of "independent" air forces, the rationale being that these forces would operate far behind the front in places that armies could not reach. However, as illustrated by the history of the V-1 and V-2, as well as that of some other ballistic missiles in other countries, even at that time this kind of organization was neither universal nor strictly necessary.

Since 1945 the situation has changed. Many antiterrorist, antiguerrilla, and counterinsurgency campaigns take place so close to home that the combatants—if that is the correct word—can see the whites of their enemies' eyes. Even when these conflicts are waged in remote countries, the difference between front and rear barely exists. Either way, there seems to be good reason to question the independence of "independent" air forces and instead to reintegrate drones in particular with the ground forces for which they work and to which they provide support. In fact this has been happening.

Within the limits of the technology that medium-sized and small powers can afford, the trend away from manned toward unmanned equipment may be more pronounced for the smaller nations than for the few large ones. Take the cases of Iran, Pakistan, and Syria. Not one of them has a powerful modern air force. Since their main enemies are their own neighbors, they do not need ICBMs. Yet they can, and do, afford and deploy sufficient medium-range missiles (armed with either nuclear or chemical warheads) to build credible deterrent forces indeed. The same goes for cruise missiles and for drones, which, though by no means cheap, are within reach of many medium-sized and small powers and even of nonstate terrorist organizations, such as the Lebanese Hezbollah. The one asset those countries lack is satellites, but even in this field the smaller powers, provided they are willing to use other nations' launchers, can build some capabilities. If a country believes that it needs an air force but as a medium-sized or small power cannot afford the tens of billions needed to build and maintain a modern one, undoubtedly unmanned systems are the way to go.

As somebody once said, it is not old views that die, but those who hold them. For both intellectual and institutional reasons, the first reaction to any attempt to show that the old is on its way out and the new on its way in is almost always rejection. As one would expect, such responses tend to be especially numerous during periods of rapid change that threatens the status and livelihood of a great number of people. Early in the twentieth century cavalrymen made quite a name for themselves by the obtuseness with which they defended their swords and horses against the onslaught of motor transport and tanks. A hundred years later their successors—the pilots working for every military around the world—are mounting a similarly forlorn campaign against a future that threatens to overwhelm them. This is probably even more true for small and medium-sized powers that cannot afford to maintain a manned air force than for the handful of larger ones that still can do so, more or less. The present essay seeks to show why, for such powers, the only way ahead is to focus on unmanned systems, such as ballistic missiles, cruise missiles, satellites, and drones, and, by so doing, help clear the rubbish of the past and make way for the future.

TEN

The Response to Uncertainty

Air Vice Marshal R. A. Mason

An Environment in Turmoil

If a soothsayer from ancient Rome could be invited in 2013 to forecast the future of European air power, he would, with good reason, observe, "The omens are not propitious." The certainties of the Cold War are long gone. The European context of air power is in disarray. The United States, under acute budgetary pressure, is increasingly looking to the Far East rather than to Europe and is exhorting its European partners to increase their contributions to the North Atlantic Treaty Organization (NATO). The majority of European states are, however, in financial difficulties and have thus accorded defense a low priority. Some are disillusioned with intervention operations and reluctant to look beyond their continent for security. The member states of the European Union have no common foreign policy, and the European members of NATO have various priorities and interests.

Within European forces, allocation of dwindling resources stimulates fierce and frequently highly subjective debate. Cyber warfare and terrorism seem more threatening than conventional conflict, although Russia remains a source of unease to her neighbors. Some commentators have offered the naive suggestion that insurgency has rendered air power obsolescent, disregarding the fact that insurgency itself is in many ways an enforced response to conventional military superiority.

The air forces must make difficult decisions on roles, force structure, and equipment despite all the imponderables. Previous chapters in this volume have explained how European air forces are preparing for an uncertain future with cautious optimism. In its short history air power has become a uniquely versatile and effective political and military instrument across the spectrum of conflict. Facing so much uncertainty, the demands on the flexibility of air power have never been greater.

The Century of Confident Assumptions

Air power was born and came of age in a century dominated by three wars: World Wars I and II and the Cold War. Two were fought between conventional armed forces on land, on sea, and in the air. The third would have been, in the shadow of nuclear escalation.

In World War I aerial reconnaissance stimulated struggle to control the air over the trenches. Wasteful competition and duplication between the Royal Flying Corps and the Royal Naval Air Service, aggravating the inadequacy of British air defenses against German attacks, not a bombing campaign, led to the creation of the independent Royal Air Force (RAF) in 1918. The potential of air power to reach far beyond front lines attracted air power theorists for the remainder of the century. Indeed, some observers came to confuse "strategic" bombing with air power itself. Command of the air, on the other hand, became—and remains—as indispensable in warfare as command of the sea to previous generations.

In World War II air power was pervasive and fully justified the confident assumption by Winston Churchill in 1949 that "for good or ill, air mastery is today the supreme expression of military power." The Battles of Britain and Midway were decided by air power. It spearheaded Blitzkrieg, closed the Atlantic to German U-boats, enabled the Normandy invasion, crippled German industrial capacity, eliminated British naval power in Southeast Asia, and ultimately applied the coup de grace to the Japanese homeland. By 1945 no armies or navies could operate effectively, if at all, in the face of enemy control of the air above them.

There were no air battles in the Cold War, but air power strongly influenced its outcome. Airlift preserved democracy in Berlin, which checked Soviet hegemony in Eastern Europe. Strategic reconnaissance continuously monitored Soviet ballistic missiles and air defenses, playing a critical role in the Cuban missile crisis. Had deterrence failed, Warsaw Pact air forces would have spearheaded an offensive in Europe, while NATO air forces held the ring as reinforcements crossed the Atlantic and North Sea.

In all three wars confrontation was symmetrical. All sides became immersed in a conflict in which fundamental national interests were perceived to be at stake. The armed forces confronted each other with similar force structures and postures, albeit with different strategies. The wars were or would have been decided by uniformed combatants. The conflicts demanded total political and economic commitment, drove procurement and force structures, and were afforded priority in the allocation of national resources. The need to gain control of the air to enable all operations on land and sea, the ability of air power to reach far beyond conventional battle lines, and the synergy of air power in cooperation with armies and navies were unquestioned.

The Exception

Meanwhile, between the wars the British government had been faced with the problem of imposing its authority on newly acquired territories in the Middle East. In 1921 it could not afford the estimated cost of army garrisons to provide internal security for the territory of Mesopotamia. Colonial Secretary Churchill reduced the army presence from twenty-two battalions to four and entrusted the RAF to enhance the reduced numbers of ground troops by establishing secure air bases and landing strips, from which aircraft could operate in every part of the protectorate. Political control was achieved by deterrence, air attack, and rapid deployment of ground forces by air, taking advantage of range, speed, responsiveness, and firepower. The opposition was unsophisticated, divided, unfamiliar with aircraft and air attack, easily located and identified, inhabiting largely barren territory, technologically inferior, and media innocent. The RAF operated under closely coordinated political control unconstrained by public opinion, media exposure, or undue humanitarian sensitivity. These operations were asymmetric, with air power used against opponents on the ground who were largely denied opportunities to fight on their own terms.

Such circumstances are unlikely to be repeated in the twenty-first century, but the principles of those RAF operations remain very relevant. Air power enabled considerable reductions in costs, in numbers of ground troops, in exposure of forces to enemy attack, and in removal of extended, vulnerable surface lines of communication. Despite considerable differences in the political and operational environment, air power offered similar advantages in Afghanistan nearly a century later.

The Impact of Asymmetry

With the collapse of the Soviet empire, the Cold War environment evaporated, exposing permanent features in the international landscape. But hopes among European states of a "peace dividend" quickly disappeared. In the following twenty years, the symmetry of twentieth-century warfare was replaced by conflicts in which political commitment, strategies, and operations were increasingly asymmetric. Air power had to adapt to very different circumstances.

In the first Gulf War, coalition air forces isolated, decimated, and demoralized numerically superior Iraqi ground forces to the extent that they were defeated in four days by coalition troops. Serbian operations in Bosnia and Herzegovina were halted when NATO air forces were finally authorized to intervene. In Kosovo NATO air power was the only practical military instrument usable because of alliance incoherence and the difficulties of deploying ground forces into the theater. In 2001 coalition aircraft, coordinated with Afghan ground forces, drove the Taliban down to the southern border areas almost to the point of extinction. In 2003 air power reprised the first Gulf War to enable ground forces to drive on to Baghdad with the minimum of opposition. In 2012 air power was again the only acceptable military instrument when, with only a handful of ground special forces, it enabled the Libyan opposition to topple Gaddafi. The impact of air power in widely differing environments in this period was enhanced by all-weather precision-guided munitions (PGMs), pervasive reconnaissance, and rapidly increasing acceleration of the target acquisition-identification-response-attack process.

Throughout the history of warfare, opponents have sought ways of countering the enemy's strategy, tactics, and weapons, causing a pendulum to swing, sometimes unexpectedly and erratically, between offense and defense. Carl von Clausewitz, however, in his reflections on the complexities of "the people in arms," identified a different kind of warfare in which one side seeks to avoid attacking or defending in the manner of its opponents at all, thus creating an asymmetric confrontation. He discussed the problems presented to conventional forces by what we would term "insurgents"[1]: they would operate in small, highly mobile groups, taking advantage of regional terrain, striking swiftly and fleetingly, avoiding set-piece battles except when locally superior, harassing lines of communication, relying on popular support for intelligence and supplies, and gradually wearing down the determination and morale of the opposition. Perhaps the Taliban studied Clausewitz?

Other features of modern insurgency operations would be unfamiliar to the Prussian theorist. In their contingency planning European air forces need to take into account national sensitivity to their own and civilian casualties, collateral damage, and the inevitable hostile exploitation of international media. They must be prepared for opposition that may lack air power but has learned how to constrain air operations by dispensing with conventional uniforms and structure while generating operational asymmetry.

In the Gulf War of 1991, the overwhelming impact of air power was widely analyzed for emulation by European air forces. Significant asymmetric features of the one-sided conflict were carefully noted by those who could be on the receiving end of future air attack. Saddam Hussein sought to exploit Western concern over the possibility of extensive allied casualties. He allowed Western journalists to remain in Baghdad in order to ensure that images of civilians killed by air attacks were transmitted in near-real time back to the allied populations. None of his measures had any strategic effect on air operations, but public sensitivity to the images of annihilation of transport on the Basra road in the closing days of the war appear to have hastened the conflict's conclusion by President George H. W. Bush.

Saddam Hussein's media management was maladroit, but in subsequent conflicts media manipulation constrained allied air power in Bosnia and Herzegovina, Kosovo, Iraq, and Afghanistan. In Bosnia and Herzegovina, Bosnian Serb forces held United Nations (UN) hostages against air attack. In Kosovo, Serbian ground forces complicated air attack by deploying among civilian communities and mingling with civilian transport. Eyewitness and other reports of destruction in the target area could reach the media much more quickly than responses from NATO headquarters. In the media battle it was a close contest between Serbian images of NATO targeting errors and Western images of brutalized refugees. In Afghanistan, reports of civilian casualties from remotely piloted vehicle (RPV) attack have received much wider publicity than the RPVs' effectiveness against insurgents. More recently, successful RPV strikes against al Qaeda leaders in Somalia and Yemen have generated similar international concern.

On the other hand, as in RAF operations between the wars, and in a different political context, air power brings its own asymmetric advantages against insurgents. In Afghanistan coalition air forces provided rapid firepower to beleaguered or isolated ground forces. Repeatedly, the presence or the imminence of combat aircraft had a visibly deterrent impact on insurgents. Persistent aerial reconnaissance enabled timely and precise attacks on Taliban forces, denying them sanctuary. Helicopters gave ground forces the mobility to reach and surprise insurgent strongholds. They provided reinforcement, resupply, and casualty evacuation, and they raised the visibility of the central government by taking officials and politicians into remote areas. In sum, air power greatly reduced the numbers of ground troops that would otherwise have been required, reduced dependence on vulnerable surface movement, and on many occasions took tactical and strategic initiative away from the insurgents. These wide-ranging operations are a reminder that air power is about far more than just bombing; it continues to be the full military exploitation of the air and space above it, as relevant in its second century as in its first.

Limitations and Constraints

Unfortunately, in Afghanistan there were also echoes of the negligible impact of air power against Jewish insurgents in Palestine and against the Vietcong in Vietnam. It is, however, disingenuous of Professor Martin van Creveld to condemn air power for failure while suggesting that comparisons with ground forces are irrelevant. The British Army and RAF were both unable to defeat the insurgency that was the genesis of the state of Israel. More than half a million U.S. troops, not just air power, failed to prevent the unification of Vietnam under the Hanoi regime. In the face of a hostile population enjoying international support, no armed force is likely to achieve anything more than transient control and influence unless applied ruthlessly, with overwhelming strength and with permanence over an extended period, as in Israel's fight for survival. Too often air power has been criticized for its inability to force a favorable conclusion when the real failure was to assume that any kind of armed force could succeed in the existing political and strategic environment.

In the later phases of conflict in Iraq and Afghanistan, insurgents exploited mobility, concealment, deception, and surprise and were indistinguishable by their dress from civilian noncombatants, thereby making target identification, discrimination, and confirmation much more difficult for ground and air forces alike. In response the UN forces, lacking the authority to impose or coordinate economic and political policies, were condemned to operations without clearly defined political objectives.

Politicians and airmen must therefore continue to be extremely sensitive to images of civilian casualties and destruction, relayed across the world in near-real time. If the object of friendly intervention is explicitly to improve the lot of a suffering civilian community, the propaganda impact of death and destruction is proportionately increased. Rules of engagement have been tightened to ensure as far as possible that air attack is proportionate, accurate, and confined. Real-time intelligence, unequivocal target identification, precise attack, and minimal collateral damage are no longer merely desirable, but essential to ensure that the operational effects of an air strike are not detrimental to the political objective and undermine the public opinion that supports it.

But however effective the rules of engagement may be in reducing civilian casualties and collateral damage, public support may become fragile because of an underlying political asymmetry between the opponents. Recent interventions have been generated by humanitarian concerns, national interest, support for international law, or any combination. They are, however, a far cry from the life-and-death conflicts of the last century. Many are optional. All are transient. None has demanded the total commitment of national resources.

The opponents of intervention, on the other hand, have been fighting for political control and the resolution of age-old ethnic and religious disputes. Such objectives encourage total commitment over an extended period. Hence the political asymmetry in a drawn-out conflict, which weakens the determination and morale of the intervening forces, encourages doubts about their objectives, magnifies the impact of costs and friendly casualties, increases concern about civilian casualties and collateral damage, and stimulates pressure to disengage. The cumulative effect on the intervening countries, evident in both Iraq and Afghanistan, is war-weariness, which in 2014 reinforces a lack of enthusiasm in Europe for making new, lengthy, and uncertain military commitments.

Managing Uncertainty

Yet amid the profusion of political, economic, and strategic uncertainties, disagreements, and pressures swirling around European security decision making in 2014, a number of confident assumptions can still be made. National security will remain a primary responsibility of government. Threats to national security may be internal, originate beyond national boundaries, or be encouraged by external support. Armed force will continue to be an instrument of international diplomacy. National interests may be perceived beyond Europe. Membership in NATO and other organizations will continue to carry commitments. Humanitarian crises may stimulate national responses. The more complex the uncertainties, the greater the need for versatile armed forces that can defend the homeland and, if required, uphold international commitments and support national interests farther afield.

The control of national air space remains paramount. Counterterrorism will remain the province of internal security services, but air power has a contribution to make. With the attacks of September 11, 2001, unlikely to be forgotten, the RAF mounted a highly visible presence in southeastern England during the London Olympics in July 2012 as a deterrent to terrorist air activity. Less obtrusive protection is maintained 24/7 elsewhere in the United Kingdom in an air defense structure that links ministerial authority through the command chain to the pilot in the cockpit. Since the terrorist attacks on London in 2006, there have been unconfirmed but well-founded reports that RAF aircraft have contributed to the collection of electronic intelligence from suspect sources within the United Kingdom.

Control of sovereign air space not only is essential for national security but may also support national foreign policy. In October 2012 a Syrian transport aircraft en route from Russia to Syria, allegedly carrying military equipment in contravention of an arms embargo, was compelled to land in Turkey by Turkish fighter aircraft.

Provision of European national air defense will remain an integrated NATO responsibility. Even the larger states will depend on partnership for early warning and defensive depth. Aircraft types and associated systems, however, will be procured from a variety of sources and operational cost-effectiveness across the alliance still requires much greater interoperability. Much can be achieved without heavy investment, especially in communications and intelligence processing. Existing multinational exercises, training, and exchange postings can be extended.

Looking only to Europe, states can confidently depend on existing partners to reinforce national forces in the air and on the ground.

Force Projection

Projecting such cooperation beyond Europe, despite a lack of common foreign policy, remains feasible. If any state chooses to retain only a defensive posture, it will concede all initiative to a potential adversary. Several states with distinguished records of participation in UN humanitarian or peace-keeping operations may continue to combine altruistic international responsibility with perceptions of self-interest. Britain and France have residual worldwide post imperial responsibilities. The four Nordic states share common security interests but have also been strong contributors to global peace-keeping and humanitarian operations. Germany, although heavily constrained by the legacy of World War II, has consistently deployed armed forces in support of UN and NATO operations in Europe and beyond. Turkey retains a direct national security interest in the Middle East as well as its alliance commitments to Europe.

Deterrence, crisis management, conflict prevention, or reaction to events outside Europe may be desirable or indeed essential. Tension in the Middle East remains of concern because of dependence on oil and in North Africa because of the impact of political upheaval there on Europe. The U.S. inclination to play a leading or major role in support of European interests cannot be assumed in the longer term.

Under such circumstances an ability to influence events beyond Europe without an entangling extended commitment of ground forces is attractive. Hitherto, the inability of aircraft to hold ground has been regarded as a liability; now their impermanence becomes an alternative political asset. Ideally, air power should be coordinated with indigenous friendly forces. Indeed, if there were no such forces, there could be serious reservations about any kind of military intervention. Participation in an interstate conflict without U.S. cooperation, with the possible exception of another Falkland Islands confrontation, would be unlikely for European states.

Aircraft procured primarily for the European theater can also deploy farther afield. Even within constrained budgets an air force can be equipped to operate with NATO in the European theater and in coalition beyond it. Priority should be given to capabilities rather than platforms. A handful of multirole combat aircraft capable of establishing air control, delivering air-to-air and air-to-ground all-weather PGMs, and carrying reconnaissance pods would make valuable partners in either European integrated air defense or in coalitions out of area. They would, however, have to be able to use common real-time intelligence, communications, and targeting systems. If financial constraints compelled a choice, European nations should favor investing in a reduced number of updated, interoperable platforms rather than purchasing new ones. The world is replete with venerable airframes whose systems effectiveness has been repeatedly updated: an evolution to be applauded, not, as in some quarters, derided.

Alternatively, a state may decide not to procure combat aircraft. Transport aircraft and helicopters have major roles in all theaters of war in addition to their availability for humanitarian operations and disaster relief. Such a choice would, however, assume dependence on partners to establish and maintain a favorable air environment.

In the Libyan intervention by NATO and friends in 2011, the United States provided 90 percent of in-flight refueling, airborne early warning, reconnaissance, and the supporting real-time command, control, communications, and intelligence network. European partners rapidly exhausted their weapon stocks. Investment in those terms, ideally cooperative, is an essential European requirement.

For deterrence to be effective, capability must be visible and determination credible. It is not necessary for every European partner to invest in entry-level equipment, but a coalition must possess it. The capabilities of the Joint Strike Fighter and Eurofighter Typhoon considerably enhance deterrence. European air power has been seen as capable of rapid response and long reach. Even humanitarian operations have faced lethal opposition in the past. Potential enemies will continue to seek to oppose aerial assaults from the ground. They already receive advanced air defense weapons from powerful friends. The impact of the U.S. Stinger missile in Afghanistan set an unhealthy precedent for aircraft engaged in counterinsurgency operations. The ability to suppress air defenses is likely to be required at all levels of conflict to enable all other roles and must be possessed by at least one partner in any coalition.

Increased procurement costs and reduced defense budgets have compelled severe reductions in all European air forces. Nevertheless, it is facile for critics simply to attack the costs of an aircraft and its supporting systems. The significant figures are opportunity costs and related operational cost-effectiveness. The current procurement programs of China, Russia, and the United States will guarantee that the importance of command of the air, demonstrated in almost every conflict in the last hundred years, will not diminish. The opportunity costs of not being able to establish and sustain command of the air would be borne by the casualties among the air, ground, and naval forces trying to operate when air superiority was held by an opponent. Operational cost-effectiveness is achieved by aircraft and systems that can deliver multiple effects in many different scenarios, from deterrence to war fighting, from counterinsurgency to high-intensity conflict.

Resource Allocation

The future roles of air power are already well defined, but even with realistic operational cost analysis, three comparatively new factors complicate European resource allocation. They are easily identified but difficult to separate in practice: satellite dependence, cyber war, and the use of RPVs or drones.

Space-based systems pervade all aspects of warfare. War games attempt with great difficulty to simulate the loss of satellite communication, navigation, and reconnaissance. RPV control other than over short ranges depends entirely on satellites. Continued investment in European satellites is essential and should be a factor in cooperative cost sharing.

Air power will likely remain marginal in cyber warfare, except when kinetic attack on a known source is desirable. Cyber warfare has already begun. Widespread, albeit unconfirmed, reports suggest that air defense suppression may already include cyber attack. Cyber warfare transcends all traditional boundaries of the armed services but is an addition, not an alternative, to conventional conflict. The vulnerability of industry and commerce as well as national security systems indicates that resource provision is no longer the exclusive responsibility of ministries of defense.

The remaining question is how far air power roles can be discharged by RPVs. The attractions of RPVs are well known. Aircrew vulnerability is removed; RPVs are commanded and controlled securely far from the war zone; production, personnel, and deployment costs are reduced, albeit not to the extent originally expected; RPVs' endurance, and hence persistence, is much greater than that of manned aircraft even when the latter are refueled in-flight; multirole combat intelligence, surveillance, target acquisition, and reconnaissance utility approaches that of manned aircraft; RPVs have potential for freight delivery; and they reduce the costs of forward deployment.

Contemporary arguments about the morality or legality of RPV use are likely to prove transient. Infringement of sovereign air space by both RPVs and manned aircraft is contrary to international law. Allegations of unfair advantage and unwillingness to risk aircrew unnecessarily reflect an unworldly view of aerial warfare. The principle of force protection afforded by distance of command and absence of aircrew is traditional and laudable. Civilian casualties from U.S. RPVs are the product of human error, system malfunction, or perhaps targeting risk assessment. The location, identification, and elimination of hostile commanders, now emotionally branded as "assassination," may not be the most chivalrous feature of warfare, but it is no novelty.

Other reservations are more substantial. The European states' attraction to RPVs is tempered by current dependence on space-based U.S. command and control systems. Use of European satellites is desirable, but the potential vulnerability of either induces caution. Jamming of communications to RPVs is still in its infancy, and remote control centers remain invulnerable, but the center of gravity of any RPV system is, and is likely to remain, its command link. That link, including its ground source, must become a prime target of any opponent. The future strategic importance of RPVs at any level of conflict is such that no opponent could afford to allow them to operate without constraint. This innovation and response mirror the impact and consequences of aerial reconnaissance in World War I. The physical sanctuary enjoyed by operators in Nevada or any other remote location will sooner or later be threatened. The static control centers, their staff, and their domestic residences will become targets as legitimate as Royal Flying Corps airfields in World War I. Above all, RPVs can only operate in a benign environment. For the foreseeable future, all their contributions will depend on the previous establishment of air control by manned aircraft. Command of the air will remain a prerequisite for all operations, with or without aircrew.

Proposals to replace manned aircraft entirely with RPVs are therefore uninformed and shortsighted, ignoring the history of warfare and making the inherent flexibility of air power a hostage to technological fortune. To ensure future Western military dominance and assured command of the air, human responsiveness and ingenuity will remain indispensable. Fine judgment will be required to secure a long-term, operationally cost-effective balance between manned and unmanned systems.

Synergy from Cooperation

Even with disagreements over foreign policy, European states are unlikely to become involved in future conflicts without partners, with the possible exception of the United Kingdom and France because of their residual imperial interests. Even in these countries, the cost of defense procurement has driven greater cooperation in recent years. The unit cost of aircraft and associated systems compels all governments to seek the greatest operational flexibility from them. Cooperative procurement of multirole aircraft, systems, and weapons that could be deployed at home and overseas is highly desirable, despite competing national industrial interests. Common secure communications are fundamental.

Operational interoperability of equipment can, however, be cobbled together in an emergency provided some commonality allows technical interfacing. Coalition foundations, on the other hand, must be laid on understanding, confidence, and trust in peacetime. Many steps may be taken by European air forces themselves without infringing on political sensitivities or implying political commitments. As much as possible, training and exercises should be multinational, attended by nonparticipating observers from potential partners with different priorities. Simulators should be shared. Successful, mainstream careers should include regular personnel exchanges at all levels. Doctrine and concept formulation should seek cooperative principles as well as identify the potential operational implications of differences. The experience of NATO cooperation should be exploited without necessarily adhering to NATO structure. Examples of regional integration, such as Nordic Defence Cooperation, should be explored. Moves to pool resources, such as the European Air Transport Command, Air Transport Force, and Nordic Joint Tactical Air Transport, should be accelerated. Niche contributions such as rotary, medical, and airfield defense should be encouraged. None of these cooperative steps are cost free, but the question facing European governments is not "Can we afford to have them?" but "Can we afford not to have them?"

Here and Now

In the past, air power proponents have sometimes promised more than air power could deliver, fueling justified criticism when it fell short of expectations. Some have peddled air power as a panacea for military victory in all circumstances. Zealots have sought to constrict it by dogma, which choked its intrinsic flexibility as a political instrument. Now, air power's fundamental attributes of responsiveness, reach, speed, over-the-hill perspective, and versatility have been enhanced by advances in communication, precision munitions, reconnaissance, and endurance. Now, for the first time, air power is demonstrating, not promising. It can be applied effectively by European states across the conflict spectrum in the twenty-first century, but only if they prepare fully in time of peace to operate as partners in crisis.

NOTES

Introduction

1. John A. Warden, "Afterword: Challenges and Opportunities," in *Air Power Confronts an Unstable World*, ed. Richard P. Hallion (London: Brassey's, 1997), 227.

2. Colin S. Gray, *Airpower for Strategic Effect* (Maxwell Air Force Base AL: Air University Press, 2012), 307.

3. Benjamin S. Lambeth, "Lessons from Modern Warfare: What the Conflicts of the Post-Cold War Years Should Have Taught Us," *Strategic Studies Quarterly*, Fall 2013, 32. For Lambeth's work, see for example *Air Operations in Israel's War against Hezbollah* (Santa Monica CA: Rand, 2011); *Air Power against Terror: America's Conduct of Operation Enduring Freedom* (Santa Monica CA: Rand, 2005); *NATO's Air War for Kosovo: A Strategic and Operational Assessment* (Santa Monica CA: Rand, 2001); and *The Transformation of American Air Power* (Ithaca NY: Cornell University Press, 2000). See also John Andreas Olsen, ed., *A History of Air Warfare* (Washington DC: Potomac Books, 2010).

4. Mark Bucknam, "Michael E. Ryan: Architect of Air Power Success," in *Air Commanders*, ed. John Andreas Olsen (Washington DC: Potomac Books, 2012), 332–33.

5. Rohan Maxwell and John Andreas Olsen, *Destination NATO: Defence Reform in Bosnia and Herzegovina, 2003–2013*, Whitehall Paper 80 (London: RUSI, 2012).

6. Robert A. Pape, "The True Worth of Air Power," *Foreign Affairs* 83, no. 2 (March/April 2004): 116–30.

7. David Gates, "Air Power: The Instrument of Choice," in *Air Power 21: Challenges for the New Century*, ed. Peter W. Gray (London: Stationery Office, 2000), 39.

8. Gates, "Air Power," 33.

9. I would like to acknowledge Dr. Alan Stephens for having suggested this framework. The shape-deter-respond frame is also presented in the Air Power Development Centre, *The Air Power Manual*, AAP 1000-D (Canberra: Australian Air Publication,

2007), 66–68. There are many fine air power doctrines, but this is one of the finest. See also Alan Stephens, "The Asia Pacific Region," in *Global Air Power*, ed. John Andreas Olsen (Washington DC: Potomac Books, 2011), 300–304.

10. Air power is of course not the exclusive domain of air forces, but this study focuses mainly on the respective air services.

11. Turkey, a Eurasian country, is included here as "European." It is part of NATO, aspires to EU membership, and works closely with European partners in training, exercises, and education, as well as in real operations.

12. The Nordic region consists of five sovereign states—Denmark, Finland, Iceland, Norway, and Sweden—and their associated territories, such as the Faroe Islands, Greenland, Svalbard, and Åland. Among the Nordic states, Iceland has no air power to speak of; its military defense is in essence the Icelandic Coast Guard, which patrols Icelandic waters and air space. The Iceland Air Defence System, founded in 1987, has four radar sites and a command and report center as part of the coast guard. NATO allies also regularly deploy fighter aircraft to patrol the country's air space as part of the Icelandic air policing mission.

13. The quote is borrowed from Gray, *Airpower for Strategic Effect*, 315.

14. Richard P. Hallion, "Technology, Air Leadership, and the Evolution of American Air Power," in *Air Power Leadership: Theory and Practice*, ed. Peter W. Gray and Sebastian Cox (London: Stationery Office, 2002), 251.

1. French Air Power

1. See Williamson Murray and Allan Millett, eds., *Military Innovation in the Interwar Period* (Cambridge, UK: Cambridge University Press, 1996).

2. Claude Carlier, "L'aéronautique militaire, de la naissance à la participation à la victoire," in *De 1940 à nos jours*, ed. André Martel (Paris: PUF, 1994), 235.

3. See Claude Carlier, "L'aéronautique militaire," 228–29.

4. See Guy Pedroncini, "L'armée française et la Grande Guerre," in Martel, *De 1940 à nos jours*, 178.

5. On the notion of "aerial knights" and its resonance for the French Air Force, see Pascal Vennesson, *Les chevaliers de l'air. Aviations et conflits au XXe siècle* (Paris: Presses de Sciences Po, 1997), 59–71. See also Pascal Vennesson, "Institution and Air Power: The Making of the French Air Force," *Journal of Strategic Studies* 18, no. 1 (1995), http://www.tandfonline.com/doi/abs/10.1080/01402399508437579.

6. Claude Carlier, "Le destin manqué de l'aéronautique française," in Martel, *De 1940 à nos jours*, 432.

7. See Karl-Heinz Frieser, *The Blitzkrieg Legend: The 1940 Campaign in the West* (Annapolis MD: Naval Institute Press, 2013).

8. See Vennesson, *Les chevaliers de l'air*, 172.

9. See Général Ely, "L'appui aérien," chap. 12 in *Les enseignements de la guerre d'Indochine (1945–1954)* (Paris: Service historique de la Défense, collection Références, 2011).

10. See Samy Cohen, *La défaite des généraux—Le pouvoir politique et l'armée sous la Ve République* (Paris: Fayard, 1994).

11. See Lucien Poirier, *Des stratégies nucléaires* (Paris: Hachette, 1977).

12. For a good presentation of French doctrine in English, see Bruno Tertrais, "'Destruction assurée': The Origins and Development of French Nuclear Strategy, 1945–1981," in *Getting MAD: Nuclear Mutual Assured Destruction, Its Origins and Practice*, ed. Henry Sokolski (Carlisle PA: Strategic Studies Institute, 2004), 51–122. For the classic exposition of the doctrine in French, see Poirier, *Des stratégies nucléaires*.

13. On post-Vietnam innovations in the U.S. Air Force, see Richard Hallion, *Storm over Iraq: Air Power and the Gulf War* (Washington DC: Smithsonian Institution Press, 1992); and Benjamin Lambeth, *The Transformation of American Air Power* (Ithaca NY: Cornell University Press, 2000).

14. See Etienne de Durand, "La "mère" de toutes nos batailles," *Guerres mondiales et conflits contemporains*, no. 244 (December 2011): 9–30.

15. See Michael Gordon and Bernard Trainor, *The Generals' War: The Inside Story of the Conflict in the Gulf* (Boston: Little, Brown, 1995), 221.

16. See Louis Gautier, "Le fait aérien et la décision politique depuis la fin de la guerre froide," in *Politique, défense, puissance: 30 d'opérations aériennes*, ed. Jérôme de Lespinois (Paris: CESA–La Documentation française, 2011).

17. See Claude Carlier, "L'aéronautique et l'espace, 1945–1993," in Martel, *De 1940 à nos jours*, 473–74.

18. In the vast literature spurred by the 1991 victory, see for instance Eliot Cohen, "A Revolution in Warfare," *Foreign Affairs*, March/April 1996, 37–54; and Benjamin Lambeth, "The Technology Revolution in Air Warfare," *Survival*, Spring 1997, 65–83.

19. On U.S. strategic culture, see Colin Gray, "Strategy in the Nuclear Age: The United States, 1945–1991," in *The Making of Strategy: Rulers, States, and War*, ed. Williamson Murray, Alvin Bernstein, and MacGregor Knox (Cambridge, UK: Cambridge University Press, 1996), 589–98. On French initial attitude to the RMA, see, for instance, Bruno Tertrais, "Faut-il croire à la révolution dans les affaires militaires?" *Politique étrangère*, no. 3 (1998): 611–29.

20. For a defense of land power and a pointed criticism of transformation and associated concepts such as effects-based operations (EBO), see Vincent Desportes, *La guerre probable*, 2nd ed. (Paris: Economica, 2008), 105–20.

21. See Michel Goya, "Dix millions de dollars le milicien-La crise du modèle occidental de guerre limitée de haute technologie," *Politique étrangère*, no. 1 (2007): 191–202.

22. For French publications on air power, see Col. Régis Chamagne, *L'art de la guerre aérienne* (Paris: Esprit Du Livre Eds, 2004); and Joseph Henrotin, *L'Air power au 21e siècle. Enjeux et perspectives de la stratégie aérienne* (Brussels: Bruylant, 2005).

23. See Etienne de Durand and Bastien Irondelle, *Stratégie aérienne comparée: France, Etats-Unis, Royaume-Uni*, Les documents du C2SD (Paris: C2SD-SGA, 2006). A counterargument that qualifies the air force's "doctrinal torpor" and presents actual doctrinal documents can be found in Jérôme de Lespinois, ed., *La doctrine des forces aériennes françaises 1912–1976* (Paris: CESA–La documentation française, 2010).

24. See Gautier, "Le fait aérien et la décision politique depuis la fin de la guerre froide."

25. See Paul Quilès and François Lamy, *Kosovo: une guerre d'exceptions*, rapport d'information no. 2022 (Paris: Commission de la défense, Assemblée nationale, 2002), 102.

26. The Harfang was previously known as the SIDM (for Système intérimaire de drone MALE).

27. Jean-Marc Tanguy, *Harmattan. Récits et révélations* (Paris: Nimrod, 2012), 114.

28. This total of around 5,600 air sorties breaks down as follows: 3,100 offensive sorties, 1,200 reconnaissance sorties, 400 for air defense, 340 for air control, and 580 for refueling. On all these figures, see http://www.defense.gouv.fr/operations/actualites/libye-point-de-situation-n-50-bilan-de-l-operation-unified-protector.

29. See Allied Joint Force Command Naples, SHAPE, NATO HQ, "NATO and Libya: Operational Media Update," Operation Unified Protector, October 31, 2011, http://www.jfcnaples.nato.int/Unified_Protector/page191573217.aspx.

30. For a detailed account of the March 19 raid to protect Benghazi, see Jean-Christophe Notin, *La vérité sur notre guerre en Libye* (Paris: Fayard, 2012), 154.

31. Notin, *La vérité sur notre guerre en Libye*, 288, 314, 368, 377, 437.

32. These figures are compiled from the information provided by the Ministry of Defense. See Ministére de la Défense, "Actualité," Operations: Mali, http://www.defense.gouv.fr/operations/mali/actualite.

33. There are three units of Commandos Parachutistes de l'Air: CPA 10 is part of the special forces, whereas CPA 20 and 30 belong to the regular armée de l'Air.

34. Sophie Lefeez, "Toujours plus chers? Complexité des armements et inflation des coûts militaires," *Focus stratégique*, no. 42 (February 2013): 8–9, claims that the difference in operating costs between the Rafale and earlier generation is threefold or higher. As the French Air Force is getting used to the Rafale, however, the costs have subsided, as they did with previous generations, such as Mirage 2000. It is therefore difficult to ascertain the exact margin of "military inflation" from one generation to the next.

35. See Etienne de Durand, "The Hidden Side of Air Power," *Défense nationale et sécurité collective*, June 2007, 27–34.

36. *Livre blanc sur la défense et la sécurité nationale* (Paris: La documentaire française, 2008), 291.

37. See Jean-Paul Paloméros, *Audition Paloméros à l'Assemblée Nationale*, October 2011, 6. See the link: http://www.assemblee-nationale.fr/13/cr-cdef/11-12/c1112004.asp.

38. *Livre blanc sur la défense et la sécurité nationale* (Paris: La documentation française, 2013), 139.

39. See Paloméros, Audition, 7.

40. See *Livre blanc* (2013), 93.

41. See Denis Mercier, in *Compte rendu, Commission de la défense nationale et des forces armées*, October 16, 2012, 8: "je souligne que le Mirage 2000D au potentiel de vie encore élevé nous permettrait de disposer d'un avion, dont il nous faut déterminer le niveau de rénovation et le format, capable d'effectuer à moindre coût une large gamme de nos missions en complément du Rafale."

42. See Mercier, in *Compte rendu*, 7.

43. See *Livre blanc* (2013), 89.

2. German Air Power

1. On the changing nature of nuclear and missile proliferation, see Paul Bracken, *The New Nuclear Age: Strategy, Danger and the New Power Politics* (New York: Times Books, 2012).

2. Karl Müllner, *Luftmacht 2030* (Berlin: Luftwaffe, September 2012), http://augengeradeaus.net/wp-content/uploads/2012/08/Luftmacht-2030.pdf, 10.

3. The CIA's recent use of UAVs to kill terrorists seems like an innovative approach. Although this tactic may be similar to terrorist tactics—the strike comes from out of the blue and the perpetrator is hard to apprehend—it clearly has different targets and intentions.

4. Robert Kaplan offers a readable, insightful discussion of geography and strategy in his many books, including, most recently, *Monsoon: The Indian Ocean and the Future of American Power* (New York: Random House, 2011); and *The Revenge of Geography: What the Map Tells Us about Coming Conflicts and the Battle against Fate* (New York: Random House, 2012).

5. German Ministry of Defense, *Defence Policy Guidelines: Safeguarding National Interests—Assuming International Responsibility—Shaping Security Together* [official English translation] (Berlin, May 27, 2011), http://www.nato.diplo.de/contentblob/3150944/Daten/1318881/VM_deMaiziere_180511_eng_DLD.pdf, 3.

6. German Ministry of Defense, *Defence Policy Guidelines*, 4.

7. German Ministry of Defense, *Defence Policy Guidelines*, 1.

8. See De Maizière: Rede zur Bundeswehrreform in Berlin, "Gravierende Mängel bei der Bundeswehr," *Süddeutsche Zeitung*, May 18, 2011, http://www.sueddeutsche

.de/politik/bundeswehrreform-rede-in-berlin-de-maizire-beklagt-gravierende-maengel-bei-armee-1.1098936.

9. German Ministry of Defense, 1994 White Paper on Defense (Bonn, 1994). The official English translation is available on the Canadian Ministry of Defense site: http://publications.gc.ca/collections/collection_2012/dn-nd/D3-6-1994-eng.pdf. The sections here refer to Par. 245–53.

10. German Ministry of Defense, *Verteidigungshaushalt 2012: Der Verteidigungshaushalt–Einzelplan 14 des Bundeshaushalts–ist der finanzielle Rahmen der Bundeswehr* (Berlin, January 4, 2012), http://www.bmvg.de/portal/a/bmvg/!ut/p/c4/Nck9doAgDEDhs3gBSkxc3lyFupCiDTb8aKDg9wUxl9_0yIdewsYOhe-EAVbYDp7tq2xsTkVOXIQyl6gaZSE-2dXkyowlc2jGrSdlujbopviizp4fj1-gd5nd8bI!.

11. NATO, "Financial and Economic Data Relating to NATO Defence," news release, April 13, 2012, http://www.nato.int/nato_static/assets/pdf/pdf_2012_04/20120413_pr_cp_2012_047_rev1.pdf, 6.

12. German Parliament, *Bundeshaushalt 2012* (Berlin, August 12, 2011), http://dipbt.bundestag.de/dip21/btd/17/066/1706601.pdf, 20.

13. "De Maizière stellt Details der Bundeswehr-Reform vor," *Die Zeit*, September 21, 2011, http://www.zeit.de/politik/deutschland/2011-09/bundeswehr-streitkraefte-maiziere.

14. Thomas de Maizière, "Der Auftrag der Bundeswehr, Ausgangspunkt und Ziel der Neuausrichtung," *Europäische Sicherheit und Technik*, January 2013, 10 (author's translation).

15. Introductory letter from Karl Müllner, *Luftmacht 2030*, 5 (author's translation).

16. On the lessons of Unified Protector, see Erica D. Borghard and Costantino Pischedda, "Allies and Airpower in Libya," *Parameters*, Spring 2012, 63–74.

17. Ulrich Rapreger, "Neuausrichtung der Luftwaffe," *Europäische Sicherheit und Technik*, January 2012, 30 (author's translation).

18. "Interview mit Generalleutnant Karl Müllner, Inspekteur der Luftwaffe, 'Unbemannte Flugzeuge werden eine wichtige Rolle spielen' [Unmanned aircraft will play an important role]," *Europäische Sicherheit und Technik*, September 2012, 28 (author's translation).

19. See Thomas de Maizière, *Dresdner Erlass*, March 21, 2012, http://www.bmvg.de/portal/a/bmvg/!ut/p/c4/NYvBCsIwEET_aDcBQfFm7UUQQT1ovUjaLGGhScq6rRc_3uTQGXgwPAZfWJrcwsEp5-RGfGI38L7_Qh-XAJETf5SE5wie5L1uEPKU8FHvnmDIibRSKSkXBnGaBaYsOlYzixQD7LEztm2MNWvsb3c_Hy_Xzda0p-aGU4yHP60iXEQ!/.

20. According to the Luftwaffe Press Office, currently valid English translations exist for the following commands: Einsatzführungskommando der Bundeswehr (Bundeswehr Joint Operations Command); Kommando Luftwaffe (Headquar-

ters of the German Air Force); Zentrum Luftoperationen (Air Operations Command); Kommando Einsatzverbände Luftwaffe (Air Force Operational Forces Command); Kommando Unterstützungsverbände Luftwaffe (Air Force Support Forces Command).

21. Müllner, *Luftmacht 2030*, 12.

22. Müllner, *Luftmacht 2030*, 11.

23. See Sven Heursch und Jörg Sievers, "Zentrum Luftoperationen: Kompetenzträger für Luftmacht," *Europäische Sicherheit und Technik*, October 2012, 34 (author's translation).

24. See German Ministry of Defense, *Die Neuausrichtung der Bundeswehr* (Berlin, March 2012), http://www.bmvg.de/portal/a/bmvg/!ut/p/c4/DcrLDYAgDADQWVygvXtzC_VWsIEGLITyWV_zrg9v_ClNCdSlKGU88fKyuwXunQFMfOQWWbrVkqVLAjf0YVscGygPGtb-04cGrOnYPha7rVM!/, 47–55.

25. German Ministry of Defense, *Die Neuausrichtung der Bundeswehr*, 52 (author's translation).

26. Müllner, *Luftmacht 2030*, 12.

27. See "NATO Air Headquarters Ramstein Passes Missile Defence Test," *NATO News*, April 4, 2012, http://www.nato.int/cps/en/natolive/news_86018.htm.

28. "NATO Declares Interim Missile Defence Capability," *NATO News*, May 20, 2012, http://www.nato.int/cps/en/natolive/news_87599.htm?selectedLocale=en.

29. Friedrich Wilhelm Ploeger, "Ballistic Missile Defense," *Europäische Sicherheit und Technik*, August 2012, 39 (author's translation).

30. Ploeger, "Ballistic Missile Defense," 39.

31. Ploeger, "Ballistic Missile Defense," 39.

32. See Autorenteam Flugabwehrgruppe, "Das Flugabwehrwaffensystem Mantis," *Europäische Sicherheit und Technik*, August 2012, 88.

33. See Norbert Bäumel, "Fregatte 124 in der Luftverteidigung," *Europäische Sicherheit und Technik*, January 2013, 78.

34. See Ulrich Rapreger, "IRIS-T SL," *Europäische Sicherheit und Technik*, April 2012, 88.

35. See Regine Friedberger, "Überlegungen zur deutschen Luftverteidigungsarchitektur," *Europäische Sicherheit und Technik*, October 2012, 70–73.

36. See Wolfgang Deffner, "Strategische Mobilität," *Europäische Sicherheit und Technik*, January 2013, 57–59.

37. Ulrich Rapreger, "Lufttransport–Zentrale Aufgabe der Luftwaffe," *Europäische Sicherheit und Technik*, April 2012, 57.

38. Luftwaffe, *Ende einer Erfolgsstory* (Berlin, December 1, 2010), http://www.luftwaffe.de/portal/a/luftwaffe/!ut/p/c4/NYu5DsJADAX_yE5SAKIjQiAajiqEzmysYGmPyJik4ePZLXgjTTN6-MBMpFlGMkmRPN6xd7J9LuAXMKY

ALPENpO41Myg7x9iV08DgUmQrNo4m2aOSJYUpqflSPqq5gAzYV_W-rVbVf_V3096O165ZN6fz4YJTCLsftXl2Vg!!/.

39. See "Heron 1: 10.000 Flugstunden über Afghanistan," *Flugrevue*, July 30, 2012, http://www.flugrevue.de/de/ luftwaffe/uav/heron-1–10000-flugstunden-ueber-afghanistan.97077.htm.

40. See "Europas größte Drohne über Deutschland getestet," www.faznet.de, January 11, 2013, http://www.faz.net/aktuell/wirtschaft/unternehmen/eurohawk-europas-groesste-drohne-ueber-deutschland-getestet-12022493.html.

41. See Peter Preylowski, "NATO Alliance Ground Surveillance: Eine neue Fähigkeit für das Bündnis," *Europäische Sicherheit und Technik*, September 2012, 78.

42. See Sven Kühberger, "Galileo—Das Europäische Satellitennavigationssystem," *Europäische Sicherheit und Technik*, June 2012, 88–91; and Thomas Beer, "GMES: Das europäische Erdbeobachtungsprogramm," *Europäische Sicherheit und Technik*, December 2012, 110–13.

43. Müllner, *Luftmacht 2030*, 15.

44. Richard Offinger and Guido Plörer, "Einsatz von Luftmacht im Rahmen von COIN," *Europäische Sicherheit und Technik*, December 2012, 23 (author's translation).

45. "Interview mit Generalleutnant Karl Müllner."

46. "Interview mit Generalleutnant Karl Müllner."

47. Müllner, *Luftmacht 2030*, 12.

48. See Ulrich Rapreger, "Air Surface Integration," *Europäische Sicherheit und Technik*, June 2012, 32.

49. "Interview mit Generalleutnant Karl Müllner."

50. See Dietmar Klos, "Unbemannte Luftfahrzeuge im Einsatz," *Europäische Sicherheit und Technik*, April 2012, 78–81.

51. See "Interview with Alexander Müller, RUAG Aerospace, 'Der Predator B erfüllt die Forderungen der Luftwaffe,'" *Europäische Sicherheit und Technik*, June 2012, 97.

52. "Afghanistan-Einsatz: Was die Bundeswehr mit bewaffneten Drohnen plant," *Süddeutsche Zeitung*, September 24, 2012, http://www.sueddeutsche.de/politik/mehr-als-gefahren-aufklaerung-bundeswehr-will-bewaffnete-drohnen-kaufen-1.1476829.

53. See Markus Becker, "Super-Drohne der Bundeswehr absolviert ersten Testflug," *Der Spiegel*, January 11, 2013, http://www.spiegel.de/wissenschaft/technik/langstrecken-drohne-euro-hawk-absolviert-ersten-testflug-a-877077.html.

54. "Interview mit Generalleutnant Karl Müllner," 34.

55. See Veit Medick, "Bundeswehr im Ausland: Regierung will zügig Kampfdrohnen anschaffen," *Der Spiegel*, January 24, 2013, http://www.spiegel.de/politik/deutschland/bundesregierung-draengt-auf-einsatz-bewaffneter-drohnen-a-879547.html.

56. See Michael Sturzbecher, "Kooperationsvereinbarung Luftwaffe-Wirtschaft," *Europäische Sicherheit und Technik*, January 2012, 53.

57. Müllner, *Luftmacht 2030*, 11.

58. See Michael Rühle, "Die Drei Herausforderungen der NATO," *Frankfurter Allgemeine Zeitung*, March 9, 2013.

3. Turkish Air Power

1. Lindsay Peacock and Alexander von Rosenbach, *Jane's World Air Forces*, no. 37 (Coulsdon, Surrey: IHS Jane's, 2013), 689, 692.

2. Nicholas de Larrinaga, "Turkey Finishes F-16 Build Programme," *Jane's Defence Weekly* 50, no. 1 (January 2, 2013): 13.

3. Lindsay Peacock and Alexander von Rosenbach, *Jane's World Air Forces*, no. 36 (Coulsdon, Surrey: IHS Jane's, 2012), 678.

4. Christian F. Anrig, *The Quest for Relevant Air Power: Continental European Responses to the Air Power Challenges of the Post–Cold War Era* (Maxwell Air Force Base AL: Air University Press, 2011), 22–23; Peacock and von Rosenbach, *Jane's World Air Forces*, no. 36, 678.

5. Turkish Air Force, "Today's Air Force: Aircraft in the Inventory," accessed October 11, 2012, http://www.hvkk.tsk.tr/en/EnvanterdekiUcaklar.aspx?id=7.

6. *The Military Balance 2012* (Abingdon, Oxfordshire: Routledge, 2012), 164.

7. Peacock and von Rosenbach, *Jane's World Air Forces*, no. 36, 678.

8. Peacock and von Rosenbach, *Jane's World Air Forces*, no. 36, 678, 681.

9. Peacock and von Rosenbach, *Jane's World Air Forces*, no. 36, 681.

10. Peacock and von Rosenbach, Jane's World Air Forces, no. 37, 689.

11. Turkish Air Force, "Firsts in the 100th Anniversary: Aviation Industry," last updated January 21, 2011, http://www.hvkk.tsk.tr/en/IcerikDetay.aspx?id=120.

12. F. Stephen Larrabee, *Turkey as a U.S. Security Partner* (Santa Monica CA: Rand, 2008), 14–15.

13. Ilter Turan, "The United States and Turkey: Limiting Unilateralism," in *Hegemony Constrained: Evasion, Modification, and Resistance to American Foreign Policy*, ed. Davis B. Bobrow (Pittsburgh: University of Pittsburgh Press, 2008), 88–89.

14. Larrabee, *Turkey as a U.S. Security Partner*, 27.

15. Larrabee, *Turkey as a U.S. Security Partner*, 26.

16. F. Stephen Larrabee, "Turkey Rediscovers the Middle East," *Foreign Affairs* 86, no. 4 (July/August 2007): 104–5.

17. Turan, "United States and Turkey," 90–91.

18. Turan, "United States and Turkey," 93–94.

19. Walter J. Boyne, *Operation Iraqi Freedom: What Went Right, What Went Wrong, and Why* (New York: Forge, 2003), 68–69.

20. Umit Enginsoy and Burak Ege Bekdil, "Turks May Give 20 Mi-17 Helos to Afghanistan," *Defense News* 24, no. 10 (March 9, 2009): 1.

21. *Strategic Survey 2010: The Annual Review of World Affairs* (Abingdon, Oxfordshire: Routledge, 2010), 183.

22. *Strategic Survey 2007* (Abingdon, Oxfordshire: Routledge, 2007), 183.

23. Larrabee, "Turkey Rediscovers the Middle East," 106.

24. Umit Enginsoy and Burak Ege Bekdil, "Turkey's Balancing Act: While Conventional Threats Remain, Asymmetric Conflict Has Dominated," *Defense News* 24, no. 16 (April 20, 2009): 11.

25. Larrabee, "Turkey Rediscovers the Middle East," 106.

26. *Strategic Survey 2008* (Abingdon, Oxfordshire: Routledge, 2008), 181.

27. Burak Ege Bekdil and Umit Enginsoy, "Syria Challenge May Force Turks to Review Procurement," *Defense News* 27, no. 39 (October 15, 2012): 21.

28. Gareth Jenkins, "Smugglers Paradise: Illegal Trade along the Turkish-Syrian Border," *Jane's Intelligence Review* 25, no. 9 (September 2013): 46.

29. Larrabee, "Turkey Rediscovers the Middle East," 109.

30. Larrabee, "Turkey Rediscovers the Middle East," 107.

31. *Strategic Survey 2007*, 183.

32. *Strategic Survey 2010*, 178.

33. Larrabee, "Turkey Rediscovers the Middle East," 107.

34. Larrabee, *Turkey as a U.S. Security Partner*, 11.

35. *Strategic Survey 2010*, 179.

36. *Strategic Survey 2011: The Annual Review of World Affairs* (Abingdon, Oxfordshire: Routledge, 2011), 240–41.

37. *Strategic Survey 2008*, 176.

38. *Strategic Survey 2008*, 176.

39. *Strategic Survey 2008*, 177–78; *Strategic Survey 2011*, 236.

40. Larrabee, *Turkey as a U.S. Security Partner*, 4.

41. *Strategic Survey 2010*, 175.

42. *Strategic Survey 2009: The Annual Review of World Affairs* (Abingdon, Oxfordshire: Routledge, 2009), 190.

43. *Strategic Survey 2010*, 182; Larrabee, *Turkey as a U.S. Security Partner*, 22–23.

44. "EU-Beitritt: Erdogan drängt Merkel zur Hilfe," *Tagesanzeiger*, February 25, 2013, http://www.tagesanzeiger.ch/ausland/europa/EUBeitritt-Erdogan-draengt-Merkel-zur-Hilfe/story/28072149.

45. Larrabee, *Turkey as a U.S. Security Partner*, 31–32; *Strategic Survey 2009*, 184.

46. *Strategic Survey 2008*, 177, 182.

47. Burak Ege Bekdil and Umit Enginsoy, "Turkey Reshapes Military after Top Leaders Resign," *Defense News* 26, no. 29 (August 8, 2011): 7; Lale Sariibrahimoglu, "Turkey Takes Legal Step to End Justification for Coups," *Jane's Defence Weekly* 50, no. 27 (July 3, 2013): 8.

48. *Strategic Survey 2011*, 243; "Turkey Hands Former CGS Life Sentence for Coup Plot," *Jane's Defence Weekly* 50, no. 33 (August 14, 2013): 5.

49. Bekdil and Enginsoy, "Turkey Reshapes Military after Top Leaders Resign," 7.

50. Peacock and von Rosenbach, *Jane's World Air Forces*, no. 36, 679.

51. Larrabee, "Turkey Rediscovers the Middle East," 110.

52. Larrabee, *Turkey as a U.S. Security Partner*, 19.

53. Ed Blanche, "Israel and Turkey Look to Extend Their Influence into Central Asia," *Jane's Intelligence Review* 13, no. 8 (August 2001): 34.

54. Blanche, "Israel and Turkey Look to Extend Their Influence into Central Asia," 35.

55. Emily Chorley and Scott Johnson, "Nuclear Fallout: Israel's Campaign against Iran," *Jane's Intelligence Review* 24, no. 4 (April 2012): 49.

56. Blanche, "Israel and Turkey Look to Extend Their Influence into Central Asia," 34.

57. Blanche, "Israel and Turkey Look to Extend Their Influence into Central Asia," 34.

58. Larrabee, "Turkey Rediscovers the Middle East," 110.

59. *Strategic Survey 2009*, 192.

60. *Strategic Survey 2010*, 177; Barak Ravid, "Israel Hits Back at Turkey over Scuppered Air Force Drill: Turkey Bans Israel from International Air Force Drill; U.S. Then Withdraws, Leading to Cancellation of Drill," *Haaretz*, October 11, 2009, http://www.haaretz.com/misc/article-print-page/israel-hits-back-at-turkey-over-scuppered-air-force-drill-1.6319?trailingPath=2.169%2c2.216%2c.

61. Burak Ege Bekdil and Umit Enginsoy, "Turkey, China in Exercises: NATO Blanches as Ankara Looks East," *Defense News* 25, no. 39 (October 18, 2010): 1, 8; *Strategic Survey 2011*, 241.

62. *Strategic Survey 2010*, 178.

63. *Strategic Survey 2010*, 177.

64. Guy Anderson and Nicholas De Larrinaga, "Turkey's Row with Israel Opens Up Opportunities," *Jane's Defence Weekly* 48, no. 37 (September 14, 2011): 38.

65. *Strategic Survey 2010*, 177.

66. Turkish Air Force, "Firsts in the 100th Anniversary: Operations Missions," last updated January 21, 2011, http://www.hvkk.tsk.tr/en/IcerikDetay.aspx?id=125; Peacock and von Rosenbach, *Jane's World Air Forces*, no. 36, 678.

67. Turkish Air Force, "Firsts in the 100th Anniversary."

68. Tim Ripley, *Air War Bosnia: UN and NATO Airpower* (Shrewsbury, UK: Airlife Publishing, 1996), 9, 18.

69. Ripley, *Air War Bosnia*, 39, 47.

70. The German contingent was relegated to support defensive actions of the multinational Rapid Reaction Force. See Anrig, *Quest for Relevant Air Power*, 179.

71. Richard L. Sargent, "Aircraft Used in Deliberate Force," in *Deliberate Force—A Case Study in Effective Air Campaigning: Final Report of the Air University Balkans*

Air Campaign Study, ed. Robert C. Owen (Maxwell Air Force Base AL: Air University Press, 2000), 209.

72. Sargent, "Aircraft Used in Deliberate Force," 219.

73. NATO air forces that had airlifters equipped with self-defense systems continued the airlift effort. See Ripley, *Air War Bosnia*, 9.

74. Mark J. Conversino, "Executing Deliberate Force, 30 August–14 September 1995," in Owen, *Deliberate Force*, 166.

75. Richard L. Sargent, "Weapons Used in Deliberate Force," in Owen, *Deliberate Force*, 258–59.

76. Anrig, *Quest for Relevant Air Power*, 177, 199.

77. Karl Mueller, "The Demise of Yugoslavia and the Destruction of Bosnia: Strategic Causes, Effects, and Responses," in Owen, *Deliberate Force*, 17.

78. John E. Peters, et al., *European Contributions to Operation Allied Force: Implications for Transatlantic Cooperation* (Santa Monica CA: Rand, 2001), 19.

79. Benjamin S. Lambeth, *NATO's Air War for Kosovo: A Strategic and Operational Assessment* (Santa Monica CA: Rand, 2001), 33–34.

80. Lambeth, *NATO's Air War for Kosovo*, 164.

81. Turan, "United States and Turkey," 89; Boyne, *Operation Iraqi Freedom*, 41; Larrabee, *Turkey as a U.S. Security Partner*, 25.

82. Anrig, *Quest for Relevant Air Power*, 29.

83. Larrabee, "Turkey Rediscovers the Middle East," 105.

84. *Strategic Survey 2008*, 180–81.

85. *Strategic Survey 2008*, 181; Peacock and von Rosenbach, *Jane's World Air Forces*, no. 36, 678.

86. *Strategic Survey 2009*, 189.

87. Umit Enginsoy and Burak Ege Bekdil, "Fallout with Israel May Hurt Turkey's War with PKK," *Defense News* 26, no. 33 (September 12, 2011): 28.

88. Umit Enginsoy and Burak Ege Bekdil, "Turks Might Cancel Long-Range Air Defense System," *Defense News* 27, no. 40 (October 22, 2012): 43.

89. *Strategic Survey 2011*, 238.

90. Elisabeth Quintana, "The War from the Air," in *Short War, Long Shadow: The Political and Military Legacies of the 2011 Libya Campaign*, RUSI Whitehall Report 1-12, ed. Adrian Johnson and Saqeb Mueen (London: Royal United Services Institute for Defence and Security Studies, 2012), 33.

91. Scott Wilson and Karen DeYoung, "U.S. Appears to Be Closer to Turning over Command of Libya Operation," *Washington Post*, March 22, 2011, http://articles.washingtonpost.com/2011-03-22/world/35208188_1_nato-role-operation-odyssey-dawn-libyan-operation.

92. Ian Traynor, "Turkey and France Clash over Libya Air Campaign," *Guardian*, March 24, 2011, http://www.guardian.co.uk/world/2011/mar/24/turkey-france-clash-libya-campaign.

93. Mary Beth Sheridan and Greg Jaffe, "Coalition Agrees to Put NATO in Charge of No-Fly Zone in Libya," *Washington Post*, March 25, 2011, http://www.washingtonpost.com/world/coalition-agrees- to-put-nato-in-charge-of-no-fly-zone-in-libya/2011/03/24/ABlZNLSB_story.html.

94. NATO, "Operation Unified Protector: Final Mission Stats," fact sheet, November 2, 2011, http://www.nato.int/nato_static/assets/pdf/pdf_2011_11/20111108_111107-factsheet_up_factsfigures_en.pdf.

95. Traynor, "Turkey and France Clash over Libya Air Campaign."

96. *Strategic Survey 2011*, 239.

97. Italian Air Force General Staff, information forwarded to the author by Gregory Alegi, journalist, historian, and lecturer at the Italian Air Force Academy, November 13, 2012.

98. Burak Ege Bekdil, Ankara-based *Defense News International* journalist, e-mail to the author, December 9, 2012.

99. Shashank Joshi, "The Complexity of Arab Support," in Johnson and Mueen, *Short War, Long Shadow*, 64.

100. "Libya Conflict: Cameron and Sarkozy Visit Tripoli," BBC *News Africa*, September 15, 2011, http://www.bbc.co.uk/news/world-africa-14926308; "Libya Conflict: As It Happened," BBC *News*, September 16, 2011, http://www.bbc.co.uk/news/world-africa-14945510.

101. Liz Sly, "Turkey Says It Will Take 'Steps' after Determining That Syria Shot Down Missing Jet," *Washington Post*, June 22, 2012, http://www.washingtonpost.com/world/middle_east/turkey-investigates-whether-syria-shot-down-missing-jet/2012/06/22/gJQAtSLdvV_print.html.

102. Greg Jaffe, "Syrian Downing of Turkish Jet Serves as Warning," *Washington Post*, June 26, 2012, http://articles.washingtonpost.com/2012-06-26/world/35461782_1_turkish-jet-syrians-president-bashar.

103. Sly, "Turkey Says It Will Take 'Steps' after Determining That Syria Shot Down Missing Jet."

104. Liz Sly, "Turkey Threatens Military Retaliation along Syria Border, Drawing Defiance from Assad," *Washington Post*, June 26, 2012, http://www.washingtonpost.com/world/nato-condemns-downing-of-turkish-jet-by-syria/2012/06/26/gJQAjZqs3v_print.html.

105. "Turkey PM Erdogan Issues Syria Border Warning," BBC *News Middle East*, June 26, 2012, http://www.bbc.co.uk/news/world-middle-east-18584872.

106. Sly, "Turkey Threatens Military Retaliation along Syria Border."

107. Sly, "Turkey Threatens Military Retaliation along Syria Border."

108. Sly, "Turkey Threatens Military Retaliation along Syria Border"; "Turkey Scrambles F-16 Jets on Syria Border," *BBC News Europe*, July 1, 2012, http://www.bbc.co.uk/news/world-europe-18666165.

109. "Turkey Hits Targets inside Syria after Border Deaths," *BBC News Middle East*, October 4, 2012, http://www.bbc.co.uk/news/world-middle-east-19822253; Lale Sariibrahimoglu, "Turkey Approves Military Action against Syria," *Jane's Defence Weekly* 49, no. 41 (October 10, 2012): 5.

110. "Turkey PM Recep Tayyip Erdogan 'Not to Start Syria War,'" *BBC News Europe*, October 4, 2012, http://www.bbc.co.uk/news/world-europe-19838470.

111. "Syrian Passenger Plane Forced to Land in Turkey," *BBC News Middle East*, October 11, 2012, http://www.bbc.co.uk/news/world-middle-east-19905247.

112. Blanche, "Israel and Turkey Look to Extend Their Influence into Central Asia," 35.

113. Edin Omanovic, "11 October 2012: Turkey's Interception of a Syrian Passenger Aircraft," Stockholm International Peace Research Institute, http://www.sipri.org/media/expert-comments/Omanovic_11oct.

114. NATO, "Statement by the NATO Secretary General on Patriot Missile Deployment to Turkey," November 21, 2012, http://www.nato.int/cps/en/sid-b21864a5–5f600c32/natolive/news_91426.htm.

115. Burak Ege Bekdil and Umit Enginsoy, "Turkish Patriot Deployment Could Derail $4B Missile Deal," *Defense News* 27, no. 46 (December 3, 2012): 1.

116. "NATO Agrees to Augment Turkey's Air-Defence Capabilities," *NATO News*, December 4, 2012, http://www.nato.int/cps/en/natolive/news_92861.htm.

117. Nick de Larrinaga, "Anatolian Ambition," *Jane's Defence Weekly* 50, no. 17 (April 24, 2013): 25.

118. Lale Sariibrahimoglu, "Turkish Defence Budget Rises by 11.8%," *Jane's Defence Weekly* 49, no. 45 (November 7, 2012): 14.

119. Guy Anderson and Nicholas de Larrinaga, "Strong Trajectory," *Jane's Defence Weekly* 48, no. 51 (December 21, 2011): 30–31.

120. Anderson and de Larrinaga, "Strong Trajectory," 32.

121. Umit Enginsoy and Burak Ege Bekdil, "Can Turkey Afford Its Extensive Defense Plans?" *Defense News* 27, no. 30 (July 30, 2012): 4.

122. Aaron Mehta, David Pugliese, and Tom Kington, "Canada Reconsiders JSF: Italy's Leading PM Candidate Would Trim F-35 Buy," *Defense News* 27, no. 47 (December 10, 2012): 6.

123. Anderson and de Larrinaga, "Turkey's Row with Israel Opens Up Opportunities," 38.

124. Burak Ege Bekdil and Umit Enginsoy, "Italy Winning Majority of Turkey's Purchases," *Defense News* 24, no. 4 (January 26, 2009): 10.

125. Lale Sariibrahimoglu, "Turkey to Buy 100 JSFs for USD 16 Billion," *Jane's Defence Weekly* 49, no. 9 (February 29, 2012): 6.

126. Burak Ege Bekdil, Ankara-based *Defense News International* journalist, e-mail to the author, January 29, 2013.

127. Peacock and von Rosenbach, *Jane's World Air Forces*, no. 36, 682.

128. Undersecretariat for Defence Industries, "Ozgur Project," last modified December 12, 2011, http://www.ssm.gov.tr/home/projects/air/originalAirVhcl/Sayfalar/OzgurProject.aspx.

129. Umit Enginsoy and Burak Ege Bekdil, "Turk-Israeli Deals Threatened by Gaza," *Defense News* 24, no. 5 (February 2, 2009): 10.

130. Enginsoy and Bekdil, "Fallout with Israel May Hurt Turkey's War with PKK," 28.

131. Peacock and von Rosenbach, *Jane's World Air Forces*, no. 36, 684.

132. Zvi Bar'el, "Strained Ties with Turkey Hurt Israeli Defense Contract with U.S. Firm," *Haaretz*, March 15, 2012, http://www.haaretz.com/news/diplomacy-defense/strained-ties-with-turkey-hurt-israeli-defense-contract-with-u-s-firm-1.418900.

133. Gareth Jennings, "South Korea Receives First Peace Eye," *Jane's Defence Weekly* 48, no. 32 (August 10, 2011): 16; Burak Ege Bekdil and Umit Enginsoy, "Syria Challenge Exposes Turkish Shortcomings," *Defense News* 27, no. 31 (August 6, 2012): 6.

134. Umit Enginsoy and Burak Ege Bekdil, "Turks, U.S. Boost Cooperation; Equipment Transfers Lags," *Defense News* 27, no. 29 (July 23, 2012): 10, 12.

135. Anderson and de Larrinaga, "Strong Trajectory," 30–31.

136. Umit Enginsoy and Burak Ege Bekdil, "Erdogan's Re-Election Means 'Buy Turkish': Government to Support Local Arms Producers," *Defense News* 26, no. 24 (June 20, 2011): 26.

137. Anderson and de Larrinaga, "Strong Trajectory," 31.

138. Lale Sariibrahimoglu, "Turkey Steps Up Critical Technologies Development," *Jane's Defence Weekly* 49, no. 16 (April 18, 2012): 20.

139. Umit Enginsoy and Burak Bekdil, "Turkish Defense Exports Top $1B, Likely to Rise," *Defense News* 27, no. 33 (September 3, 2012): 9.

140. Sariibrahimoglu, "Turkey Steps Up Critical Technologies Development," 20.

141. Umit Enginsoy and Burak Ege Bekdil, "Raytheon Touts Local Benefits in Turkish Missile Defense Bid," *Defense News* 26, no. 23 (June 13, 2011): 24.

142. Bekdil and Enginsoy, "Italy Winning Majority of Turkey's Purchases," 10; Umit Enginsoy and Burak Ege Bekdil, "Turkey's Largest Helo Program Is Faltering," *Defense News International* 27, no. 32 (August 20, 2012): 14; Burak Ege Bekdil, "Indigenous Tank, Professional Army Backbone of Turkish Efforts," *Defense News International* 1, no. 20 (October 21, 2013): 16.

143. Burak Ege Bekdil, "A Plethora of Firsts for Turkey: Development of 'National Systems' Moves at Full Speed," *Defense News International* 1, no. 7 (April 29, 2013): 18.

144. Umit Enginsoy and Burak Ege Bekdil, "Turkey Remains Short of Helicopter Gunships," *Defense News* 24, no. 17 (April 27, 2009): 15.

145. Bekdil and Enginsoy, "Italy Winning Majority of Turkey's Purchases," 10.

146. Usman Ansari, "Turkey, Pakistan Seek Better Ties: But Money Short for Defense Deals," *Defense News* 27, no. 45 (November 26, 2012): 1, 8.

147. "Airbus Military and TAI to Support Turkey's A400M," *airforce-technology.com*, July 2, 2012, http://www.airforce-technology.com/news/newsairbus-military-tai-turkey-a400m.

148. Umit Enginsoy and Burak Ege Bekdil, "Turkey's Only Non-U.S. Fighter Option?" *Defense News* 26, no. 19 (May 16, 2011): 18.

149. Umit Enginsoy and Burak Ege Bekdil, "Turkey Delays Fighter Program," *Defense News* 27, no. 17 (April 30, 2012): 25.

150. Bekdil and Enginsoy, "Syria Challenge May Force Turks to Review Procurement," 21.

151. Enginsoy and Bekdil, "Turkey's Only Non-U.S. Fighter Option?" 18.

152. Enginsoy and Bekdil, "Turkey Delays Fighter Program," 25.

153. Burak Ege Bekdil and Umit Enginsoy, "Analysts Skeptical as Turkey, Brazil Pursue Defense Cooperation," *Defense News* 27, no. 21 (May 28, 2012): 7.

154. Bekdil and Enginsoy, "Italy Winning Majority of Turkey's Purchases," 10.

155. Enginsoy and Bekdil, "Turkey's Only Non-U.S. Fighter Option?" 18.

156. Bekdil e-mail, January 29, 2013.

157. Nicholas de Larrinaga, "TAI Reveals Three Concepts for Fifth-Gen Fighter," *Jane's Defence Weekly* 50, no. 20 (May 15, 2013): 6.

158. Burak Ege Bekdil, "Turkey Aims to Synch Air and Space Firepower," *Defense News International* 1, no. 11 (June 17, 2013): 14.

159. Lale Sariibrahimoglu and Nicholas de Larrinaga, "Turkey's Hürkuş Conducts Maiden Flight," *Jane's Defence Weekly* 50, no. 36 (September 4, 2013): 13; de Larrinaga, "Anatolian Ambition," 26.

160. Burak Ege Bekdil, "Turkey to Reissue F-35 Order: Ankara Must Also Choose Engine for Indigenous Fighter," *Defense News International* 1, no. 20 (October 21, 2013): 10.

161. Peacock and von Rosenbach, *Jane's World Air Forces*, no. 36, 684.

162. David Donald, "Turkey's Stand-Off Missile Revealed," *Jane's Defence Weekly* 48, no. 38 (September 21, 2011): 5; Burak Ege Bekdil and Umit Enginsoy, "Turkey Demonstrates 1st Locally Made Cruise Missile," *Defense News* 26, no. 24 (June 20, 2011): 26.

163. Huw Williams, "Tübitak-Sage Unveils Latest Ordnance-Guidance System," *Jane's International Defence Review* 46 (June 2013): 6.

164. Peacock and von Rosenbach, *Jane's World Air Forces*, no. 36, 678, 683.

165. Burak Ege Bekdil and Umit Enginsoy, "Turks Devise Ambitious Satellite Roadmap," *Defense News* 27, no. 4 (January 30, 2012): 14.

166. Bekdil and Enginsoy, "Turks Devise Ambitious Satellite Roadmap," 14.

167. Bekdil and Enginsoy, "Turks Devise Ambitious Satellite Roadmap," 14.

168. Murad Bayar, "Opening Speech" (presented at the International Conference on Air and Space Power [ICAP] 2013, Istanbul, March 28–29, 2013).

169. Bekdil, "Turkey Aims to Synch Air and Space Firepower," 15.

170. Bekdil, "Turkey Aims to Synch Air and Space Firepower," 15.

171. Anderson and de Larrinaga, "Strong Trajectory," 32; Enginsoy and Bekdil, "Turks Might Cancel Long-Range Air Defense System," 43.

172. Lale Sariibrahimoglu and Nicholas de Larrinaga, "Turkey to Build Armed Anka UAV as T-Loramids Decision Delayed," *Jane's Defence Weekly* 49, no. 30 (July 25, 2012): 15.

173. Bekdil and Enginsoy, "Syria Challenge May Force Turks to Review Procurement," 21.

174. Enginsoy and Bekdil, "Turkey Remains Short of Helicopter Gunships," 15; and Bekdil, "Indigenous Tank," 16.

175. Bekdil and Enginsoy, "Syria Challenge Exposes Turkish Shortcomings," 6.

176. Sariibrahimoglu and de Larrinaga, "Turkey to Build Armed Anka UAV as T-Loramids Decision Delayed," 15.

177. Burak Ege Bekdil, "Turkey Aims at 'Big Data,' Shared Tactical Picture," *Defense News International* 1, no. 16 (August 19, 2013): 12.

178. Huw Williams, "Anka Unaffected by Thielert Takeover," *Jane's Defence Weekly* 50, no. 39 (September 25, 2013): 12.

179. Bekdil and Enginsoy, "Turkey Demonstrates 1st Locally Made Cruise Missile," 26.

180. "Anka MALE Unmanned Aerial Vehicle (UAV), Turkey," *airforce-technology.com*, http://www.airforce-technology.com/projects/anka-male-unmanned-aerial-vehicle-uav-turkey; Bekdil and Enginsoy, "Turkey Demonstrates 1st Locally Made Cruise Missile," 26.

181. Peacock and von Rosenbach, *Jane's World Air Forces*, no. 36, 682.

182. Jeremy Binnie and Andy Dinville, "IMINT Shows Iranian Missile Accuracy," *Jane's Defence Weekly* 49, no. 44 (October 31, 2012): 6.

183. *The Military Balance 2012* (Abingdon, Oxfordshire: Routledge, 2012), 349.

184. "200-km Range Turkish Missile," *Defense News* 27, no. 41 (October 29, 2012): 3.

185. Burak Ege Bekdil and Umit Enginsoy, "Turkey Seeking Ballistic Missiles," *Defense News* 27, no. 3 (January 23, 2012): 11.

186. Bekdil and Enginsoy, "Turkey Seeking Ballistic Missiles," 11.

187. Larrabee, "Turkey Rediscovers the Middle East," 108.

188. Jung Sung-Ki, "S. Korea Unveils Cruise, Ballistic Missiles," *Defense News* 27, no. 16 (April 23, 2012): 16; James Hardy, "Seoul Confirms Plans to Extend Its Missile Ranges," *Jane's Defence Weekly* 49, no. 13 (March 28, 2012): 15.

189. Enginsoy and Bekdil, "Turks Might Cancel Long-Range Air Defense System," 43.

190. Burak Ege Bekdil and Umit Enginsoy, "Turkish Patriot Deployment Could Derail $4B Missile Deal," *Defense News* 27, no. 46 (December 3, 2012): 9.

191. Peacock and von Rosenbach, *Jane's World Air Forces*, no. 36, 683.

192. Sariibrahimoglu and de Larrinaga, "Turkey to Build Armed Anka UAV as T-Loramids Decision Delayed," 15.

193. Enginsoy and Bekdil, "Turks Might Cancel Long-Range Air Defense System," 43.

194. Burak Ege Bekdil, "Turkey May Adopt Chinese Air Defense System," *Defense News International* 1, no. 12 (June 24, 2013): 1.

195. Lale Sariibrahimoglu and Nicholas de Larrinaga, "Turkey Abandons USD4 Billion T-Loramids SAM System Buy," *Jane's Defence Weekly* 50, no. 5 (January 30, 2013): 5.

196. Nicholas de Larrinaga, "Ankara's T-Loramids SAM Contest Nears Conclusion," *Jane's Defence Weekly* 50, no. 20 (May 15, 2013): 8.

197. Lale Sariibrahimoglu and Nicholas de Larrinaga, "Turkey Selects Chinese HQ-9 SAM for T-Loramids," *Jane's Defence Weekly* 50, no. 40 (October 2, 2013): 5.

198. Burak Ege Bekdil, "Controversy Deepens over Chinese Air Defenses for Turkey," *Defense News International* 1, no. 19 (October 7, 2013): 8.

199. Jon Grevatt, "Turkey's Selection of Chinese SAMs Seen as 'Stepping Stone' to Europe," *Jane's Defence Weekly* 50, no. 41 (October 9, 2013): 20.

200. Lale Sariibrahimoglu, "Turkey Sticks by Its Chinese T-Loramids Choice," *Jane's Defence Weekly* 50, no. 41 (October 9, 2013): 5.

201. Bekdil, "Controversy Deepens over Chinese Air Defenses for Turkey," 8.

202. Umit Enginsoy and Burak Ege Bekdil, "Turkey to Buy $5.5B in Weapons: NATO Concerned by Russian, Chinese Interest," *Defense News* 27, no. 23 (June 11, 2012): 6.

203. Enginsoy and Bekdil, "Raytheon Touts Local Benefits in Turkish Missile Defense Bid," 24.

204. Umit Enginsoy and Burak Ege Bekdil, "Options Complicate Turkish Role in NATO Plan," *Defense News* 25, no. 45 (November 29, 2010): 8.

205. Bekdil, "Controversy Deepens over Chinese Air Defenses for Turkey," 8.

206. de Larrinaga, "Anatolian Ambition," 25–26.

207. Lale Sariibrahimoglu, "Turkey Tests Low-Altitude Air Defence Missile," *Jane's Defence Weekly* 50, no. 42 (October 16, 2013): 17.

208. Bekdil and Enginsoy, "Syria Challenge Exposes Turkish Shortcomings," 6.

209. Yaakov Katz, "Israel Worried by Improved Syrian Air Defences," *Jane's Defence Weekly* 49, no. 22 (May 30, 2012): 17.

210. Enginsoy and Bekdil, "Erdogan's Re-Election Means 'Buy Turkish,'" 26.

211. Bekdil and Enginsoy, "Syria Challenge Exposes Turkish Shortcomings," 6.

212. Bekdil e-mail, January 29, 2013.

213. *Military Balance 2012*, 164.

214. Sebnem Arsu, "Jailed Leader of the Kurds Offers a Truce with Turkey," *New York Times*, March 21, 2013, http://www.nytimes.com/2013/03/22/world/europe/kurdish-leader-declares-truce-with-turkey.html?ref=abdullahocalan&_r=0.

215. Burak Ege Bekdil, "Peace Deal Would Alter Turkish Procurement," *Defense News International* 1, no. 3 (March 4, 2013): 16.

216. Soli Ozel and Charles A. Kupchan, "A Turkey-Israel Opening," *New York Times*, April 1, 2013, http://www.nytimes.com/2013/04/02/opinion/global/a-turkey-israel-opening.html.

217. Burak Ege Bekdil, "Thaw Could Restore Turk-Israeli Arms Trade," *Defense News International* 1, no. 5 (April 1, 2013): 6.

218. Burak Ege Bekdil, "Turkey's New Security Threat: Turks," *Defense News International* 1, no. 10 (June 10, 2013): 6.

219. Larrabee, *Turkey as a U.S. Security Partner*, 29.

220. Larrabee, "Turkey Rediscovers the Middle East," 111.

221. Burak Ege Bekdil and Umit Enginsoy, "Syrian Uprising Heightens Turkish—U.S. Intel Cooperation," *Defense News* 27, no. 32 (August 20, 2012): 16.

222. Abidin Ünal, "Future of Our Air and Space Power and Training Perspective" (briefing presented at the International Conference on Air and Space Power [ICAP] 2013, Istanbul, March 28–29, 2013).

223. Jung Sung-Ki, "Tech Transfer Vital to Seoul's Fighter Contest," *Defense News* 26, no. 39 (October 24, 2011): 16.

224. Cooperative arrangements in the domain of European F-16 operations culminated in the creation of the European Participating Air Forces' Expeditionary Air Wing (EEAW), facilitating combined training among the Belgian, Danish, Dutch, Norwegian, and Portuguese F-16 forces, as well as providing a framework for common deployed operations. The European Participating Air Forces (EPAF) concept originally was conceived as a means of pooling national procurement requirements. In the 1990s EPAF specified a common requirement for the midlife update of the Belgian, Danish, Dutch, and Norwegian F-16A/B Block 15 fighter-bombers. See Anrig, *Quest for Relevant Air Power*, 235–36, 255.

225. "Turkey PM Recep Tayyip Erdogan 'Not to Start Syria War.'"

4. British Air Power

1. See, for example, the comment at "UK's World Role: Punching above Our Weight," Open Politics, *BBC News*, accessed January 29, 2013, http://news.bbc.co.uk

/hi/english/static/in_depth/uk_politics/2001/open_politics/foreign_policy/uks_world_role.stm.

2. Michael Hannan, "Punching above Their Weight," *New Atlanticist* (blog), October 1, 2012, http://www.acus.org/new_atlanticist/punching-above-their-weight. This assessment includes Norway, Sweden, Denmark, and the Netherlands. The "original" comment was Douglas Hurd, "The New Disorder" (speech at the Royal Institute for International Affairs [Chatham House], January 27, 1993).

3. Hurd, "New Disorder."

4. "Alliances and Partnerships," Part 5 of *Securing Britain in an Age of Uncertainty: The Strategic Defence and Security Review*, CM 7948 (London: Her Majesty's Government, October 2010), http://www.official-documents.gov.uk/document/cm79/7948/7948.pdf, 59.

5. "Alliances and Partnerships," paragraphs 5.2 and 5.6.

6. See, for example, John Dumbrell, "The U.S.-UK Special Relationship: Taking the 21st-Century Temperature," *British Journal of Politics and International Relations* 11, no. 1 (February 2009): 64–78.

7. *Securing Britain in an Age of Uncertainty*, paragraphs 1.5 and 1.6.

8. The tribalism need not be endemic; see, for example, the UK National Defence Association list of patrons, accessed November 3, 2013, http://www.uknda.org/uploads/1/5/3/0/15302742/uknda_list_vice_presidents_-_revsied_for_9th_may_2013.pdf. For a joint, as opposed to parochial, view of the debate, see UKNDA *Calls for National Debate on Defence*, September 18, 2012, http://www.uknda.org/uknda-reports.html.

9. UK defense spending is traditionally expressed in terms of gross domestic product and often cited in comparison with world or NATO partners. See MOD, *Management of Defence*, accessed February 12, 2013, http://www.armedforces.co.uk/mod/listings/l0012.html#ukdefence expenditure. Great effort is made to portray this expenditure as being as high as possible.

10. See Tony Mason, *Air Power: Centennial Appraisal* (London: Brassey's, 1994), 150.

11. House of Commons Defence Committee, *Ninth Report: Operations in Libya* (London: UK Parliament, February 8, 2012), http://www.publications.parliament.uk/pa/cm201012/cmselect/cmdfence/950/95003.htm, paragraphs 117–27.

12. House of Commons Defence Committee, "Defence Equipment 2009," February 26, 2009, http://www.parliament.the-stationery-office.co.uk/pa/cm200809/cmselect/cmdfence/107/10703.htm. See also Archie Hughes, "Regeneration Point," *Defence Management Journal*, no. 61 (Summer 2013): 48–49, http://www.dsg.mod.uk/pdf_archive/DMJ_Issue61_Summer13.pdf.

13. House of Commons Defence Committee, *Helicopter Capability*, HC 434 (London: Stationery Office, July 16, 2009), http://www.publications.parliament.uk/pa/cm200809/cmselect/cmdfence/434/434.pdf, 3.

14. Defence Committee, *Helicopter Capability*, 10.

15. Defence Committee, *Ninth Report*, paragraph 74.

16. Defence Committee, *Ninth Report*, paragraph 81.

17. Defence Committee, *Ninth Report*, paragraphs 90–91.

18. Tony Mason's chapter follows later in this volume. See also Graham Pitchfork, *The Sowreys* (London: Grub Street, 2012), 216–17, for notes on the origins of this post.

19. *British Air Power Doctrine*, AP 3000, 3rd ed. (London: Stationery Office, 1999), 3.12.9. The RAF *War Manual* was still in use, along with a lot of other outdated material, in the late 1970s as fodder for promotion examinations.

20. Andrew Valance, *Air Power: Collected Essays on Doctrine* (London: Stationery Office, 1990).

21. See J. J. G. Mackenzie and Brian Holden Reid, eds., *The British Army and the Operational Level of War* (London: Tri-Service Press, 1989), and the foreword by Sir Nigel Bagnall.

22. *UK Air and Space Doctrine*, JDP 0-30 (London: Ministry of Defence, July 2013), https://www.gov.uk/government/publications/uk-air-and-space-doctrine-jdp-0-3.

23. *British Air and Space Power Doctrine*, AP 3000, 4th ed. (London: Air Staff, 2009), http://www.raf.mod.uk/rafcms/mediafiles/9e435312_5056_a318_a88f14cf6f4fc6cE.pdf, 8.

24. *British Air and Space Power Doctrine*, 30.

25. See, for example, Sebastian Cox and Peter Gray, eds., *Air Power History: Turning Points from Kitty Hawk to Kosovo* (London: Cass, 2002); and Peter Gray, ed., *Air Power 21: Challenges for the New Century* (London: Stationery Office, 2000).

26. See *British Defence Doctrine*, JDP-0-01, 4th ed. (London: Ministry of Defence, November 2011), chap. 4.

27. See MOD, "Armed Forces Covenant Published for the First Time," announcement, May 16, 2011, https://www.gov.uk/government/news/armed-forces-covenant-published-for-first-time.

28. See MOD, "The Armed Forces Covenant," last modified June 28, 2013, https://www.gov.uk/the-armed-forces-covenant.

29. MOD, "Standing Commitments," December 12, 2012, https://www.gov.uk/standing-commitments.

30. See John Keegan, "A Real Turning Point," *Sunday Telegraph*, June 6, 1999. For a more detailed approach, see Stephen T. Hosmer, *Why Milosevic Decided to Settle When He Did* (Santa Monica CA: Rand, 2001).

31. John Kiszely, "Thinking about the Operational Level," *JRUSI*, December 2005, 38.

32. Kiszely, "Thinking about the Operational Level," 42.

33. David T. Zabecki, *The German 1918 Offensives: A Case Study in the Operational Level of War* (Abingdon, Oxfordshire: Routledge, 2006), 11.

34. Zabecki, *German 1918 Offensives*, 12.

35. Edward N. Luttwak, "The Operational Level of War," *International Security* 5, no. 3 (Winter 1980/1981): 61.

36. Shimon Naveh, *In Pursuit of Military Excellence: The Evolution of Operational Theory* (Abingdon, Oxfordshire: Cass, 1997), 9.

37. See Hosmer, *Why Milosevic Decided to Settle.*

38. See H. Rittell and M. Webber, "Dilemmas in a General Theory of Planning," *Policy Sciences* 4, 155–69. For the application of this typology to the military environment, see Keith Grint, *Leadership, Management and Command: Rethinking D-Day* (Basingstoke: Palgrave Macmillan, 2008), 11–18.

39. MOD, "Dr. Liam Fox Responds to Defence Committee Report on SDSR," announcement, December 14, 2012, https://www.gov.uk/government/news/dr-liam-fox-responds- to-defence-committee-report-on-sdsr.

40. *Securing Britain in an Age of Uncertainty*, 27.

41. See Andrew Brooks, "Life after Nimrod," *Defence Management Journal*, March 1, 2011.

42. Brooks, "Life after Nimrod."

43. *Securing Britain in an Age of Uncertainty*, 38.

44. Brooks, "Life after Nimrod." See also Alex Barker, "Navy Chief Attacks Nimrod Cuts," *Financial Times*, November 9, 2010, http://www.ft.com/cms/s/0/a965264c-ec3d-11df-9e11-00144feab49a.html#axzz2k23dohAu.

45. For a historical perspective, see Gjert Lage Dyndal, *Land Based Air Power or Aircraft Carriers: A Case Study of the British Debate about Maritime Air Power in the 1960s* (Farnham, Surrey: Ashgate, 2012).

46. Annette Amerman, "Integration of U.S. Marine Corps Aviation in First World War: A Case Study; the Court Martial of Captain Edmund Chamberlain" (unpublished PhD research, University of Birmingham). This ongoing research looks at the integration U.S. Marine Corps aviation into the U.S. Navy and more broadly into Allied cooperation during the First World War.

47. *Securing Britain in an Age of Uncertainty*, 23.

48. *Securing Britain in an Age of Uncertainty*, 23.

49. Defence Committee, *Ninth Report*, paragraphs 103 and 106. Note also the First Sea Lord's assurance that the new carriers would also have been used had they been available (paragraphs 115–16).

50. *Securing Britain in an Age of Uncertainty*, 23.

51. "Government in £100m U-turn over F35-B Fighter Planes," *BBC News*, May 10, 2012, http://www.bbc.co.uk/news/uk-politics-18008171.

52. "Joint Strike Fighter Decision Was Flawed, MPs Say," *BBC News*, February 5, 2013, http://www.bbc.co.uk/news/uk-21332054. See also "MOD Errors Blamed for Fiasco That Cost Millions," *The Times*, February 5, 2013, 14.

53. *Securing Britain in an Age of Uncertainty*, 23. Readers should note that in the carrier context "strike" does not mean nuclear attack.

54. *Securing Britain in an Age of Uncertainty*, 23.

55. National Audit Office, *Carrier Strike*, HC 1092 (London, July 7, 2011).

56. National Audit Office, *Carrier Strike*, 8.

57. National Audit Office, *Carrier Strike*, 9.

58. National Audit Office, *Carrier Strike*, 28.

59. James Bosbotinis, "The Strategic Utility of the Queen Elizabeth Class Carriers," *Defence IQ*, January 3, 2012, http://www.defenceiq.com/naval- and-maritime-defence /articles/the-strategic-utility-of-the-queen-elizabeth-class/.

60. National Audit Office, *Carrier Strike*, 32.

61. See P. W. Singer, "YouTube War: The Public and Its Unmanned Wars," chap. 16 in *Wired for War* (London: Penguin, 2009).

62. See, however, Kenny Fuchter, "The First Drone War: Air Power for Strategic Effect" *Royal Air Force Air Power Review* 15, no. 3 (Autumn/Winter 2012): 17–35.

63. There is a growing literature on the subject, with the term RPA being used along with unmanned aerial vehicle (UAV) and drone (which can also be land-borne). As a reminder that there are operators in the loop, this chapter will use RPA.

64. See, for example, Peter W. Gray, "The Myths of Air Control and the Realities of Imperial Policing," *Royal Air Force Air Power Review* 4, no. 2 (Summer 2001). Also published in the *Aerospace Power Journal*, Fall 2001.

65. Fuchter, "First Drone War," 21.

66. Fuchter, "First Drone War," 26–28. See also Nick Tucker-Lowe, "RPAs and the Ethical Landscape of Contemporary Conflict," *Royal Air Force Air Power Review* 15, no. 3, 2–16; and Singer, *Wired for War*, chap. 20.

67. Michael Isikoff, "Department of Justice Memo Reveals Legal Case for Drone Strikes on Americans," *NBC News*, February 6, 2013, http://openchannel.nbcnews.com/ _news/2013/02/04/16843014-exclusive-justice-department-memo-reveals-legal-case -for-drone-strikes-on-americans?lite.

68. See, for example, "Iran 'Fends Off New Stuxnet Cyber Attack,'" *BBC News*, December 25, 2012, http://www.bbc.co.uk/news/world-middle-east-20842113.

69. See, for example, "U.S. Law Permits Pre-emptive Cyber Strikes," *Sydney Morning Herald*, February 5, 2013, http://www.smh.com.au/it-pro/security-it/us-law -permits-preemptive-cyber-strikes-20130204-2dutf.html.

5. Norwegian Air Power

1. Norwegian Ministry of Defence, *Capable Force: Strategic Concept for the Norwegian Armed Forces* (Oslo, 2009), 8–11.

2. Target categories for the 588 expended bombs: tanks (45), aircraft shelters (11), artillery (29), ammunition storage (248), Scud missile (1), command and control facilities (113), landlines of communication (12), air defense (12), armored personnel vehicles (19), other vehicles (28), and infrastructure (70).

7. Swedish Air Power

1. Tommy Petersson, *Med invasionen i sikte* [With the Invasion in Focus] (Stockholm: University of Stockholm, 2009), 169–71.

2. Swedish foreign minister Carl Bildt in the Swedish Parliament, February 15, 2012, from Ann-Sofie Dahl's "NATO Defense College in Rome," NATO *Research Paper* 82 (September 2012).

9. Approaching the End?

1. See, above all, Martin van Creveld, *The Age of Airpower* (New York: PublicAffairs, 2011), 423–42.

2. See, for some figures, Enzo Angelucci, *The Rand-McNally Encyclopedia of Military Aircraft, 1914 to the Present* (New York: Gallery Books, 1990), 29.

3. Winston Churchill, quoted in M. J. Armitage and R. A. Mason, *Airpower in the Nuclear Age* (Urbana: University of Illinois Press, 1983), 1.

4. Stanley Sandler, *The Korean War: No Victors, No Vanquished* (Lexington: University Press of Kentucky, 1999), 185.

5. The best account of the Arab Revolt and the role British air power played in it is R. Yermiash, "The Wings of Empire: The Royal Air Force in Palestine and Transjordan, 1919–39" [in Hebrew] (PhD dissertation, Hebrew University, 2008), 196–252.

6. Malaysia is a disputed case, so I shall not discuss it here.

7. This and subsequent figures from James S. Corum and Wray R. Johnson, *Airpower in Small Wars: Fighting Insurgents and Terrorists* (Lawrence: University Press of Kansas, 2003), 262–63.

8. The total was 96,318, which works out at 263 per day. Richard J. Overy, *The Air War, 1939–1945* (London: Europa, 1980), 77 (table 5).

9. See, for a recent specimen of the literature on the question, Richard P. Hallion, "Precision-Guided Munitions and the New Era of Warfare," APSC Paper 53 (Fairbairn, Australian Capital Territory, Australia: Air Power Studies Center, 1995), http://www.fas.org/man/dod-101/sys/smart/docs/paper53.htm.

10. D. D. Jackson, "Warbirds and Airshows," accessed August 24, 2013, http://www.warbirdsandairshows.com/historicsites.htm.

11. Robert M. Gates, speech to the Economic Club of Chicago, July 16, 2009, http://www.defenselink.mil/speeches/speech.aspx?speechid=1369.

12. W. Wheeler, "How the F-35 Nearly Doubled in Price," *Time*, July 9, 2012, http://nation.time.com/2012/07/09/f-35-nearly-doubles-in-cost-but-you-dont-know-thanks-to-its-rubber-baseline/.

13. See on this Martin van Creveld, *Technology and War* (New York: Free Press, 1989), 265–96.

14. See P. de Souza, "Naval Forces," in *The Cambridge History of Greek and Roman Warfare*, eds. Peter Sabin, Hans van Wees, and Michael Whitby (Cambridge UK: Cambridge University Press, 2008), 1:358; and J. S. Morrison, "Hellenistic Oared Warships, 399–31 BC," in *Age of the Galley: Mediterranean Oared Vessels since Pre-Classical Times*, ed. R. Gardiner (London: Conway Maritime Press, 2004), 73–74.

15. See in general Bernard Brodie, *Naval Strategy* (Princeton NJ: Princeton University Press, 1943).

16. M. J. Neufeld, *The Rocket and the Reich* (New York: Free Press, 1993), 1–2, 147–48.

10. The Response to Uncertainty

1. Carl von Clausewitz, *On War*, ed. Michael Howard and Peter Paret (Princeton NJ: Princeton University Press, 1976), 479–83.

SELECTED BIBLIOGRAPHY

Angelucci, Enzo. *The Rand-McNally Encyclopedia of Military Aircraft, 1914 to the Present*. New York: Gallery Books, 1990.

Anrig, Christian F. *The Quest for Relevant Air Power: Continental European Responses to the Air Power Challenges of the Post–Cold War Era*. Maxwell Air Force Base AL: Air University Press, 2011.

Armitage, M. J., and R. A. Mason. *Airpower in the Nuclear Age*. Urbana: University of Illinois Press, 1983.

Boyne, Walter J. *Operation Iraqi Freedom: What Went Right, What Went Wrong, and Why*. New York: Forge, 2003.

Bracken, Paul. *The New Nuclear Age: Strategy, Danger and the New Power Politics*. New York: Times Books, 2012.

Brodie, Bernard. *Naval Strategy*. Princeton NJ: Princeton University Press, 1943.

Corum, James S., and Wray R. Johnson. *Airpower in Small Wars: Fighting Insurgents and Terrorists*. Lawrence: University Press of Kansas, 2003.

Cox, Sebastian, and Peter Gray, eds. *Air Power History: Turning Points from Kitty Hawk to Kosovo*. London: Cass, 2002.

Dyndal, Gjert Lage. *Land Based Air Power or Aircraft Carriers: A Case Study of the British Debate about Maritime Air Power in the 1960s*. Farnham, Surrey, UK: Ashgate, 2012.

Frieser, Karl-Heinz. *The Blitzkrieg Legend: The 1940 Campaign in the West*. Annapolis MD: Naval Institute Press, 2013.

Gray, Colin S. *Airpower for Strategic Effect*. Maxwell Air Force Base AL: Air University Press, 2012.

Gray, Peter W., ed. *Air Power 21: Challenges for the New Century*. London: Stationery Office, 2000.

Gray, Peter W., and Sebastian Cox. *Air Power Leadership: Theory and Practice*. London: Stationery Office, 2002.

Grint, Keith. *Leadership, Management and Command: Rethinking D-Day*. Basingstoke, Hampshire, UK: Palgrave Macmillan, 2008.

Hallion, Richard P., ed. *Air Power Confronts an Unstable World*. London: Brassey's, 1997.

———. *Storm over Iraq: Air Power and the Gulf War*. Washington DC: Smithsonian Institution Press, 1992.

Hosmer, Stephen T. *Why Milosevic Decided to Settle When He Did*. Santa Monica CA: Rand, 2001.

Johnson, Adrian, and Saqeb Mueen, eds. *Short War, Long Shadow: The Political and Military Legacies of the 2011 Libya Campaign*, RUSI Whitehall Report 1-12. London: Royal United Services Institute for Defence and Security Studies, 2012.

Kaplan, Robert. *Monsoon: The Indian Ocean and the Future of American Power*. New York: Random House, 2011.

———. *The Revenge of Geography: What the Map Tells Us about Coming Conflicts and the Battle against Fate*. New York: Random House, 2012.

Lambeth, Benjamin S. *Air Operations in Israel's War against Hezbollah*. Santa Monica CA: Rand, 2011.

———. *Air Power against Terror: America's Conduct of Operation Enduring Freedom*. Santa Monica CA: Rand, 2005.

———. *NATO's Air War for Kosovo: A Strategic and Operational Assessment*. Santa Monica CA: Rand, 2001.

———. *The Transformation of American Air Power*. Ithaca NY: Cornell University Press, 2000.

Larrabee, F. Stephen. *Turkey as a U.S. Security Partner*. Santa Monica CA: Rand, 2008.

Mackenzie, J. J. G., and Brian Holden Reid, eds. *The British Army and the Operational Level of War*. London: Tri-Service Press, 1989.

Mason, Tony. *Air Power: Centennial Appraisal*. London: Brassey's, 1994.

Murray, Williamson, and Allan Millett, eds. *Military Innovation in the Interwar Period*. Cambridge, UK: Cambridge University Press, 1996.

Naveh, Shimon. *In Pursuit of Military Excellence: The Evolution of Operational Theory*. London: Cass, 1997.

Neufeld, M. J. *The Rocket and the Reich*. New York: Free Press, 1993.

Olsen, John Andreas, ed. *Air Commanders*. Washington DC: Potomac Books, 2012.

———, ed. *Global Air Power*. Washington DC: Potomac Books, 2011.

———, ed. *A History of Air Warfare*. Washington DC: Potomac Books, 2010.

Olsen, John Andreas, and Rohan Maxwell. *Destination NATO: Defence Reform in Bosnia and Herzegovina, 2003–2013*, RUSI Whitehall Paper 80. London: Royal United Services Institute for Defence and Security Studies, 2012.

Overy, Richard J. *The Air War.* London: Europa, 1980.

Owen, Robert C., ed. *Deliberate Force—A Case Study in Effective Air Campaigning: Final Report of the Air University Balkans Air Campaign Study.* Maxwell Air Force Base AL: Air University Press, 2000.

Peters, John E., Stuart E. Johnson, Nora Bensahel, Timothy Liston, and Traci Williams. *European Contributions to Operation Allied Force: Implications for Transatlantic Cooperation.* Santa Monica CA: Rand, 2001.

Ripley, Tim. *Air War Bosnia: UN and NATO Airpower.* Shrewsbury, UK: Airlife, 1996.

Sabin, Phil, Hans van Wees, and Michael Whitby, eds. *The Cambridge History of Greek and Roman Warfare.* Cambridge, UK: Cambridge University Press, 2008.

Sandler, Stanley. *The Korean War: No Victors, No Vanquished.* Lexington: University Press of Kentucky, 1999.

Singer, Peter W. *Wired for War.* London: Penguin, 2009.

Valance, Andrew. *Air Power: Collected Essays on Doctrine.* London: Stationery Office, 1990.

Van Creveld, Martin. *The Age of Airpower.* New York: Free Press, 2011.

———. *Technology and War.* New York: Free Press, 1989.

Zabecki, David T. *The German 1918 Offensives: A Case Study in the Operational Level of War.* Abingdon, UK: Routledge, 2006.

CONTRIBUTORS

Christian F. Anrig is deputy director of doctrine research and education in the Swiss Air Force. From early 2007 until September 2009, he was a lecturer in air power studies in the Defence Studies Department of King's College London, while based at the Royal Air Force (RAF) College. He was one of two leading academics who created the distance-learning master's degree program on Air Power in the Modern World, and he served on the editorial board of the RAF *Air Power Review*. In 2009 he became a member of the RAF Centre for Air Power Studies academic advisory panel. Dr. Anrig began his professional career in the field of defense studies as a researcher at the Center for Security Studies at the Swiss Federal Institute of Technology (ETH Zurich) in January 2004. He has published various articles, covering topics from European military transformation to modern air power and its ramifications for small nations. He served in the mountain artillery of the Swiss Army and is currently a reserve major assigned to the Air Staff of the Swiss Air Force. Christian F. Anrig holds a PhD from King's College London. He is the author of *The Quest for Relevant Air Power: Continental European Responses to the Air Power Challenges of the Post–Cold War Era* (2011).

Micael Bydén is the chief of staff of the Swedish Air Force, a position he has held since 2012. Born in Gnarp, he began his military career at the Coastal Artillery Academy (1983–85), KA4, Gothenburg, before entering Basic Flying Training at the Swedish Air Force Flying Training

School. He was a fighter pilot at F 21 Wing, Norbotten, from 1989 to 1995; upon finishing the Staff Course at the Swedish National Defence College, he was promoted to major and assigned as deputy squadron commander at F 21 Wing. After the Advanced Command Course (1997–99), Bydén was assistant air attaché at the Swedish embassy in Washington DC for two years; then he spent a year as the air attaché. From 2002 to 2003 he was a staff officer at the Air Force Branch of the Swedish Armed Forces Headquarters; from 2003 to 2005 he was commanding officer of the Air Force Flying Training School (Linköping); from 2005 to 2008 he was deputy commanding officer of the Helicopter Wing (also Linköping); and from 2008 to 2009 he was commanding officer of that wing. Promoted to brigadier general in 2009, he became head of training and procurement for the Swedish Air Force.

Henrik Røboe Dam is the commander of the Royal Danish Air Force. Born in Tøder, he entered the Non-Commissioned Officers' School in 1977 at the Air Force Station in Værløse. Upon graduation from the Officers' Basic Course, Air Force Flying School, in Aalborg, in 1984, he became platoon leader, second in command, and acting squadron commander at Karup. In 1986–89 he was intercept controller, flight allocator, and head of the Operations Platoon at Squadron 601, Skagen, and next head of the Operations Platoon and second in command of Squadron 605, Tórshavn. After a short tour as staff officer at the Policy Division of the Policy Branch of the Defence Staff, he served in the First Office of the Ministry of Defence from 1992 to 1995. Promoted to lieutenant colonel, he spent the next three years as commander of the Air Force Station Bornholm. In 1998 he became chief of the Plans Branch of the Plans Division in the Defence Staff; in 2000 he became commander of the Control and Reporting Group; and the following year he also became commander of the Air Force Surface-to-Air Missile (SAM) Group. From 2001 to 2004 he was commander of the Control and Air Defence Group. Promoted to major general in 2004, he became deputy chief of staff for operations, budget, and finance at the Defence Command. In 2008 he was appointed commander of Combined Air Operations Center 1, Findrup, and in 2009 commander of the Tactical Air Command. From 2012 his responsibilities in that position also included command of the Combined Air Operations Centre, Findrup. His military education has included several courses at the Defence College: Junior Staff Course (1987), Senior Joint Staff Course (1989–90), Management Course (1997), Personnel and Resource Management Course (1999), and Executive Leadership Course (2002).

Etienne de Durand is an analyst of strategic and military affairs, a senior research fellow at the French Institute of International Relations (Ifri), and since 2006 the director of Ifri's Security Studies Center. He is also assistant professor at the Institut d'Etudes Politiques de Paris (Sciences Po). He has taught international relations and security studies at the Université Jean Moulin–Lyon III, the Ecole Militaire Spéciale de Saint-Cyr Coëtquidan, and the Collège Interarmées de Défense. Etienne de Durand regularly performs analyses for the French Ministries of Defense and Foreign Affairs. He was part of the group of civilian advisers for Gen. Stanley McChrystal's Afghanistan review in July 2009 and contributed to the 2012 Defense White Paper in France. At Ifri, Etienne de Durand concentrates specifically on French and U.S. defense and security policy, European security and transatlantic issues, nuclear deterrence and proliferation, and current military issues, such as ongoing interventions and military transformation. He has authored numerous monographs and articles on these issues (including *Stratégie aérienne comparée* with Bastien Irondelle, which analyzes and compares the air doctrine in the United States, Britain, and France). He is also the editor of the *Proliferation Papers* and *Focus stratégique* electronic series.

Peter W. Gray retired from the Royal Air Force in June 2008, having reached the rank of air commodore; he took up the position of senior research fellow in air power studies at the University of Birmingham on September 1, 2008. Immediately prior to his retirement from active duty, Dr. Gray was director of the Defence Leadership and Management Centre, taking up post in September 2004. Gray spent his early career as a navigator on the F-4 Phantom aircraft, and more recently, he commanded 101 Squadron flying VC-10K tanker aircraft. He spent two staff tours in the personnel field, followed by a lengthy sojourn in the Cabinet Office and several appointments in the Ministry of Defence, and he has served as director of defence studies for the Royal Air Force. Gray holds degrees from the Universities of Dundee, London, Cambridge, and Birmingham (PhD). He is a fellow of the Royal Aeronautical Society, the Royal Historical Society, and the Institute of Leadership and Management. His latest book, *Leadership, Direction and Legitimacy of the RAF Bomber Offensive*, was published in June 2012.

Finn Kristian Hannestad is the chief of staff of the Royal Norwegian Air Force. He began basic officers training in 1980 and completed pilot training in 1983. He served at Ørland Main Air Station from 1984 to 1997, first as an F-16 pilot, next as flight commander, deputy squadron commander, and squadron commander. During his service as operations group commander at Bodø Main Air Station in 1997–99, he was appointed detachment commander for the Norwegian F-16 unit operating out of Grazzanise in Italy during Operation Allied Force. Hannestad served as a staff officer from 1999 to 2002 and then spent a year as director for operations in the Plans and Policy Division of the Joint Headquarters (HQ), planning the Norwegian F-16 support to Operation Enduring Freedom. From 2003 to 2004 he was the chief of staff's primary spokesperson, next moving to Ramstein as deputy chief of staff for operations (DCOS OPS) at Component Command Air HQ. Before becoming chief of staff of the air force in 2010, he spent two years as DCOS OPS at the Norwegian Joint Operational HQ, responsible for national and international operations. Major General Hannestad is a graduate of the Norwegian Air Force Academy (1989), the Joint Command and Staff College in Oslo (1997), and the Air War College at Maxwell Air Force Base (2002).

R. A. Mason, Air Vice Marshal (ret.), Royal Air Force (RAF), holds an honorary chair at the School of Social Sciences at the University of Birmingham. His academic field of specialization is the interaction of diplomacy and armed forces, with particular reference to air power.

His last RAF appointment was as air secretary from 1986 to 1989. He is a former director of the Centre for Studies in Security and Diplomacy at the University of Birmingham, was specialist air adviser to the House of Commons Defence Committee from 2001 to 2006, and is a frequent media commentator on defense issues. In 2007 he was appointed an honorary fellow of the Royal Aeronautical Society. Professor Mason has contributed to policy studies for the RAF, the U.S. Air Force, and the Australian, New Zealand, German, Swedish, Netherlands, Swiss, Norwegian, Omani, Indian, Thai, South Korean, and Chinese Air Forces. He has published several books, articles, and papers on air power and related defense subjects, including *Air Power in the Nuclear Age, 1945–1985* (1985) and *Air Power: A Centennial Appraisal* (1994). He is a graduate of the RAF Staff College and the U.S. Air War College and holds degrees from the University of St. Andrews, the University of London, and the University of Birmingham.

Holger H. Mey, born in Flensburg, Germany, is head of advanced concepts, Airbus Defence and Space (Munich). Before joining what now became Airbus in June 2004, Professor Mey worked for twelve years as a self-employed security policy analyst and consultant in Bonn and was a frequent television and radio commentator, publisher, and lecturer. Professor Mey began his professional career in 1986 as a research associate at the Stiftung Wissenschaft und Politik (Foundation for Science and Politics) then at Ebenhausen. From 1990 to 1992 he served as a security policy analyst on the Policy Planning Staff of the German Ministery of Defense. In 1992 he founded the Institute for Strategic Analyses and became chair and director; for two years he was also the security policy adviser to the chair of the Defense Committee in the German parliament. Professor Mey directed and conducted over thirty studies for various ministries and government agencies. He is an honorary professor at the University of Cologne and a member of many international and national foreign and security policy associations, including the International Institute for Strategic Studies (IISS, London) and the Deutsche Gesellschaft für Auswärtige Politik (the German Council on Foreign Relations, Berlin). Professor Mey has published well over one hundred and fifty articles in major security policy journals, newspapers, and books. He is editor, coauthor, and author of many books, including *Deutsche Sicherheitspolitik 2030* (2001).

John Andreas Olsen is currently assigned to the Norwegian Ministry of Defence and is a visiting professor of operational art and tactics at the Swedish National Defence College. He was the deputy commander and chief of the North Atlantic Treaty Organization (NATO) Advisory Team at NATO Headquarters, Sarajevo, from 2009 to 2012. Previous assignments include tours as dean of the Norwegian Defence University College and head of its division for strategic studies. Colonel Olsen is a graduate of the German Command and Staff College and has served both as liaison officer to the German Operational Command in Potsdam and as military assistant to the Norwegian embassy in Berlin. He has a doctorate in history and international relations from De Montfort University, a master's degree in contemporary literature from the University of Warwick, and a master's degree in English from the University of Trondheim. Professor Olsen is the author of *Strategic Air Power in Desert Storm* (2003) and *John Warden and the Renaissance of American Air Power* (2007); coauthor of *Destination NATO: Defence Reform in Bosnia and Herzegovina, 2003–2013* (2013); editor of *On New Wars* (2006), *A History of Air Warfare* (2010), *Global Air Power* (2011), and *Air Commanders* (2012); and coeditor of *The Evolution of Operational Art: From Napoleon to the Present* (2011) and *The Practice of Strategy: From Alexander the Great to the Present* (2012).

Lauri Tapio Puranen is the commander of the Finnish Air Force. He started his military career as an air force cadet in 1980. Upon graduation three years later, he served at Fighter Squadron 11, Lapland Wing, from 1983 to 1989. After a one-year captain course, he was assigned to Lapland Air Command, first as deputy flight commander (1990–95) and next as flight commander. Upon graduation from the General Staff Officer Course, he began service at the Air Command Headquarters, first as senior staff officer and then as chief of operations. In 1997–2001 he was senior staff officer at the Finnish Defence Staff Operations Division. Upon completing the Senior Command Course, then colonel Puranen served as chief of the Finnish Defence Staff, Army Aviation Division; after completing the High Command Course, he became the commander of Lapland Air Command. In 2008–12, now brigadier general Puranen was assistant chief of staff at the Defence Command as the chief of the C4 Division, chief of staff of the Air Force Command, and chief of logistics at the Defence Command. Major General Puranen has flown the Saab 91 Safir, Fouga CM-170 Magister, Valmet L-70 Vinka, BAE Systems Hawk 51, Saab 35 Draken, Piper PA-31-350 Chieftain, Pilatus PC-12, and the MD Helicopters MD 500.

Martin van Creveld was born in the Netherlands but was raised and educated in Israel. After receiving his master's degree at the Hebrew University in Jerusalem, he obtained a PhD in history at the London School of Economics and Political Science. Since 1971 he has been on the faculty of the History Department at the Hebrew University, where he is currently a professor. He is one of the world's leading experts on military history and strategy, with a special interest in the future of war. Professor van Creveld has been a consultant to the defense establishments of several countries and has taught or lectured at defense colleges, both military and civilian, from Canada to New Zealand and from Norway to South Africa. He has also appeared on countless television and radio programs as well as written for, and been interviewed by, hundreds of papers and magazines around the world. He has authored twenty books, including *Supplying War* (1978), *Command in War* (1985), *The Transformation of War* (1991), *The Rise and Decline of the State* (1999), *The Changing Face of War: Lessons of Combat from Marne to Iraq* (2006), *The Culture of War* (2008), and *The Age of Airpower* (2011).

INDEX

Other works by John Andreas Olsen

John Warden and the Renaissance of American Air Power

Edited Volumes

A History of Air Warfare

Global Air Power

Air Commanders